From Goosecreek to Gandercleugh

England and America are both at this moment supplied, in a great measure, with a literature of Scottish manufacture. We should not be much surprised were we to live to see the day when we, in our turn, shall be gaping for new novels and poems from the other side of the Atlantic, and when, in the silence of our own bards and romancers, we shall have Ladies of the Lake from Ontario, and Tales of My Landlord from Goose-creek, as a counterpart to those from Gandercleugh.

(Constable's *Edinburgh Magazine*,
September, 1819)

ANDREW HOOK

From Goosecreek to Gandercleugh:
Studies in Scottish-American Literary and Cultural History

TUCKWELL PRESS

Published with support from the University of
Glasgow Publications Committee and from the
MacFie Fund

First published in Great Britain in 1999 by
Tuckwell Press
The Mill House
Phantassie
East Linton
East Lothian EH40 3DG
Scotland

Note

Listed here are earlier published versions of some of the essays in this book.

'Scotland and the Invention of the USA,' in Mario Materassi and Maria Irene Ramalho de Sousa Santos (eds.) *The American Columbiad, "Discovering" America, Inventing the United States*, Amsterdam: VU University Press, 1996, pp. 149–61.

'Philadelphia, Edinburgh and the Scottish Enlightenment,' in Richard B. Sher and Jeffrey R. Smitten (eds.) *Scotland and America in the Age of Enlightenment*, Edinburgh: Edinburgh University Press, 1990, pp. 227–41.

'Hogg, Melville and the Scottish Enlightenment,' *Scottish Literary Journal*, 4 (December, 1977), pp. 25–39.

'Carlyle and America' *Occasional Papers No. 3*, The Carlyle Society, Edinburgh, 1970.

'Macaulay and America,' *Journal of American Studies*, 9 (December, 1975), pp. 335–46.

'The Scottish Landscape of Southern Literature' in Tony Badger, Walter Edgar, Jan Nordby Gretlund (eds.) *Southern Landscapes*, Tubingen, Stauffenburg Verlag, 1996, pp. 41–53.

'Scottish Academia and the Invention of American Studies' in Robert Crawford (ed.) *The Scottish Invention of English Literature*, Cambridge: Cambridge University Press 1998, pp. 164–79.

ISBN 1 898410 58 5

British Library Cataloguing in Publication Data

A catalogue record for this book is available
on request from the British Library

Typeset by Hewer Text Ltd, Edinburgh
Printed and bound by Cromwell Press, Trowbridge

For all my friends
in America

Contents

Preface

My own study of Scottish-American literary and cultural relations began in the Witherspoon Collection at Princeton University in the late 1950s. At the time I had good reason for regarding myself as something of a pioneer. Of course there was an existing literature on Scotland and America but its frequent filiopietism was not entirely misrepresented by a *Reader's Digest* article, published in 1955 and entitled 'The Scots Among Us', which largely consisted of long lists of Americans, from generals to golfers, who could lay claim to Scottish blood somewhere in their past. (The article was for many years made available in U.S. Consulates in Scotland.) Admittedly 1954 had seen the publication of the ground-breaking *William and Mary College Quarterly* issue devoted to the topic of Scotland and America and marking a new academic seriousness in the study of the field. But the *William and Mary Quarterly* did not address the literary dimension of the Scottish-American connection, and, much more significantly, the editors of *The Reader's Digest* clearly remained innocent of its contents.

The situation today, I believe, is different but hardly transformed. In the introductory chapter of this book, by focusing on the reception of Garry Wills's controversial study of Jefferson and the Scottish Enlightenment called *Inventing America*, I make a case for the view that a kind of *Reader's Digest* innocence often continues to surround the topic of Scotland and America. What this means is that despite all that has been achieved by scholars working in the decades subsequent to the publication of the *William and Mary Quarterly* articles, particularly in the field of the Scottish-American Enlightenment, a specifically Scottish dimension to the mainstream of American cultural history largely continues to go unrecognised. The position appears to be that in these years the Scottish case

1

has been put, but, as I suggest in my introductory chapter, neither judge nor jury appears to have been paying much attention.

Why this should be so is not a simple matter to explain. Academic conservatism has undoubtedly been a factor; old historical orthodoxies are always reluctant to give way to new ideas. But attempting to look at this particular example from the widest of possible perspectives, I am inclined to the view that the identification of what precisely *is* 'Scottish' lies at the heart of the problem: the Scottish dimension of American culture has rarely been consciously denied, but it has frequently gone unrecognised. All too often, it seems to me, scholars working in the field of Scottish Studies in general assume that what is or is not 'Scottish' is self-evident; because the scholars themselves find no difficulty, it is assumed that none exists. But might it not be the case that their own familiarity with the material upon which they work makes their perspective untypical? At the final plenary session of a meeting of the Eighteenth-Century Scottish Studies Society, held in Brown University in Providence, Rhode Island, in 1994, the issue of 'Scottishness' came up. Most of those who spoke felt there was no problem even in the eighteenth century: everyone knew that the provisions of the Treaty of Union of 1707 between Scotland and England, leaving Scottish law, Scottish education, and the Scottish Church untouched, meant that Scotland retained its separate national identity. Some of us, however, including perhaps the most distinguished contemporary American colonial historian, were not persuaded that the outside world in particular necessarily recognised this, then or now. The truth about Scotland may well be its distinctive separateness, but in the post-Union situation what is that truth worth? Even today, when, for a variety of political and cultural reasons, recognition of a Scottish identity is more widespread than at any time in the modern period, is it not true that Scotland and Scottishness are still regularly subsumed under England and Englishness?

I would suggest that at least since the eighteenth century, and the emergence of the United Kingdom, the definition of 'Scottishness' has been immensely difficult for Scottish culture itself; the division between Highlands and Lowlands, the existence of different languages, not to mention the crucial relationship with England, have all complicated the issue. Now if the Scots themselves find their cultural identity problematical, it is hardly surprising that Americans, and others, frequently fail to recognise even its existence. Nor is it hard to understand why, in the period since the eighteenth century, 'Scottishness' should often have largely disappeared in the cracks between Englishness and Britishness.

I would argue that as the lively debate over the nature of Scottish cultural identity in the eighteenth century–often conducted in terms very similar to those that resurfaced in the course of the twentieth century–gave way to narrower, more provincial, concerns in the nineteenth, the distinctiveness of a separate Scottish voice, particularly as far as the outside world was concerned, became increasingly obscured. Thus by the 1920s, when the serious study of American literary history was becoming established, any general awareness of Scottish culture had more or less disappeared from the American consciousness. Inevitably, then, when markers were being set down for the guidance of early scholars of American literature and culture, there was little surviving sense of a separate Scottish dimension to what was seen as the Anglo-American relationship. This was perhaps the situation that produced the problems faced by those scholars who, in the decades after 1954, struggled seriously to raise America's Scottish consciousness.

Since 1954 much, I agree, has been achieved–particularly by American scholars. Certainly there is now in existence a substantial body of work focusing on the Scottish contribution to America's intellectual and cultural history. But whether one thinks of Scottish Studies in general, – at, say, the University of South Carolina, or Guelph in Canada – or of the specific topic of the Scottish-American connection, the scale and consequences of this achievement remain rather modest. Is it unfair to draw a comparison with the situation of Irish Studies? In recent years, both in Britain and the USA, Irish Studies as an academic subject has expanded enormously: there are major programmes at Liverpool, Bath, the University of North London, and St Mary's University College, Strawberry Hill; at Notre Dame, New York University, Boston College, and Wake Forest in North Carolina: and a multiplicity of smaller-scale courses at a huge number of American and British institutions. There is an American Conference for Irish Studies (which publishes a booklet listing all the American universities and colleges that offer undergraduate or postgraduate Irish Studies courses), and a British Association for Irish Studies. The *Irish Studies Review* has been appearing since 1992. It would be difficult to argue that the profile of Scottish Studies either in Britain or the US is at present even remotely parallel.

Yet there are good reasons for believing that the future for Scottish Studies (including Scottish-American studies) is reasonably bright: and I mean more than the new politics that will produce a Scottish parliament in 1999. The theorising that has gone on in recent years in cultural studies has developed concepts which have relevance to the Scottish case. Both cultural and literary history now, for example, take a particular interest in the nature of the relationship between 'centres', where political, economic and hence cultural power originates, and what are variously termed 'provinces', 'regions', 'margins' or 'peripheries'. The notion that the cultural interchange between the two should necessarily be viewed from the perspective of the centre, the dominant power-structure, is frequently called in question because such a perspective simply reinscribes the inferior status of what lies outside the centre. In the context of English Studies, the alternative is to challenge what a recent scholar called 'the Anglocentric notion of English literature', by reading the English literature of the periphery–be it Scottish, Irish, American, West Indian or whatever–in relation to its own concerns, its own identity. The debate over centres and peripheries is in turn related, in a literary context, to another contentious theoretical issue: that of the so-called 'canon'. The assumption is that what is defined as 'canonical' is very much a question of what is seen to be central to a tradition and what is

4

merely marginal. To destabilise the centre is thus inevitably to destabilise the canon.

In the recent study of American literary history in particular, the impact of these new theoretical positions is very much in evidence. Indeed in the context, say, of women's writing, or of African-American or other kinds of ethnic literature, that impact is frequently manifested with a polemical urgency. Chapters on such writing in the comprehensive *Columbia History of American Literature* (1988) provide an excellent example. Equally to the point, however, is Tony Hilfer's well-considered conclusion in his more recent *American Fiction Since 1940* (1992) to the effect that one of the major cultural patterns in America in the period since 1940 has been 'the play between the margins and the unstable centre'.

What the 1990s are showing is that such developments in cultural theory, relevant as they are to any analysis of Scottish culture, are indeed providing a major stimulus to the specific field of Scottish-American studies. Crucial here is Robert Crawford's 1992 study, *Devolving English Literature*. Attempting to de-centre what has traditionally been called 'English literature', Crawford examines American, Australian, and of course Scottish writing, in a brilliant re-assessment of what is now to be seen as 'English' literature. For Crawford the peripheries are invading–have always been invading–the ground of the centre. In this context, his chapter entitled 'Anthologizing America', concerned mainly with Cooper, Emerson, and Whitman, is evidence of the fruitfulness of a lively scholarly focus on the Scottish dimension of the literary culture of nineteenth-century America.

Published two years earlier in 1990, Susan Manning's study *The Puritan-Provincial Vision* will perhaps come to be seen as representing a still more important watershed. Subtitled *Scottish and American Literature in the Nineteenth Century*, at last a book had been written involving a fully-developed comparative study of Scottish and American literature. Using the concepts of Puritanism and provincialism, not so much as indications of types of subject-matter as of 'a state of mind, a predisposition to view the world in certain ways', Dr Manning's book is a subtle exploration of the Scottish-American literary symbiosis. Even if it is true that the precise meaning of the 'provincial' vision is less securely anchored and defined than the 'Puritan' one, the book represents a major contribution to a scholarly area that has been calling out for attention at least since 1954 and the *William and Mary Quarterly's* Scottish-American issue. Taken together, what these books by Crawford and Manning indicate is that, in considering the formation and development of American literature, attention is at last beginning to be paid to the specifically Scottish dimension. What they herald, perhaps, is a process of assimilation into the mainstream of American cultural history of almost half a century's wide-ranging scholarly activity in the Scottish-American field. That conclusion, however, must remain tentative; past experience, as I indicate, makes it clear that such assimilation is more than a little difficult to achieve.

In the later chapters of this book I try to add some further detail to the map of the Scottish-American cultural relationship. I make no grander claim for these essays, some of which have appeared in earlier versions and over several decades. They do not emerge out of any single theoretical approach to the nature of cultural history–though notions of marginality and forms of postcolonialism are frequently relevant–nor do they advance a single thesis or a consistent critical argument. Inevitably originally conceived of as free-standing, self-explanatory pieces, to a substantial degree that is what they remain–which is why the same or similar points may recur in different essays. What they do all reflect is my own belief that the specifically Scottish element in America's cultural history is more various and enduring than has been generally recognised. Ranging from a consideration of the importance of eighteenth-century Scottish rhetoric in America to the Scottish inheritance of William Faulkner, what these essays do provide is an account of literary connections between Scotland and America which an understandable scholarly preoccupation with America's debt to the Scottish Enlightenment has to some degree obscured. The essays focusing on Scott, Carlyle, Hogg and Melville, Macaulay, and

Preface

Faulkner are all obviously relevant in this context. Those on Philadelphia and Edinburgh, on Scottish rhetoric, on Samuel Miller, on American visitors to Scotland, and on John Nichol's history of American literature, also to varying degrees involve aspects of the literary connection. The Henry George chapter, while primarily demonstrating how in the nineteenth century the Scottish-American link was such that influence could flow in either direction, also argues that the tone of George's writing is best understood in the context of one of the key figures in the nineteenth-century Scottish-American literary exchange: Thomas Carlyle.

I like to think, then, that the material in this book helps to give voice to a still too silent chapter in American literary historiography. The study of American literature has come a long way from the time when the original British edition of the *Cambridge History of American Literature* (1917–21) was happy to describe itself as 'supplementary' to the *Cambridge History of English Literature*. But there is still room for a Scottish supplement to the history of America's literary culture.

CHAPTER ONE

Introductory:
The Scottish Invention of the USA

In the Preface I allude to the development in recent cultural theory which emphasises the tension between what are called 'centres' and 'peripheries'. The idea is a simple one. Culture and its transmission inevitably involve questions of power. It is centres of power that set the standards, establish the norms of cultural values. The peripheries, whether defined geographically, or historically as colonies, or socially as groups outside the dominant mainstream, are positioned in relation to these established values. Thus American literature was long regarded as an off-shoot of English literature; so too was what used to be called Commonwealth literature, or indeed any literature written in English anywhere in the world. From the perspective of the centre, English literature is about commonality, the continuity of conventions and traditions; otherness and distinctiveness are elided; it is what is shared that is recognised, not what separates. The literature of the periphery, that is, is read in terms of the interests and concerns of the centre. To challenge such a reading, the power of the centre has to be recognised and resisted by whatever means; only then does American literature become the literature of America, and no longer a transatlantic branch of English literature.

Some readers may object that the example of American literature is inappropriate: who could possibly dispute the distinctiveness, the separate identity of American literature? But the historical evidence makes it clear that the American periphery had to fight long and hard for recognition. Centres of power are never anxious to cede their authority. While the case for the periphery against the centre may be a strong one in theory, in practice to bring about changes in perspective that are real and enduring may prove to be difficult indeed.

Introductory

The essay that follows charts the case of a periphery demanding recognition from a centre. On this occasion America is the centre—the American academy and American historiography in particular – and the Scottish Enlightenment – specifically its influence on the mind of Thomas Jefferson—is the periphery. Despite the essay's title, which employs the attention-seeking language of the periphery, the subject may seem a narrow one; but I believe it illuminates with some vividness recurring problems in the debate between centres and peripheries.

I

Scotland discovered America late in the seventeenth century. That was the time when the mercantile community in the west of Scotland, in Glasgow and the other towns and ports around the estuary of the River Clyde, began to appreciate the geographical advantages of their position in terms of trade with the English colonies down the eastern seaboard of North America. The result was that by the opening of the eighteenth century a lucrative contraband trade between Scotland and America already existed; and after the legitimising Treaty of Union of 1707, that Scottish-American trade went on rapidly expanding down to the outbreak of the American Revolution in 1776. For the material and economic development of the west of Scotland, nothing was of greater significance than the American trade; the wealth it created helped to make Glasgow, in Daniel Defoe's memorable phrase, 'the cleanest and beautifullest and best built' of British cities, London excepted.

Its importance for the Scottish economy, however, is not the true measure of the ultimate significance of Scotland's discovery of America. The Scottish discovery of America was no more than a prologue to the Scottish invention of the USA. What Scotland imported from the American colonies was tobacco; what she exported to the American colonies was ideas. The result was that in terms of the ideological invention of the USA, and its subsequent cultural definition, no external source of influence compared with that of eighteenth-century Scotland.

Scottish intellectual and cultural influence upon America developed rapidly through the eighteenth century, was of major importance in the Revolutionary period, continued to grow in the decades after the Revolution, and was still a significant presence well into the nineteenth century. Over the last forty years a handful of scholars, many of them American, have been busily exploring Scotland's contribution to the invention of the USA, but they have had little or no success in compelling general recognition of that contribution. The Scottish case has been put, but, as it were, to an empty courtroom. Thus American historians–and American historiography–have remained largely unaware of the Scottish dimension to the origins of their national identity and culture. This is why for most Americans today Scotland means, if anything, 'Brigadoon' and golf, rather than the thinkers of the Scottish Enlightenment.

Only once in these last forty years has the Scottish genie threatened to escape from its ignored and sidelined bottle. That was in 1978 when Garry Wills published *Inventing America*. Wills's study of Jefferson's drafting of the Declaration of Independence was received as a kind of historical bombshell by the American historical establishment. In the whole tradition of American historiography no notion seemed more widely accepted and more securely grounded than that of John Locke's crucial influence on Jefferson's drafting of the Declaration of Independence. Wills, however, dared to disagree. The tablets of stone had been misread. The Englishman Locke was only one, and not the most important, of the British thinkers who influenced Jefferson. Pride of place should rather go to the Scots. The primary influences on Jefferson, according to Wills, were Francis Hutcheson, Lord Kames, Thomas Reid, and other philosophers of the Scottish Enlightenment. Locke was out and the Scots were in. A Scottish cat had been set among the established English pigeons, and inevitably feathers flew. In recent times only *Time on the Cross*, perhaps, has created more of a scholarly uproar.

10

Introductory

Now let me make it clear at once that it is not my purpose here to discuss Wills's book or to debate its strengths and weaknesses. I am not an expert in American constitutional history, nor in political science or philosophy. But even if I were, that would not be the point. Within the wider context of Scottish-American eighteenth-century studies in general, it is the manner in which *Inventing America* was received that I find highly significant. Wills's book contends that through its formative influence on the intellectual life of Thomas Jefferson, the Scottish Enlightenment made an absolutely crucial contribution to the political invention of the USA. The response of American reviewers–many of them leading academic historians–to this idea was initially one of amazement and astonishment, subsequently modulating into incredulity and even outrage. Wills's insistence on the importance for Jefferson of the Scottish Enlightenment seems to have struck the original reviewers like some kind of extraordinary bolt from the blue. David Brion Davis in the *New York Times Book Review* described *Inventing America* as 'the best and most thorough analysis of the Declaration ever written' and insisted that its 'conclusions will startle' the reader. Edmund S. Morgan in the *New York Review of Books* opened his review by asking, 'Who would think it possible to redirect historical scholarship by explaining what Thomas Jefferson said in the Declaration of Independence?'– and went on to decide that the results of Wills's investigations 'are little short of astonishing'. In the *Saturday Review*, Arthur Schlesinger, Jr., wrote of Wills's 'discursive but often brilliant book' whose 'striking contention' is sustained 'persuasively'. Even subsequent, much less favourable, accounts share this sense of the radical originality of Wills's thesis. For example, in a hostile review essay in the *William and Mary Quarterly* to which I shall return, Ronald Hamowy described the book as "nothing short of revolutionary", and Garry J. Schmitt, in an equally hostile account in the *Political Science Review*, stated that 'Wills' argument is quite novel'. All the reviewers noted that if Garry Wills were right, then a great many other people were wrong. Carl Becker's classic study *The Declaration of Indepen-*

dence had appeared in 1922; and Becker's conclusions had been accepted and repeated unquestioningly by subsequent generations of American historians. As the reviewer of *Inventing America* in *Reviews in American History* put it, 'the idea that the Declaration was an eloquent paraphrase of Locke and that the signers assumed Locke had the last word on the subject appears to be founded chiefly on the endless reiteration of it by Carl Becker and other historians". But of course the point was that if Wills was right about the primacy of the Scottish Enlightenment's influence upon Jefferson, then Becker and all those other historians who had accepted Becker's views were wrong. Perhaps it is here that one begins to understand why it was so important for so many people that Wills be shown to be a less than reliable intellectual historian, and why the attempt to discredit him was sometimes conducted with more than normal critical animus.

II

The first line of attack on Garry Wills was more than a little disreputable. This was a straight-forwardly *ad hominem* argument that attempted to destroy Wills's credibility by insisting that *Inventing America* was a fundamentally unacademic and politically motivated book. As a British reviewer put it in the *Times Literary Supplement, Inventing America* 'seems in the US to have raised ideological as well as scholarly temperatures'. An egregious example of this form of personal attack is provided by Kenneth S. Lynn who wrote in *Commentary* as follows: 'Far from being a careful work of scholarship, *Inventing America* is the tendentious report of a highly political writer whose unannounced but nonetheless obvious aim is to supply the history of the Republic with as pink a dawn as possible'. Lynn is equally bitter–and he will be followed in this by other right-wing reviewers–about those who have lavishly praised the book. Such 'unearned acclaim' tells us only 'about modern-day intellectuals and their terrible need for radical myths'. Even allowing for a kind of post-Vietnam intellectual sourness, such views now seem somewhat hysterical. But they do crop up in other reviews, even if not always expressed with Lynn's out-spokenness. Judith Shklar, for example, opens her *New Republic* review by insisting that Garry Wills is 'an investigative reporter'–one of Wills's more obvious crimes was not to be an academic historian–'uncovering a conspiracy to distort the Declaration of Independence'. The book, she suggests attacks 'a self-serving liberal myth . . . devised by historians and politicians'. Whether Lynn's pinko writer should be so concerned about dislodging liberal myths is a moot point but Shklar goes on to accuse Wills of using evidence selectively 'to score points'–the assumption seems to be it is only investigative reporters who do this, not academic historians–in a tone 'that is generally sly and snide'. The outcome 'is terrible intellectual history', even if, oddly, 'a convincing picture of Jefferson does emerge'. Even Arthur Schlesinger, Jr., in the course of his generally favourable *Saturday Review* account, feels it is necessary to remind us that Wills is a gifted amateur rather than a professional historian who has moved from a position on the New Right to one on the New Left. When reviews began to appear in academic journals, the suggestion that *Inventing America* is a book with a hidden agenda did not entirely disappear. Thus Wills's suggestion that Jefferson may have admired the Scottish Enlightenment's emphasis on social cohesion and communal responsibility rather more than Lockean individualism – the point that alarmed and infuriated his right-wing critics – continues to be seen as merely a reflection of Wills's own political preferences. Paul Conkin in the *American Historical Review*, for example, tells us that '[D]espite the depth and subtlety of his insights, despite his often ungenerous but telling attacks on earlier historians, his final product is as self-revealing and as sharply colored by present concerns as any I have ever read'. And even James M. Cox in the *Sewanee Review* believes that Wills's contemporary experience as a political commentator weakens his book: the entire first section, he writes, 'displays too much of the shrewd political journalist who knows the ins and outs of contemporary Washington'.

The most blatantly revealing of the *ad hominem* attacks on

Wills, however, occurs in the concluding section of Garry Schmitt's account in the *Political Science Review*. 'Under the guise of scholarship', writes Schmitt, 'Wills attempts to interpret the American founding in terms more consonant with his own political views . . .' 'Instead of real scholarship', he continues, 'we are taken on a sentimental journey'. The problem with this– apart from the fact that the opening of his piece suggests that Schmitt is confused over whether the journey leads to Edinburgh or Glasgow–is the extraordinary naiveté with which he replaces what he sees as Wills's political prejudices with his own. The proverbial pot calling the kettle black, Schmitt is simply deter- mined to go on interpreting America's founding in accordance with his own political views.

III

In terms of my present purpose, the attempt to discredit *Invent- ing America* as the work of a politically-motivated writer is not important in itself. But of course the political reading does become important when it is seen as part of a wider strategy to undermine the seriousness of Wills's challenge to an estab- lished American historiographical orthodoxy. The point is not that there is no basis at all for a political reading of *Inventing America*. Only that there is nothing unique about *Inventing America* in this regard: is there anyone today who believes that *any* work of historical scholarship is entirely neutral or objec- tive? It may even be the case that Garry Wills wanted his readers to recognise the political implications of his reinterpretation of Jefferson and the Declaration of Independence. But this should in no way be allowed to detract from the seriousness of his arguments. And the same point holds for the more specific errors and weaknesses in Wills's book.

The most comprehensive attack on *Inventing America* was launched by Ronald Hamowy in his 'Critique' in the *William and Mary Quarterly*. Hamowy is able to damage Wills's case by pointing to flaws in the detail of some of his arguments, challenging unsupported claims and exaggerations, and expos- ing his less than accurate grasp even of the chronology of the

Scottish Enlightenment. Yet Hamowy's article, powerful as it is, is the work of an advocate of the Lockean 'free-market' interpretation of the Declaration of Independence, and is not without its own errors and significant weaknesses. His assertion that Thomas Reid 'was to have no influence across the Atlantic until his philosophical system was introduced to America by John Witherspoon of Princeton at the end of the century' is chronologically askew by at least three decades. John Witherspoon began his teaching career at Princeton in 1768. His statement that David Hume was an 'internationally respected philosopher' by the 1750s is highly dubious: if Hume was internationally respected as anything it was as an historian. And when Hamowy describes Wills's characterisation of Jefferson's years of study under Small as 'the most intellectually . . . influential years of his life' as 'a piece of hyperbole for which no evidence exists' he is surely being wholly disingenuous. Wills's comment, based as it is on Jefferson's own tribute in the *Autobiography* to William Small, his Scottish teacher at the College of William and Mary, is a great deal less hyperbolic than Hamowy's rejection of it, springing as the latter so obviously does from a need to discount one of the most obvious indicators that Jefferson had indeed been exposed, at a formative stage in his intellectual life, to the influence of the Scottish Enlightenment.

Admittedly, the points I have made are questions of detail only. The more basic weakness running through Hamowy's critique is encapsulated in his opening statement that Wills's thesis is 'nothing short of revolutionary'. In other words, Hamowy regards Wills's central notion of Jefferson's debt to the Scottish Enlightenment as something quite new and extraordinary. The fact that in the end he thinks he has proved Wills totally wrong does not alter this. Like many other reviewers, Hamowy simply finds Wills's reassessment of Jefferson's intellectual history much too radical to be true. Among those who take this position, few go so far as George W. Carey who, in a lengthy attack on both *Inventing America* and Wills's subsequent work *Explaining America* in the right-wing *Modern Age*, seeks to undermine Wills's thesis by appearing to cast doubt on the very existence of the Scottish Enlightenment. 'Wills', writes Carey, 'does dwell on an "enlightenment" which, so to speak, burst forth from, of all places, Scotland and influenced key leaders of our founding period'. That phrase, 'of all places', whether intended to be a witticism or not, gives the game away: clearly we are meant to agree that it is simply a joke to suggest that anywhere as obscure as Scotland could possibly have had any influence on America's great men.

But Carey, as I have indicated, is not alone among reviewers in sharing Hamowy's sense of the unacceptable novelty of Wills's account of Jefferson's–and by implication America's– intellectual history. The damaging consequences of this assumption are most clearly revealed in Schmitt's attack on Wills in the *Political Science Review* to which reference has already been made. Schmitt cites Hamowy's article approvingly, but his own account is fatally weakened by his very uncertain grasp of the evidence of Scottish intellectual influence on eighteenth-century America generally. Thus Schmitt, like Hamowy, finds it necessary to discount the full significance of Jefferson's tribute to William Small in the *Autobiography*. And he believes that the curriculum Witherspoon introduced at Princeton represented an attack on the Scottish Enlightenment. 'According to Wills', he writes, 'Witherspoon created a curriculum whose core element was the Scottish Enlightenment. The problem with this bit of evidence is that while it is true that Witherspoon was Scottish and that he had been educated at Edinburgh, his reputation in America was actually based on an attack he had made on the Scottish Enlightenment, especially as expressed by Hume'. It is a relief to know that Schmitt realised that Witherspoon was Scottish, but such extraordinary intellectual naiveté as this hardly leaves him in a position to complain about Garry Wills's scholarship. But what is really telling about such comments is the basic unfamiliarity with the material under review that they reveal. And this in turn is the crux of the matter. It is quite simply the fundamental lack of knowledge on the part of so many reviewers that made *Inventing America* appear to be so novel and revolutionary a work. In fact it is nothing of the kind.

Introductory

IV

Long before the appearance of *Inventing America*, a number of scholars had been arguing that Colonial and Revolutionary America had been highly susceptible to the influence of the Scottish Enlightenment. In 1989, introducing an article on the usefulness of the Scottish Enlightenment to the framers of the American constitution, Daniel Walker Howe makes exactly this point: 'A large body of research conducted over a period of many years has demonstrated the enormous contribution that Scottish thought made to early America'. Then, however, Howe goes on to confirm my own analysis that, pre-Wills, no one inside or outside the academic community appears to have been paying very much attention. 'Curiously enough', he writes, 'the evidence for this important influence accumulated gradually without attracting widespread attention until 1978, when Garry Wills published a book on the Declaration of Independence orienting that document within the context of Scottish thinking'. Howe agrees that *Inventing America* made a dramatic difference: 'All of a sudden, eighteenth-century Scottish moral philosophy was being discussed in the *New York Times*, the *New York Review of Books*, and all the major relevant professional journals'. Wills's book, however flawed, 'aroused a storm of controversy' and 'proved to be a landmark of a certain kind: it focused attention on the relevance of the Scottish Enlightenment to the American Revolutionary generation'. In fact one at least of the original reviewers of *Inventing America* had made the crucial point, repeated by Howe, that there was an existing body of scholarship on America's debt to Scottish thought well predating Wills. This was Gilman M. Ostrander writing in *Reviews in American History*.

Ostrander's review is broadly sympathetic. He agrees with Wills that Jefferson's intellectual world was deeply influenced by the philosophers of the Scottish Enlightenment, but argues that Hutcheson and Reid were less important for Jefferson than others among the Scottish thinkers: in particular Lord Kames and William Duncan, one of William Small's teachers at Aberdeen. Despite this disagreement, Ostrander suggests that Wills

17

has 'done much ... to establish Jefferson's and America's intellectual debt to the Scottish philosophers'. But Ostrander is aware that Wills is a long way from being the first scholar to make this connection. He cites Herbert Schneider's *History of American Philosophy*, published in 1946, which had recognized the importance of Scottish thought for the American Enlightenment. Other scholars had read and digested Schneider's work, but—and this is the crucial point—'Wills is apparently able to startle the profession by saying the very same thing more than thirty years later'. Ostrander is absolutely correct. Easily the most striking feature of the reception of *Inventing America* is the surprise with which its central thesis was greeted. The reviews in general are dotted with phrases such as 'uniquely fresh', 'refreshing perspectives', 'fresh insights', 'new insights', 'fresh perspectives', J. H. Plumb, doyen of British eighteenth-century historians, in the course of his review in the *Guardian Weekly*, described Wills's book as subtle, brilliant, absorbing, luminous, exciting—and original.

Now it has to be admitted that Garry Wills himself is partly responsible for the level of surprise in reader responses to his book. *Inventing America* makes only the briefest and most selective allusions to the work of earlier scholars in the field of Scottish-American intellectual and cultural history. Even more damagingly, the Scottish theme of *Inventing America* remains oddly decontextualised. As a result, the book has something of the quality of a conjuring trick: the Scottish thought which influenced Jefferson is produced rather like a rabbit out of a hat. Despite a few paragraphs about the distinction of the Scottish universities in the eighteenth century, about the presence of Scottish teachers in America, and about Scottish influence on the early American colleges, Wills fails utterly to indicate the wider context of Scottish intellectual and cultural contributions to colonial and Revolutionary America. Had he provided that context, Wills might well have been able to argue that a failure on Jefferson's part to register Scottish ideas would have been much more surprising than his actual assimilation of them. Yet when Wills was writing, much of the groundwork to establish this position had already been done. Had he capitalised upon it, the central thesis of *Inventing America* would have been much more soundly based, would have appeared a great deal less surprising, and therefore would have been more generally persuasive.

Two important publications provide useful parameters for the continuing scholarly investigation of the wider cultural ties between Scotland and America in the eighteenth century. These are the special issue of the *William and Mary Quarterly* in April 1954, devoted to the topic of Scotland and America, and the 1990 Eighteenth Century Scottish Studies Society publication entitled *Scotland and America in the Age of Enlightenment*. In the years between these two publications a number of scholars published works which in whole or in part throw light on almost every aspect of the Scottish-American Enlightenment and its ramifications. Examples are: George S. Pryde's *The Scottish Universities and the Colleges of Colonial America* (1957), Terence Martin's *The Instructed Vision: Scottish Common Sense Philosophy and the Origins of American Fiction* (1961), Douglas Sloan's *The Scottish Enlightenment and the American College Ideal* (1971), Donald H. Meyer's *The Instructed Conscience: The Shaping of the American National Ethic* (1971), my own *Scotland and America: A Study of Cultural Relations 1750–1835* (1975), Henry F. May's *The Enlightenment in America* (1976), and William R. Brock's *Scotus Americanus: A Survey of the Sources for Links between Scotland and America in the Eighteenth Century* (1982). Surveying the entire field of Scottish-American studies since the appearance of the *William and Mary Quarterly* special issue, the editors of *Scotland and America in the Age of Enlightenment* note 'a host of studies' on how the Scottish *literati* viewed the American question in the period of the Revolution, and on how Scottish thought may have influenced America's founding fathers; and they go on to quote James T. Kloppenberg saying, 'In the 1970s Henry F. May and Morton White led a squadron of intellectual historians who emphasised the importance of Scottish common sense philosophy in the complex ideas that constituted America's version of the Enlightenment'.

From Goosecreek to Gandercleugh

What the popular response to Wills's *Inventing America* vividly demonstrates, however, is the failure of all this work to make its presence felt in the mainstream of American historiography, not to mention in any more general American consciousness. To suggest in 1978 that Thomas Jefferson was deeply influenced by the Scottish Enlightenment was still regarded as a quite revolutionary idea. One may come to no other conclusion than that the work done in the field of Scottish-American studies has been unable to break through into the received historical understanding of the nature of eighteenth-century America. I propose to finish by offering some tentative explanations for this failure.

V

From the widest of perspectives, the lack of recognition of the Scottish contribution to eighteenth-century America is no more than a particular example of a general American reluctance to acknowledge fully the contributions of other national groups to America's development. Immigration studies generally, for example, remain in a sense ghettoised within their individual nationalisms: a wide range of countries are acknowledged to have made a contribution to America, but theirs is no more than a contribution from the periphery to the centre which is the truly American. American historiography, that is, remains thirled to the notion of the uniqueness of America and the American experience. American history, even American intellectual history, is essentially American. Thus Richard Rabinowitz, in his review of *Inventing America* in *The Nation*, while praising Wills's brilliant account of Jefferson's accommodation of European Enlightenment ideas, complains that 'he has virtually nothing which connects our third President to his own country'.

Within this nativist context, the Scots of course are at a double disadvantage. As a subdivision of the British–which effectively means the English as far as the outside world is concerned–the Scots lack the national distinctiveness of other groups such as the Irish, or even the so-called 'Scotch-Irish'. Hence Americans are often not especially alert to the crucial differences between, say, English and Scottish intellectual and educational, religious, and cultural traditions. If, on the other hand, the distinctiveness of the Scots is acknowledged, then they become just another peripheral national group occasionally impinging upon native America's historical development: in Jefferson's notorious phrase in the draft of the Declaration of Independence, the Scots in the British army in America become 'Scotch and foreign mercenaries' rather than 'soldiers of our common blood'.

The recognition and definition of Scottishness is a problem for Scottish culture itself. There are other more specific factors which may have worked against a wider American acknowledgement of the Scottish contribution to eighteenth-century America. Scholars have tended to focus either on the colonial period, or the Revolutionary period, or the early nineteenth century. A sense of the continuity of Scottish influence has not always been present, and this has perhaps helped to weaken the significance of the separate periods or areas of influence that have been studied. Scotland's contribution to America concerns a great deal more than the influence of Francis Hutcheson on Jefferson. Indeed it is about a great deal more than the philosophy of the Scottish Enlightenment. Perhaps it is this failure to bring out the range and diversity of Scottish intellectual and cultural influence, and its continuity in terms of chronology, that best explains why the Scottish invention of America has not been more widely recognised.

The area of Scottish cultural activity which the existing tradition of Scottish-American scholarship, however disregarded, has paid least attention to is that of imaginative literature. Jefferson's enthusiasm for James Macpherson's *Ossian* is well-documented and widely known. Andrew Jackson's equal enthusiasm for Jane Porter's novel *The Scottish Chiefs* has never been remarked upon. But the admiration of the two presidents for these Scottish texts is a wholly accurate reflection of a general American enthusiasm for Scottish literary romanticism that lasted from the later decades of the eighteenth century well into the nineteenth. Allan Ramsay's pastoral comedy *The Gentle Shepherd*, John Home's sentimental tragedy *Douglas*, the Ossianic poems of Macpherson, the poetry of Burns and of course, overwhelmingly, the Waverley Novels of Sir Walter Scott, all of these major works of Scottish romantic literature, as well as more minor ones like *The Scottish Chiefs*, enjoyed a tremendous vogue in America. Apart from the case of Scott, scholars have failed to recognise either this vogue or its true significance. What Scottish literary romanticism is ultimately about is the invention of Scotland. If Scotland had any identity for the outside world at the beginning of the eighteenth century it was as a country of poverty, backwardness, and religious fanaticism. By the end of the century, however, a dramatic change had occurred; the achievements of the Scottish Enlightenment had transformed Scotland into a land of learning, recognized everywhere as a model of national Progress and Improvement. Despite this success, however, it was not the Scottish Enlightenment that created Scotland's national identity. For better or for worse, it was the popular triumph of Scottish literary romanticism throughout the western world that reinvented Scotland as an archetypal land of romance. It was the mythopoetic identity of Scotland, created in the eighteenth and consolidated in the nineteenth century by her poets and novelists and dramatists, that captured the imagination of the world.

For the new republic of the United States the Scottish message was clear–and widely understood at the time. What a new nation needed to invent itself, to create a national identity and gain cultural recognition and international respect, was above all a distinctively national literature. In a remarkably short space of time Scott and the others had produced for Scotland just such a literature; thus theirs was the model American writers should emulate. There had been a time–and this is a topic intellectual historians need to pay more attention to–when Scottish books were less popular in America. At the height of the Revolution, American hostility towards the Scots as a national group–because the Scots in America were universally regarded as Tories and Loyalists–was so great that the Library Society of Charleston proposed that Adam Ferguson's *Essay on Civil Society* by 'one of the kingdom of Scotland' should be condemned to be burnt. By the time, however, that James Fenimore Cooper, 'the American Scott', began writing in the 1820s, Scottish books were very much back in demand. Scotland's share in the invention of the USA had occurred and was occurring in a variety of modes, political, intellectual, and literary, that would surprise Garry Wills–not to mention his reviewers.

Reviews cited or consulted

A. J. R. Rev. of *Inventing America*. *Review of Metaphysics* **32** (March 1979): 573–74.

Ashby, John H. Rev. of *Inventing America*. *Library Journal* **103** (June 15 1978): 1275.

Brasington, George F. Rev. of *Inventing America*. *Journal of Politics* **42** (August 1989): 905.

Carey, George W. "On Inventing and Explaining America". *Modern Age* **26** (Spring 1982): 122–35.

Conkin, Paul. Rev. of *Inventing America*. *American Historical Review* **84.2** (1979): 530–31.

Cox, James M. "Inventing America", *Sewanee Review* **87.3** (1979):475–80.

Cunliffe, Marcus. "The Enlightenment Type". *Times Literary Supplement* 13 Oct. 1978: 1161.

Davis, David Brion. "Jefferson's Monument". *New York Times Book Review* 2 July 1978: 1, 17.

Detweiler, Philip D. Rev. of *Inventing America*. *Journal of Southern History* **45** (Feb. 1979): 111–12.

Hamowy, Ronald. "Jefferson and the Scottish Enlightenment. A Critique of Garry Wills' *Inventing America*: Jefferson's Declaration of Independence". *William and Mary Quarterly* 3rd ser., **36.4** (1979): 503–23.

Howe, John. Rev. of *Inventing America*. *William and Mary Quarterly* 3rd ser., **36.3** (1979): 462–64.

Rev. of *Inventing America*. *Choice* **15** (November 1978): 1277.

Rev. of *Inventing America*. *New York Times Book Review* 24 July 1979: 41.

Rev. of *Inventing America*. *Publishers Weekly* 24 Apr. 1978: 77.

Lynn, Kenneth S. "Falsifying Jefferson". *Commentary* **66.4** (1978): 66–71.

Morgan, Edmund S. "The Heart of Jefferson". *New York Review of Books* 17 Aug. 1978: 38–40.

Morrison, Malcolm F. Rev. of *Inventing America*. *English Historical Review* **97** (October 1982): 853–56.

Morrow, Lance. "Lost Language", *Times* 31 July 1978: 78–[79].

Ostrander, Gilman. "New Lost Worlds of Thomas Jefferson". *Reviews in American History* June 1979: 183–88.

J. R. Pole. Rev. of *Inventing America* (and Morton White, *The Philosophy of the American Revolution*). *Journal of American Studies*, **13** (August

1979): 271–74.

Plumb, J. H. "Insight into the Declaration". *Guardian Weekly* July 9 1979: 18

Rabinowitz, Richard. "At Jefferson's Feast". *Nation* 31 March 1979: 342–44.

Schlesinger, Arthur. Jr. "After the Revolution". *Saturday Review* Aug. 1978: 42–43.

Schmitt, Garry J. Rev. of *Inventing America. Political Science Review* **12** (Fall 1982): 99.

Shklar, Judith N. Rev. of *Inventing America. New Republic* Aug. 26–Sept. 2 1978: 32–34.

Simmons, R. C. "Sociability Before Reason". *Times Literary Supplement* 16 Jan. 1981: 55.

Welter, Rush. Rev. of *Inventing America. Journal of American History* **66**.2 (1979): 380–81.

The article by Daniel Walker Howe, to which reference is made on p. 17, is 'Why the Scottish Enlightenment was useful to the Framers of the American Constitution' in *Comparative Studies in Society and History, 31.3 (1989),* 572–87. The passages quoted are all from the article's opening paragraph.

CHAPTER TWO

Philadelphia, Edinburgh, and the Scottish Enlightenment

The eighteenth-century Enlightenment developed and flourished above all in the cities of Europe; Enlightenment culture was pre-eminently urban culture. Significantly, however, the Enlightenment was in no way the exclusive prerogative of capital cities such as Paris or London; rather the social and intellectual attitudes and institutions characteristic of the Enlightenment may be seen emerging quite as readily in provincial cities such as Naples, Bordeaux, Dublin, Edinburgh or Philadelphia. But the last two, the subject of this chapter, had much more in common than a shared investment in Enlightenment values. As part of an Atlantic community, an English-speaking world whose culture was inevitably dominated by metropolitan London, they were both in this context, peripheral cities. That may well be an important factor in helping to explain why, like Scotland and America more generally perhaps, they were often prepared to listen to each other.

In an essay originally published in 1977, Carl Bridenbaugh asked some searching questions about the export of the European Enlightenment to eighteenth-century Philadelphia: 'By whom were the Enlightened ideas and programs chosen, and how did they make the selection? What auxiliary ideas and programs were sent off at the same time? How and when did they cross the ocean'. And was the Enlightenment 'being exported in any organized or institutional forms, or was the transit to America merely a series of random occurrences or the chance work of a few individuals'?[1] Bridenbaugh did not attempt to

25

answer all these questions – and it would be easy enough to add others to his list–but merely by asking them he indicated the kinds of problems facing anyone interested in how cultural and intellectual values are transmitted from one society to another. The difficulty is not just in finding answers to the questions raised; it is in agreeing on what might be seen as the 'evidence' upon which an answer could be based. Facts and statistics are hard to come by in this field; and even those that seem to be available tend to lose credibility the closer they are examined. In the eighteenth century large numbers of Europeans, including many from Scotland, left their own countries and settled in America, not a few of them in Philadelphia. Every one of them was potentially a source of cultural influence, but immigration statistics hardly amount to proof that in fact they were. Even books, including the Scottish books that were readily available to readers in eighteenth-century Philadelphia, are less reliable evidence than they seem. Books certainly contain ideas, but for those ideas to exert any influence the books have not only to be available but also to be read, and read in a receptive frame of mind. The 'facts' of cultural history once again seem to raise more questions than they answer.

To write on the cultural history of Philadelphia in the eighteenth century is thus no simple matter. That the city was a primary focus of American intellectual life in the colonial and Revolutionary periods is not disputed: the evidence is there in Philadelphia's institutions designed to encourage intellectual enquiry and development, in the achievements and publications of its writers and thinkers and in the contributions of its leading citizens to every aspect of America's developing cultural life. Philadelphia was a city receptive to ideas, a place where the life of the mind was seen to be important. Given its intellectual pre-eminence, Philadelphia could not be other than the major transatlantic recipient of the exciting configuration of ideas that constituted the eighteenth-century Enlightenment in Europe. In so far as Scotland in the eighteenth century participated in, and in no minor way contributed to, that European Enlightenment, it would not be unreasonable to suggest that Philadelphia was influenced by the Scottish Enlightenment. I am convinced it was. But the evidence, however substantial it may appear, has to be seen for what it is: an interpretation of the past rather than an assembly of incontrovertible fact.

The difficulty in identifying a specifically Scottish contribution to the Philadelphia Enlightenment is demonstrated by the fact that in 1977 Bridenbaugh recognised no need to allude to any such contribution. In attempting to provide an answer to the important questions he had begun by raising, he drew attention solely to the dissenting, anti-Establishment tradition within the Enlightenment in Great Britain, arguing that this tradition provided a distinctive coloration to the forms of Enlightenment exported to Philadelphia. Seen in this perspective, the Scots, rather than making any distinctive contribution of their own, are simply to be assimilated within this dissenting tradition: as Presbyterians, they are assumed to share the radical Protestantism of the English dissenters and so, like them, to have contributed to 'the industrial, educational, and humanitarian, and scientific activities' of the Enlightenment in Great Britain.[2] The problems with such an account are obvious enough. The Church of Scotland was the established church in Scotland; the Scots, unlike the dissenters, were not debarred from their own country's universities or from public office. Nor was the Scottish Enlightenment wholly the preserve of Presbyterians: from the end of the seventeenth until well into the eighteenth century, the Scottish Episcopal Church was a significant force in the country's intellectual and cultural life.[3]

Yet Bridenbaugh's analysis does help to explain why the Enlightenment ideas exported to Philadelphia might well have had a distinctive Scottish coloration. He notes the dominant place occupied by dissenters in the English merchant class trading with America. Hence dissenters 'owned and freighted most of the ships that transported people, books, news, letters, ideas, and sentiments to colonial seaports, and especially, after 1720, to Philadelphia; they also controlled most of the news coming in from their counterparts in the New World'.[4] Such a reminder will almost inevitably trigger a sympathetic response from those of us who have long seen in the Scottish-American trading link a highly significant circumstance for the transmission of Scottish ideas across the Atlantic. Analysing Glasgow's rise to dominance in the tobacco trade with the American colonies, Jacob Price, as long ago as 1954, assessed the significance of this Scots-American connection in terms very similar to those of Bridenbaugh. Of the Scottish mercantile community in the Chesapeake Bay area, he wrote: 'they were there, and twice a year their ships came to them from the Clyde–ships as numerous as those from all Britain besides. For many a Virginian, this must have meant that mail, news, reading matter, ideas, religion, politics came to him via Glasgow'.[5] It is true that Scottish merchants never dominated Philadelphia as they did the tobacco-exporting ports to the south, but Philadelphia was nonetheless part of the close-knit network of Scottish trading activities stretching from New York down the entire seaboard of the mid-Atlantic colonies. Hence Bridenbaugh's analysis, just as much as Price's, indicates that Philadelphia was almost ideally placed to be a potential recipient of those enlightened ideas that formed a central part of Scotland's cultural exports from the mid-eighteenth century onwards. The realisation of that potentiality is well illustrated by a single image: the well known portrait of Benjamin Rush by Charles Willson Peale. In the background of this painting appear a number of scholarly volumes, including the *Essay on Truth* by James Beattie. That Rush, one of Philadelphia's leading intellectuals, should choose to associate himself with a work in which an Aberdeen moral philosopher tried to combat the dangerous scepticism of David Hume clearly demonstrates how the concerns of the Scottish Enlightenment came to inform Philadelphia's intellectual life in the late eighteenth century.

II

But how had it happened? Why should Philadelphia have taken an interest in the concerns of the Enlightenment and of the Scottish Enlightenment in particular? If, as I have suggested, Scottish trading links with the eastern seaboard of America provided a viable means for the transmission of Scottish ideas to Philadelphia, why should Philadelphians have been willing to absorb such ideas? What factors might have inclined Philadelphia to pay attention to Enlightenment ideas originating in Scotland?

Of first importance are the cultural parallels between Philadelphia and a Scottish city such as Edinburgh. Both Philadelphia and Edinburgh in the eighteenth century were provincial cities, and it has been frequently noted that the European Enlightenment flourished in provincial cities such as Dublin, Bordeaux and Naples almost as readily as in metropolitan capitals. Thus, it is no cause for surprise that at least some of the attitudes and values associated with the Enlightenment began to emerge within the societies of Edinburgh and Philadelphia at roughly the same time. But in fact Philadelphia had rather more in common with Edinburgh than with the other provincial cities just mentioned, and it is this common ground that may help most in explaining the American city's responsiveness to the Scottish Enlightenment. The nature of these cities' shared experience may be identified and explained in two ways: one sociopolitical, the other sociopsychological. The sociopolitical explanation draws in particular on the work of Nicholas Phillipson, who has argued that the Enlightenment provided the social and intellectual élites of provincial societies with an ideology affording them identity and coherence of purpose.[6] The parallel sociopsychological explanation simply takes over the older Clive and Bailyn thesis on the similarities between the provincial cultures of Scotland and America and applies it to the particular circumstances of Philadelphia and Edinburgh.[7]

Obviously, for most of the eighteenth century Philadelphia's cultural situation was more like Edinburgh's than that of metropolitan London. Neither provincial city was a centre of ultimate political authority, yet both had developed institutions and assemblies that wielded very considerable power, were locally run and usually enjoyed considerable freedom from outside interference. Both cities could and did support an important and powerful ruling élite that had a more or less free hand in determining the direction of their growth and development. In Philadelphia's case one suspects that this sense of being in a position to shape and guide, even to create, the city's destiny must often have seemed particularly strong and clear. In this situation what the Enlightenment provided was a direction in which to go, a road to follow. The sign-posts were marked with words such as 'progress', 'improvement' or 'politeness', and these were accepted as the desirable destinations. Both Edinburgh and Philadelphia aimed to create a society that was modern and progressive, at least in the eyes of significant sections of their controlling élites, rather than provincial and backward—a society that might in the end command the approval, rather than the disdain, of the metropolitan capital that remained the standard of a mature and civilised culture. The very smallness and compactness of the intellectual society in cities such as Philadelphia and Edinburgh made such a coherence of purpose and sharing of aims easier to achieve. Throughout the eighteenth century Edinburgh's population was substantially larger than that of Philadelphia: in the 1790s, for example, Edinburgh's total was well over eighty thousand while Philadelphia's was just over forty thousand. Nonetheless, neither city was large enough to sustain a series of separate intellectual groups; the pattern in both was rather for the same range of individuals to be involved in a variety of intellectual and cultural activities.

The best evidence of this latter similarity is the prevalence in both cities of clubs or societies, and other corporate and civic institutions, which became major agencies for advancing the kinds of progressive change that signal the spread of Enlightenment values. As is well known, Philadelphia's first public effort in this area proved abortive: Franklin's American Philosophic Society of 1744 survived for only a year or two. But even this Philadelphian failure suggests an Edinburgh parallel: the *Edinburgh Review* of 1755 proved equally short-lived, despite the fact that its contributors included such distinguished literati as Hugh Blair, Adam Smith and William Robertson. The year 1766 saw the rebirth of Franklin's Philosophic Society as the

American Society for Promoting and Propagating Useful Knowledge, Held in Philadelphia. Whereas Franklin's original society had concentrated mainly on scientific observation, the new society emphasised invention and agricultural improvement. The focus of a rival organisation founded three years later–the American Philosophical Society–was the study of pure science and astronomy. But it was not long before the two organisations, in a move characteristic of the impulse towards unity in the city's intellectual life, amalgamated under the title American Philosophical Society Held at Philadelphia for Promoting Useful Knowledge. Thus was created the single most important organisation for the development of science in America both before and after the Revolution.[8]

Of course, by the end of the 1760s some of Edinburgh's most famous societies had been in existence for several decades: the Rankenian Club had been formed as early as 1716, and the Philosophical Society of Edinburgh (forerunner of the Royal Society of Edinburgh of 1783) had first met in 1737. The Select Society, however, bringing together nearly all of Edinburgh's literati, was not founded until 1754. And in the 1760s the impulse to create clubs and societies as a focus of intellectual debate and enquiry was as strong as ever: the Poker Club, the Tuesday Club and the vitally important Speculative Society were all founded in that decade. Of special significance is the emphasis placed by all these organisations, both in Edinburgh and Philadelphia, on 'useful knowledge'. The Scottish Enlightenment had always been characterised by a strong emphasis on the practical, social benefits of progress and improvement: the Scottish clubs and societies mentioned had their social, convivial side, but rather than the pursuit of knowledge for its own sake they frequently had quite specific, practical aims. Self-improvement and civic advancement seemed to go hand-in-hand. No emphasis could have been more to the taste of the Philadelphia improvers. From the earliest days of the Junto, in 1727, Franklin had been emphatic on this point: the Junto was 'a Club for Mutual Improvement'. The parallel with Allan Ramsay's Easy Club, founded in Edinburgh in 1712 'in order that by a Mutual

Improvement in Conversation' its members might 'become more adapted for fellowship with the politer part of mankind and learn also from one anothers happy observations', is almost exact. And Franklin's later comment–'what signifies Philosophy that does not apply to some Use?'–could well stand as a motto for the advancement of the intellectual life of both Edinburgh and Philadelphia.[9] That Edinburgh's Society for Improvement in the Knowledge of Agriculture should thus be matched by Philadelphia's Society for the Promotion of Agriculture hardly comes as a surprise.

The social structures of the intellectual life of Philadelphia and Edinburgh clearly had much in common; but how are we to understand the similar emphasis on the need for knowledge to be useful? Bridenbaugh probably provides the correct answer. Of the citizens of Philadelphia he says: 'Progress for them was not an idea, not a dream; it was a visible reality'.[10] The remark could apply equally to the citizens of Edinburgh. At the end of the eighteenth century Edinburgh, just as much as Philadelphia, was a dramatically new city. At the beginning of the century, when Philadelphia was just beginning to grow, Edinburgh was the capital of one of the poorest, most backward and least familiar countries in Europe; by the end of the eighteenth century Edinburgh and Philadelphia had both become capitals of thriving, progressive countries, increasingly more than holding their own as contributors to Western culture. Enlightenment values had been given tangible social and civic embodiment in the development of both cities.

III

These parallels between Edinburgh and Philadelphia go some way towards explaining why both cities should have shared an active interest in Enlightenment values. The economic tie between Scotland and the American colonies provided an accessible route whereby Scottish ideas could be exported across the Atlantic. But there remains the question of receptiveness: why should Philadelphians have been open to influence from the Scottish dimension of the European Enlightenment? The Clive and Bailyn thesis provides part of an answer to this question. By the middle of the eighteenth century, at a time when the intellectual life of Philadelphia was still in the process of formation, Edinburgh was already making some of its most significant contributions to the wider world of the Enlightenment. There is no question as to which city was more likely to learn from the other. But by allowing us to see that Edinburgh and Philadelphia may have shared a complex sense of intellectual and cultural inferiority (a consequence of their provincial status in relation to standard-setting London), Clive and Bailyn help us to understand why some Philadelphians at least, like Americans elsewhere, might have been particularly interested in Scottish responses and solutions to shared problems.

It is these 'shared problems' that need to be emphasised. There is no evidence that Philadelphians regarded Scottish culture itself as in any sense 'inferior'; on the contrary, respect and admiration for Scotland's cultural achievements clearly continued to grow in Philadelphia throughout the eighteenth century. In other words, it is not primarily an awareness of its provincial status that explains Philadelphian responsiveness to the Scottish Enlightenment; a shared sense of 'cultural provincialism' could only have been a single dimension of that wider pattern of similarities between Philadelphia and Edinburgh, already alluded to, which ensured a Philadelphian interest in Scottish cultural progress.

There remains the question of evidence in support of the theoretical Philadelphian response to the Scottish Enlightenment. In my view the area of intellectual activity most relevant is education, and the decisive period the 1740s. Specific Scottish contributions to education in Philadelphia were the result of two factors: influential Scottish educators present in the city on the one hand, Philadelphians travelling to Scotland for educational purposes on the other. In the first category the key figure is William Smith, Episcopal clergyman and graduate of King's College, Aberdeen. But Smith's appointments, first as head of the Philadelphia Academy in 1753 and, two years later, as provost of the College of Philadelphia, into which the academy developed, are themselves to be seen as the consequence of increasing Scottish influence in Philadelphia around the mid-century. By the 1740s the old Quaker hegemony over most aspects of Philadelphia's political and social life had broken down and, as Henry F. May argues, the powerful Presbyterian element in the city was simultaneously split over the issues created by the Great Awakening. In the consequent power vacuum it was, in May's view, the largely upper-class Episcopalian party that benefited the most: Smith's appointment is thus evidence of their rise to a position of dominance in Philadelphia life and culture.[11]

But Smith's Scottishness may have mattered as much as his Episcopalianism. The 1740s had seen a consolidation of Scottish influence in Philadelphia. In 1747 the St Andrews Society of Philadelphia had been founded, thus providing all the Scots in the city with a meeting-ground that was almost certainly used for purposes extending beyond the purely charitable aims of the organisation. The society's original membership of twenty-five included Thomas Graeme, a physician from Perthshire who was the St Andrews Society's first president and also a founding member of the American Philosophical Society; James Hamilton, lieutenant governor of Pennsylvania, the society's second president and subsequently also president of the American Philosophical Society; Alexander Alexander, who later taught at the College of Philadelphia; Alexander Barclay, comptroller of customs in Philadelphia; and Franklin's business partner David Hall. It is true that the Scots were caught up in the debate over the Great Awakening and its consequences, but the resurgence of evangelical Scottish Presbyterianism should not be allowed to obscure the significance of the Scottish Episcopalian tradition that a man like Smith represents. Thus, the coincidence of the founding of the St Andrews Society and the rise to dominance of the Anglican faction suggests a potential increase in Scottish influence on Philadelphia's intellectual and cultural life.

What is the nature of that influence as defined by the appointment of William Smith? Franklin was largely responsible for securing Smith's initial appointment, so perhaps the question should be rephrased to ask what it was about Smith that appealed to Franklin. The answer probably is that Smith appealed as a new man, with innovative enlightened and progressive ideas, who would nonetheless be entirely acceptable to upholders of conventional moral and religious orthodoxies. Smith had set out his educational theories in *A General Idea of the College of Mirania*, first published in New York in 1753. Among the distinctive features of his programme were its recognition that a college need not be seen only as a school for clergymen, and its emphasis on the need for the future leaders of civic society to be trained in the arts and graces of polite living as well as in the traditional scholarly disciplines. The main point here is that Smith's programme derives from his experiences as a student at Aberdeen, and particularly from the changes introduced there in the 1740s.

Franklin's sympathy for an educational programme such as Smith's was guaranteed. In his own *Proposals for the Education of Youth* (1749) he had in fact drawn largely upon the very same Aberdonian tradition that Smith represented. In the writings of the Aberdeen regents George Turnbull and David Fordyce, and perhaps also in Alexander Gerard, Franklin had found an educational ideology that exactly suited his own predilections.[12] This ideology can be defined as a vision of a liberal university education, dedicated to the promotion of civic virtue and the protection of liberty. The ideal polite academy would further these aims by including in its pattern of education first the old commonwealthman Whig tradition of Toland and Molesworth, which had always emphasised virtue and liberty as primary aims of education; second, an emphasis on the superiority of the empirical, Baconian method over older scholastic traditions; and third, Shaftesbury and Molesworth's desire to bring out the moral and aesthetic faculties inherent in human nature.[13] These were the kinds of educational objectives that Franklin himself sought to promote, and it is therefore easy to understand his support for Smith, who in *Mirania* agreed with Tillotson 'that the knowledge of what tends neither directly nor indirectly to make better men, or better citizens, is but a knowledge of trifles'.[14] In supporting Smith, Franklin must have believed he was taking practical steps to promote the realisation in Philadelphia of the ideals of college education to which he was committed. Hence both in theory and practice Scottish models played a highly significant role in the development of Philadelphia's major educational institution.

At the college, Smith himself taught courses in logic, rhetoric (that favourite Scottish topic) and moral and natural philosophy, all subjects he had studied at Aberdeen in the 1740s. And Smith was not without considerable additional Scottish support. Francis Alison, an Ulster Scot who had studied at Edinburgh and Glasgow Universities, had run a school in New London for nine years before becoming vice-provost of the College of Philadelphia. Alison, a classical scholar, was an Old Side Presbyterian—the college had been established on an interdenominational basis—and soon, as assistant to Robert Cross in the First Presbyterian Church, became the Old Side leader in the complex Presbyterian politics of the city. At least two other Scots, Alexander Alexander and John Beveridge, held teaching posts at the college in its early years; and James Wilson himself, after his brief initial stint as a Latin tutor, retained a teaching connection with the college. Wilson's own philosophical sympathies lay with the common sense, anti-Humean side of the Scottish Enlightenment—and this perhaps reinforces one's sense that the progressive modernism of the Scottish Enlightenment, as it was presented by Philadelphia's college, was unlikely to be too dangerously radical.

The emergence of the College of Philadelphia's medical school represented another major infusion of Scottish influence into Philadelphia's educational and intellectual life, but any understanding of this development requires a preliminary glance at Franklin's own Scottish connections. These are sufficiently significant to justify the assertion that, even if there had been no other factors, the Scottish Enlightenment would have played some part in Philadelphia's culture through the person of the city's own leading intellectual. Franklin and Scotland were tightly linked; moreover, it was Franklin above all who brought Philadelphia and Edinburgh into a close and creative relationship. Within Philadelphian society, Franklin's Scottish friendships were numerous. David Hall, his partner in the printing business, was a Scot who had come out to Philadelphia in 1744 from the London office of William Strahan, himself a Scot and long one of Franklin's closest friends. Hall, as has been noted, was a founding member of the Philadelphia St Andrews Society and therefore closely associated with all the most influential members of the Scots colony in the city: Thomas Graeme, James Hamilton (and his father Andrew Hamilton, a leading lawyer), Alexander Alexander, Alexander Barclay and Robert Smith, the builder and architect. When Franklin was first contemplating a trip to Scotland in 1759, he doubtless had heard much of their native land from these Philadelphian Scots, and by then, through William Strahan, he had already come into contact with nearly all the leading members of the Scottish circle in London.

More important than these encounters, however, were Franklin's actual trips to Scotland in 1759 and 1771. These visits brought Franklin into immediate personal contact with all the leading members of those intellectual groups whose joint efforts had made the Enlightenment flower in Scotland.[15] In 1759 in Edinburgh–and most of these contacts were renewed in 1771, despite the changed political circumstances–he met Hume, Kames, Sir Alexander Dick, William Robertson, Adam Ferguson, Joseph Black, William Cullen, the two Monros and Adam Smith; in Glasgow, Robert Simson, Alexander Wilson, the Foulis brothers and John Anderson (John Millar was a new contact in 1771); in St Andrews, David Gregory and Patrick Baird, a doctor who had practised for a time in Philadelphia. Such a list is practically a roll-call of the luminaries of the Scottish Enlightenment. And Franklin's respect for them is well documented. In a letter to Jonathan Potts and Benjamin Rush, young Philadelphians proposing to study medicine at Edinburgh in the 1760s, he wrote: 'You have great Advantages in going to study at Edinburgh at this Time, where there happens to be collected a Set of as truly great Men, Professors of the several Branches of Knowledge, as have ever appeared in any Age or Country'.[16]

Such a view would soon be commonplace among American intellectuals, but Franklin's position in Philadelphia's intellectual world was so central that his words gain much more than a personal significance: if in Scotland he was a kind of intellectual ambassador for his own country, then he was inevitably a channel of the most significant kind for the conveyance of almost every aspect of the Scottish Enlightenment into Philadelphia's cultural scene.

The tangible evidence of Franklin's importance is apparent in what I earlier suggested was a second specifically Scottish contribution to Philadelphia's educational life: the experience of Philadelphians who travelled to Scotland for educational purposes. In the spring of 1760 John Morgan arrived in London from Philadelphia undecided whether to pursue his medical education at Leyden or Edinburgh. A member of the first graduating class of the College of Philadelphia, Morgan applied to Franklin for advice, and Franklin, no doubt recalling his recent Scottish experience, recommended Edinburgh. Morgan did not in fact proceed to Edinburgh until the autumn of 1761; by then William Shippen, another Philadelphian and a graduate of the College of New Jersey, had already completed his first year of study at the Edinburgh Medical School. Both Morgan and Shippen arrived in Edinburgh bearing letters of introduction from Franklin to William Cullen. They were soon followed by a succession of other American medical students, among whom students from Philadelphia were always prominent: for example, Benjamin Rush, Jonathan Potts, Adam Kuhn and Hugh Williamson in the 1760s; George Logan and Thomas Parke in the 1770s. By 1800 no less than forty-one Philadelphians had studied medicine at the University of Edinburgh.[17]

How much influence their Scottish experience exerted on the intellectual lives of these students is, of course, not quantifiable. But it is very hard to believe that a period of study in Edinburgh in the late eighteenth century could have done other than produce a significant widening of intellectual horizons. When Benjamin Rush looked back on his student experience at Edinburgh, he had no doubt of the value of the 'halcyon days' spent there: 'The two years I spent in Edinburgh I consider as the most important in their influence upon my character and conduct of any period of my life'.[18] When these Edinburgh-trained doctors returned to Philadelphia, it was more or less inevitable that the Enlightenment they brought back with them should have had a distinctly Scottish dimension. Rush, for example, who had joined the Edinburgh Medical Society and probably attended meetings of the Philosophical Society, testified to the immense intellectual value of such institutions when he wrote to John Morgan in 1768 urging the advantages that would arise from the founding of a 'literary and physical society' in Philadelphia.[19] Morgan and Rush would be among the active founding members of the reactivated American Philosophical Society in Philadelphia in 1769.

By that year the Edinburgh-Philadelphia medical connection had produced an even more tangible result. On his return from Edinburgh in 1761, William Shippen began to deliver lectures on anatomy in his father's house. When Morgan returned in 1764, he and Shippen became the founders of the first American medical school, set up in the College of Philadelphia in 1765; they were soon joined by Rush and Adam Kuhn. Inevitably the school was modelled on that of Edinburgh, and up to the end of the eighteenth century all its professors save one were Edinburgh-trained.[20] Philadelphia's medical education was very much a question of Edinburgh in America.

IV

I have attempted to show how the pattern of education in Philadelphia owed a specific debt to aspects of the Scottish Enlightenment. But in assessing Philadelphia's overall debt to Scottish intellectual life, such precision, as I have already suggested, cannot be achieved. In the Revolutionary and post-Revolutionary periods, Philadelphia's debt to the Scottish Enlightenment continued to grow. Immensely relevant here is John

Witherspoon's assumption of the presidency of the College of New Jersey in 1768. No other Scot came to exercise such a profound influence over American educational, intellectual and political life. And Witherspoon's Philadelphian connections were strong: Benjamin Rush, for example, played an important part in persuading the Scottish clergyman to accept the Princeton appointment; and once in New Jersey, Witherspoon worked closely with the Presbyterian synod in Philadelphia. Given the extraordinary speed and success with which he transformed the struggling College of New Jersey into one of America's leading educational institutions, Witherspoon's presence meant the channelling of a new wave of Scottish Enlightenment values into the cultural life of his adopted country. The only Scot, apart from James Wilson, to sign the Declaration of Independence, Witherspoon's political allegiance was never in doubt; but there was nothing revolutionary about the moral and religious philosophy he taught at Princeton. Despite the anti-Moderate tendency of his theology, he embodied in his teaching both the modernity and the moderation that characterised central aspects of the Enlightenment in Scotland. These were precisely the aspects of the Scottish Enlightenment that appealed increasingly to many Philadelphians in the late eighteenth century.

An ideology that was both modern and moderate was particularly to the taste of a Philadelphian cultural élite, one of whose characteristics had always been a successful resistance to the extremes of religious and political factionalism. In this connection it is important to stress how far Enlightenment was bound up with questions of taste, decorum and politeness for provincial societies like those of Scotland and America. Enlightenment learning was polite learning. In Philadelphia we have already seen how this emphasis was present in William Smith's College of Philadelphia, indeed how Smith himself, minor poet and man of letters, embodied just such an ideal. But Philadelphia offers other Scottish examples.

Just like their counterparts in Edinburgh, Philadelphia's literati were not very productive in the area of creative, imaginative writing. Brockden Brown did not appear until the eighteenth century was almost over. But a respect for literature, drama, music and painting had always been present among the city's élite. Here the Scottish connection in eighteenth-century Philadelphia is once again evident; for example, in Franklin's enthusiasm for the Scots songs sent to his family by Sir Alexander Dick's daughter in 1763, in the production in Philadelphia of John Home's *Douglas* as early as 1759, and in the influence on Philadelphia of the Edinburgh Musical Society. Moreover, Philadelphia possessed at least one literary salon, established in the 1760s by Elizabeth Graeme Ferguson, that had much in common with later establishments in Edinburgh. Elizabeth Graeme was the daughter of Dr Thomas Graeme, and her home became a fashionable resort for those in Philadelphia, particularly in Episcopalian circles, with a taste for polite literature. William Smith himself was one of her circle; John Morgan, Benjamin Rush and William Franklin were also regular visitors.[21] But despite her strong Scottish connections, which make one wonder whether her description of Philadelphia as 'the Athens of North America' was a conscious echo of the description of Edinburgh as 'the Athens of the North', her own minor verse suggests a greater affinity with the English Augustan poets and their Scottish imitators than with eighteenth-century Scottish vernacular writers. Several decades would have to pass before Philadelphia would share in the general American enthusiasm for Scottish writing. When that taste did develop, however, Philadelphia played a major role: in the early nineteenth century Matthew Carey's *American Museum* and Brockden Brown's *Literary Magazine* both contained frequent laudatory references to the 'Scottish literati', while Joseph Dennie's *Port Folio* was even more consistently favourable towards all aspects of Scottish literature.

In the late eighteenth century, however, the Scottish Enlightenment's linking of progress and the advancement of polite society could well have been a major source of its continuing appeal for most of Philadelphia's ruling élite. In the period of the Revolution the polite, intellectual consensus that had been successfully established in Philadelphia broke down. The ultra-democratic Pennsylvania constitution of 1776 was seen by the property-conscious, anti-radical élite as a serious threat from below: modern progressiveness carried to a revolutionary extreme. Smith's College of Philadelphia was closed as too Tory and Episcopalian; the theatres were shut down; and James Wilson's house was stoned by a mob. But in the 1780s the more conservative forces regained control of the city, and the status quo–including even Smith–was more or less restored.

But Philadelphia had had a taste of what revolutionary change could mean, not in this case for the British but for its own leading citizens. Perhaps it is not then surprising that it should have continued to be attracted by the most powerful, modern and progressive, but broadly conservative ideology available, that of the Scottish Enlightenment in its post-Humean, common sense phase. In that phase what the Scottish Enlightenment offered was above all an acceptable spirit of moderation and compromise by means of which traditional morality and progressive thinking, social order and civic development, religious faith and scientific enquiry, could all be reconciled. Such a philosophy exactly suited the progressive, tolerant but anti-revolutionary élite of America's cultural capital. Writing of Philadelphia's cultural life in the post-Revolutionary period, Henry May has suggested that 'history had produced a delicate balance between the Moderate and the Revolutionary forms of Enlightenment'.[22] Both in producing that balance and in helping to sustain it, the Scottish Enlightenment played a crucial role.

Notes

1. Carl Bridenbaugh, 'Philosophy Put to Use: Voluntary Associations for Propagating the Enlightenment in Philadelphia, 1727–1776', in his *Early Americans* (New York, 1981), 151.
2. Ibid., 152.
3. Hugh Ouston, 'Cultural Life from the Restoration to the Union', in *The History of Scottish Literature, 1660–1800*, ed. Andrew Hook (Aberdeen, 1987), 11–30.
4. Bridenbaugh, 'Philosophy Put to Use', 152.
5. Jacob M. Price, 'The Rise of Glasgow in the Chesapeake Tobacco Trade, 1707–1775', *William and Mary Quarterly*, 11 (April, 1954), 198.

6. Nicholas T. Phillipson, 'Culture and Society in the Eighteenth Century Province: The Case of Edinburgh and the Scottish Enlightenment', in *The University in Society*, ed. Lawrence Stone, 2 vols. (Princeton, 1974), 2:407–48.
7. John Clive and Bernard Bailyn, 'England's Cultural Provinces: Scotland and America', *William and Mary Quarterly*, 11 (April, 1954), 200–13.
8. See Henry F. May, *The Enlightenment in America* (New York, 1976), 84. The American Philosophical Society soon became a focus of the cultural exchange between Philadelphia and Scotland. When the first volume of that society's *Transactions* was published, William Smith directed Franklin to send a copy to the librarian of King's College, Aberdeen. In 1786 Benjamin Rush arranged James Beattie's admission as a member of the society. See *Letters of Benjamin Rush*, ed. L. H. Butterfield, 2 vols. (Princeton, 1951), 1:394.
9. Bridenbaugh, 'Philosophy Put to Use', 150.
10. Ibid., 155.
11. May, *Enlightenment in America*, 80.
12. Caroline Robbins, *The Eighteenth-Century Commonwealthman* (Cambridge, Mass., 1959), 100.
13. See Peter Jones, 'The Polite Academy and the Presbyterians, 1720–1770', in *New Perspectives on the Politics and Culture of Early Modern Scotland*, ed. John Dwyer et al. (Edinburgh, 1982), 156–78, and 'The Scottish Professoriate and the Polite Academy, 1720–46', in I. Hont, M. Ignatieff (eds.), *Wealth and Virtue* (Cambridge, 1983), 89–117. See also M. A. Stewart, 'George Turnbull and Educational Reform', in *Aberdeen and the Enlightenment*, ed. Jennifer J. Carter and Joan H. Pittock (Aberdeen, 1987), 95–103.
14. Quoted in May, *Enlightenment in America*, 81.
15. J. Bennett Nolan, *Benjamin Franklin in Scotland and Ireland, 1759 and 1771* (Philadelphia, 1938).
16. L. W. Labaree (ed.) *The Papers of Benjamin Franklin* (New Haven, 1959–), **15**: 530.
17. William R. Brock, *Scotus Americanus: A Survey of the Sources for Links between Scotland and America in the Eighteenth Century* (Edinburgh, 1982), 119.
18. *The Autobiography of Benjamin Rush*, ed. G. W. Corner (Princeton, 1948), 43.
19. *Letters of Benjamin Rush*, ed. Butterfield, **1**: 51.
20. Brock, *Scotus Americanus*, 119.
21. See Martha C. Slotten, 'Elizabeth Graeme Ferguson, a Poet in "The Athens of North America",' *Pennsylvania Magazine of History and Biography* 108 (1984): 259–88. In possessing a literary salon run by a woman in the 1760s, Philadelphia may well have had an edge over Edinburgh: Mrs Archibald Fletcher and Mrs Anne Grant of Laggan and their literary salons did not emerge upon the Edinburgh scene until several decades later.
22. May, *Enlightenment in America*, 198.

CHAPTER THREE

Rhetoric and Politeness
in Scotland and America

*In eighteenth-century Scotland and America there were power-
ful pressures which, rather than resistance to England's cultural
dominance, promoted emulation of its norms and values. The
preface to the first, short-lived* **Edinburgh Review** *of 1755,
whose contributors included Hugh Blair, William Robertson,
and Adam Smith, suggested, for example, that 'If countries
have their ages with respect to improvement, North-Britain
may be considered as in a state of early youth, guided and
supported by the more mature strength of her kindred country'.
For the developing civic societies of Scotland and America,
continuing Progress and Improvement meant the ability to
match English society on its own terms. Specifically, that is,
to use the language of the dominant centre to create the
peripheries' own, recognisable credentials. In terms of today's
cultural nationalisms, and the valorisation of resistance to the
imperial centre implicit in much postcolonial theory, such an
approach may appear flawed or worse. But, as this chapter
attempts to show, it was the approach broadly taken in both
Scotland and America. In the Scottish case justification, in so
far as it was thought to be required, took the form of enthusiastic commitment to the idea of the new nation Great
Britain—as scholars such as Linda Colley (in her 1992 book*
The Britons) *and others have shown, and as the use of the term
North Britain, instead of Scotland, in the* **Edinburgh Review**
*preface just quoted, exemplifies. In colonial America no doubt
a sense of belonging to and sharing in an extended English
nationhood was often equally strong. Of course after the
Revolution America's cultural situation was radically changed.
But the notion of belonging to an English-speaking Atlantic*

community, particularly in cultural terms, was destined to persist.

It is now quite normal to see the Scottish Enlightenment as a widely-ranging social and cultural movement rather than as simply an episode in the history of philosophy. It is generally agreed that Enlightenment thinking in Scotland encouraged changes in society and in individual behaviour. Thus the kinds of political and religious controversy which at the opening of the eighteenth century were still liable to produce violence, bloodshed, and death, were by its close able to be resolved in less dramatic but more civilised fashion.

James Boswell provides us with a classic illustration. In November, 1773, at the conclusion of the tour to the Hebrides, Boswell and Dr Johnson visited Lord Auchinleck, Boswell's father, at the family seat in Ayrshire. Lord Auchinleck and Dr Johnson were mighty embodiments of two opposing cultures: Scottish and English; Presbyterian and Anglican; Whig and Tory. Boswell reports that the two champions soon came into violent dispute over Oliver Cromwell, Charles I, Toryism and the merits of Scottish Presbyterian theologians. Boswell informs the reader that he refuses 'to exhibit my honoured father, and my respected friend, as intellectual gladiators, for the entertainment of the public'. But he lets us see that each man in the contest gave as good as he got: 'Whiggism and Presbyterianism, Toryism and Episcopacy, were terribly buffeted'.[1] Nonetheless, a day or two later, the two men parted with the profoundest courtesy and civility. As Gordon Turnbull puts it: 'Times are now such that cultural collisions are conversational and end civilly; they do not, as they did for the generation who fought in the Pretender's cause, take the form of war'.[2]

What this example illustrates is the nature of the changes in society that the proponents of Enlightenment in Scotland desired—and perhaps it also suggests why they achieved some degree of success. Few Scots seem to have wished to return to the ways of the past–certainly few of those who had any kind of status or power in a developing society. Just as the English we are told in 1660 had had enough of wars and revolutions, so the Scots had no wish to remain locked into a society in which fanaticism and bigotry, violence and bloodshed, were distinguishing features. If progressive change meant a movement into a more moderate and tolerant world, then it is easy to recognise its appeal.

But the implications of Enlightenment did not operate only on the fanatical fringes of society. Change and what was regarded as improvement occurred in a whole range of areas of social conduct. Even the world of scholarship and learning was affected. Douglas Duncan has shown how early in the eighteenth century an older Scoto-Dutch tradition of learning was gradually replaced by a newer Anglo-French one, with a new emphasis on civility and politeness as constituents of the pursuit of learning. More significantly, after the Union of the Parliaments in 1707, Scottish representatives had to measure themselves in every way including manners and deportment against the English members, and early in the century they did not seem to come off too well. Thomas Somerville in his autobiography reports that William Robertson believed that the weakness of the new Scots MPs in the House of Commons in London was largely a question of their lack of polish in speech and manners: 'the want of the English language, and their uncouth manners, were much against them'.[3] The difficulty was that in the early eighteenth century neither Scottish speech nor Scottish prose style was entirely consonant with received English usage. Some comments by Robert Wodrow serve to illustrate the problem. Wodrow, author of the *History of the Sufferings of the Church of Scotland*, published in 1721, recognised that as a country minister in Eastwood, a village near Glasgow, he had no need to speak or write in correct English style. 'I write just as words offer' he said, and went on, 'no corrections will make anything I write answerable to the English taste. Could I get it good grammar, and free of obvious Scotticisms, so as people might fully understand it, I should be easy as to its politeness'.[4] But

Wodrow's is a special case. His *History* is a committed, passionate work, a patriotic defence of the Church of Scotland against those who in the seventeenth century had attempted to suppress and destroy it. Wodrow is fighting or re-fighting the battles of the past, of the old, unenlightened world. Thus his rejection of 'politeness' is understandable, but atypical. Perhaps he sensed that to assent to the demands of politeness in terms of language and style would have entailed a betrayal of the values and traditions that his book was meant to preserve. Nonetheless, even Wodrow agrees that if his book is to be comprehensible to a wider audience then he has to attend to questions of grammar and the problem of Scotticisms.

For Scottish writers anxious to espouse the enlightened values that Robert Wodrow rejects, the problem of language is still more acute. For them grammatical accuracy according to English norms, and the absence of Scotticisms, are indeed evidence of a desirable politeness. I would suggest that it is as a means towards the attainment of that kind of politeness that the Scottish Enlightenment's preoccupation with rhetoric is best understood. As Thomas Miller accurately puts it, 'Rhetoric is both a practical art and an intellectual discipline', and for Scots in the eighteenth century the study of rhetoric clearly had a strongly pragmatic basis.[5] When Franklin asked the question, 'what signifies Philosophy that does not apply to some Use'? he was voicing one of the major strains in all Enlightenment thinking; however, both in Scotland and, as we shall see, in America, students of the philosophy of rhetoric would have no problem in affirming the usefulness of their studies. Thus Thomas Sheridan's famous 1761 lecture series on the correct speaking of English, with his audience of 300 Edinburgh gentlemen, and the Select Society's follow-up creation of 'The Society for promoting the Reading and Speaking of the English Language in Scotland' are manifestations of the same impulse as lay behind the university courses the Scottish rhetoricians developed for their students.[6] Good taste and politeness in the areas of literature, language, and style are bound up with good taste and politeness in modern, civilised society as a whole. Self-improvement in the first can lead to advancement in the second. Thus one of John Stevenson's pupils in Edinburgh wrote that 'the History of our own Country' shows that the 'art of making himself agreeable by the charms of a well regulated conversation' is 'the most natural and certain method of rising in the world and making one's fortune'. And the student goes on to insist that politeness in conversation is incompatible with political or religious disputation and controversy: 'We should further be carefull how far we enter into disputes, especially upon delicate subjects where our religious, or even political principles may too far interest our positions in the argument'.[7] Similarly Adam Smith, lecturing on rhetoric to his students at the University of Glasgow in the 1750s and '60s, advised them that a decorous restraint in manner of expression was a prerequisite for gentlemanly conduct:

> The order and decorum of behaviour which is now in fashion will not admit of any the least extravagancies. The behaviour which is reckoned polite in England is a calm, composed, unpassionate serenity noways ruffled by passion. Foreigners observe that there is no nation in the world which use so little gesticulation in their conversation as the English.[8]

Thomas Miller uses such comments to support his argument that the Scottish rhetoricians, and Hugh Blair in particular, by linking the study of rhetoric so closely to the development of good taste and a belletristic sense of polite style, were diluting the subject's traditional links to a wider classical concept of civic humanism. Miller of course acknowledges that Blair recognised the basic assumptions of classical civic rhetoric, and accepted the view that the ideal orator was a person of public virtue and practical wisdom. 'In order to be a truly eloquent or persuasive speaker' Blair wrote in his *Lectures*, 'nothing is more necessary than to be a virtuous man'.[9] Nevertheless, in Miller's view, Blair's emphasis in practice is on social and aesthetic, rather than civic or political, improvement. David Daiches, however, argues that Miller exaggerates the gap between the two approaches to the study of rhetoric–and I am inclined to agree.[10] In

48

the Scottish Enlightenment generally, the personal is the political, and so personal, social, and political forms of improvement are difficult to disentangle. Blair maintained that 'Nothing . . . is more necessary for those who would excel in any of the higher kinds of oratory, than to cultivate habits of the several virtues, and to refine and improve all their moral feelings'.[11] In his unpublished *Treatise of Rhetoric* William Leechman agreed. 'Corruption of the human heart', Leechman argued, 'is as bad for style as false taste and want of genius'.[12] Sincerity and honesty of feeling on the part of the preacher are essential if the hearts of the congregation are to be justly moved. Miller would no doubt argue that there is still a gap here between individual feelings and civic action, but in the context of the struggle for Moderation in the Church of Scotland the practical implications of these attitudes are real enough.

There are grounds, then, at least for qualifying Miller's view that Hugh Blair moved decisively away from the traditional classical association of eloquence with civic humanism, but what is not in question is that the work of the eighteenth-century Scottish rhetoricians generally is very much part of the pattern of cultural change, alluded to by Douglas Duncan, in which the world of scholarship and learning and expression is increasingly integrated with that of politeness and good manners. In the early part of the eighteenth century, classical oratory, and especially that of Demosthenes and Cicero, was widely recognised as a model of eloquence supporting the ideals of civic virtue. For the so-called Country Whig opponents of Walpole's long-enduring administration in particular, this classical form of eloquence was seen as a patriotic ideal. However, as Adam Potkay shows in his *The Fate of Eloquence in the Age of Hume* (1994), this ideal of eloquence, with its strong infusion of political commitment, was slowly displaced as the century went on by a more refined style of language use reflecting an ideology of social politeness rather than civic action. In Scotland in particular, Potkay acknowledges, the rhetorical analysis of language was linked to an emphasis on politeness as the *sine qua non* for social and individual improvement.

From Goosecreek to Gandercleugh

Potkay's book-length study clearly confirms that the study of rhetoric in eighteenth-century Scotland had a strongly pragmatic basis: it contributed to the development of politeness within society. Was the study of rhetoric in eighteenth-century America in any way different? Thomas Miller implies that to a degree it was. His example of a Scottish teacher of rhetoric who retained the traditional classical emphasis on the link between eloquence and civic freedom and virtue is the transatlantic Scot, John Witherspoon. Witherspoon became president of the College of New Jersey in Princeton in 1768 and soon after his arrival in his new country he took up the cause of the patriots in the dispute with the mother-country. Hence according to Miller it is Witherspoon's own civic awareness and political concerns that inform his lectures on rhetoric to his Princeton students. Witherspoon does of course consider questions of taste and style very much in the language and manner of Blair, but his overall emphasis is different. For Witherspoon, much more than for Blair, rhetoric is concerned with the practices of political oratory and debate, and Witherspoon also keeps very much in mind the traditional link between rhetoric and moral philosophy essential to the creation of the ideal public-minded citizen. Thomas Miller undoubtedly does draw attention to an important difference in emphasis in the courses on rhetoric taught by Blair and Witherspoon. Witherspoon's lectures on rhetoric must indeed have played a part in making Princeton into an extraordinarily successful school for patriotic politicians and statesmen. Under Witherspoon's tutelage the college produced a future president of the United States; a vice-president; 10 cabinet officers; 21 United States senators; 39 members of the House of Representatives; 12 state governors; 56 state legislators; and 33 judges.[13] It is an amazing record, and one which seems to support the view that in America at least, Scottish rhetoric retained its traditional link with civic virtue.

Nevertheless, despite the example of Witherspoon, I do not believe that American enthusiasm for the Scottish rhetoricians can be explained by the political needs of the colonies in the

Revolutionary period. The evidence against such a view is simple enough. What Miller sees as Blair's lack of interest in what might be called the politics of rhetoric, in no way detracted from his American popularity. In fact of all the Scottish writers on rhetoric, Blair remained far and away the most popular. Again the American vogue for Scottish rhetoric went on growing long after the Revolution was over and was at its height in the early decades of the nineteenth century. Blair first appeared as a textbook at Yale in 1785 and at Harvard in 1788. His *Lectures on Rhetoric and Belles Lettres* was first published in America at Philadelphia in 1784, but for the following fifty years or so editions, some complete, some abridged, simply poured from American presses–between 1805 and 1823 alone some 56 editions appeared. By comparison Kames's *Elements of Criticism* so admired by Jefferson–appeared in ten editions, and Campbell's *Philosophy of Rhetoric* in five. The publishing history, then, hardly supports the view that the general American interest in Scottish rhetoric had any specific political basis–which is not to deny that many American budding politicians may have learned a great deal from their study of Blair and the others.[14]

In my view the best explanation of American interest in Scottish rhetoric once again centrally concerns the concept of politeness. The Americans, just like the Scots, felt a powerful need to learn about good taste in literature and correctness in speaking and writing. American English, like Scottish English, needed to be kept up to the mark of English English. The old Clive and Bailyn thesis about the common provincial identity of Scots and Americans, that is, seems to work particularly well in the area of language: because language was an area in which Scots and Americans faced a common problem in meeting the standards of taste and accuracy set by metropolitan London. In these circumstances it is hardly surprising that Americans should have taken a special interest in Scottish solutions to what was a shared problem. In this connection the case of John Witherspoon is once again particularly instructive.

Witherspoon's transformation of the College of New Jersey

from an ailing and shaky foundation into one of America's leading educational institutions was widely recognised at the time–as was his contribution to the whole educational, intellectual, and political life of his adopted country. But it is significant that in assessments of his specifically educational influence, his role in developing the study of rhetoric is seen as of almost equal importance to his introduction to America of Scottish common sense philosophy. Even more significant is the nature of the influence that contemporaries saw his course on rhetoric as possessing: taste and elegance in writing and speaking are in question, not the area of civic and political awareness. Thus Benjamin Rush, a Princeton graduate, wrote: 'He gave a new turn to education, and spread taste and correctness in literature throughout the United States. It was easy to distinguish his pupils every where when ever they spoke or wrote for the public'.[15] A detailed account of Witherspoon's impact upon the College of New Jersey is given by Samuel Miller in his *Brief Retrospect of the Eighteenth Century* (1803); it ends thus: 'And finally, under his presidency, more attention began to be paid than before to the principles of taste and composition, and to the study of elegant literature'.[16] The same emphasis is apparent as late as 1825 in an article on Witherspoon which appeared in the Philadelphia magazine the *Port Folio*: 'He caused an important revolution in the system of education, whereby literary inquiries and improvements became more liberal, more extensive, and more profound'.[17]

All of these tributes underline the belletristic dimension of Witherspoon's Princeton lectures on rhetoric. It is abundantly clear that his main aims in instructing his students were the development of good taste, and improvements in the accuracy of spoken and written English. In other words, Witherspoon did after all share in the polite, progressive, socially improving, dimension of the Scottish Enlightenment. What provides a final confirmation of this is an article on the use of language that he contributed to the *Pennsylvania Journal* on 9 May 1781. Having in mind no doubt the curriculum he had introduced at Princeton, he wrote: 'We may certainly infer, that the education, must be very imperfect in any seminary where no care is taken to form the scholars to taste, propriety, and accuracy, in that language which they must write and speak all their lives'. And to these comments he adds this most telling of conclusions: 'To these reflections it may be added, that our situation is now, and probably will continue to be such, as to require peculiar attention upon this subject'. By referring thus to 'our situation' Witherspoon clearly has in mind the particular linguistic position of Americans. American students are in special need of developing taste, propriety, and accuracy in the English they speak and write. American English–like Scottish English–needs to be kept under constant critical review. Otherwise the Americans, like the Scots, will be betrayed by their language, appearing as provincial inferiors before the cultural bar of metropolitan London. Given his understanding of the Scottish-American linguistic problem, it is no surprise that in his article on language, Witherspoon coined the term 'Americanism'–strictly analogous to 'Scotticism'–to indicate native American linguistic usages that had to be avoided.

Witherspoon is frequently credited with being the first teacher in America to offer formal instruction in rhetoric. However, according to Jefferson's *Autobiography*, William Small was giving regular lectures on Ethics, Rhetoric, and Belles Lettres at the College of William Mary at the beginning of the 1760s, several years before Witherspoon's arrival at Princeton. Small was a graduate of Marischal College, Aberdeen, where one of his teachers had been William Duncan, professor of natural philosophy, whose *Elements of Logick* (1748) had included a strong emphasis on rhetoric. In any event what is clear is that from the 1760s on, rhetoric became an increasingly popular course of study in America; that the textbooks from which the subject was taught in schools and colleges where wholly Scottish in origin; and that the main thrust in all these courses was in the direction of *politeness*. Attention to elegant literature, added to a concern for taste, propriety, and accuracy in written and spoken American English, were ways of improving in English for Americans, just as Sheridan's lectures in Edinburgh had been a means of improvement in English discourse for Scottish gentlemen.

It is very easy today to be contemptuously dismissive of the kinds of impulse in eighteenth-century Scotland and America which led to the crucial linking of rhetoric and politeness I have been describing. In the present climate of cultural nationalisms, of resistance to and rejection of any kind of centralised cultural authority, of democratic insistence on the equal validity of any form whatsoever of spoken or written English, the whole eighteenth-century rhetorical enterprise is liable to be rejected out of hand as an obsequious acceptance of artificial, anglicised, middle-class, colonial or imperial attitudes and habits of mind. From this perspective the study of rhetoric is no more than a form of social control, one of the many ways of continuing English cultural dominance over Scots and Americans. Perhaps there is a degree of truth in this view, and in one area at least both Scotland and America suffered a serious cultural loss as a result of their uncritical acceptance of a link between rhetoric and politeness.

In both Scottish and American societies in the eighteenth century English English became the unchallenged norm. Correctness and accuracy, polish and elegance were determined by exclusively English models: Addison and Steele, and especially Swift. The result was a total devaluing of any kind of alternative vernacular mode. Hugh Blair's comment on the Scots language of Ramsay's *The Gentle Shepherd* is typical: 'It is a great disadvantage to this beautiful poem, that it is written in the old rustic dialect of Scotland, which, in a short time, will probably be entirely obsolete, and not intelligible'.[18] And the similar views of the Edinburgh *literati* on Burns's use of the vernacular are even more familiar. But at least Scottish literature in the eighteenth century had in Ramsay, Fergusson, and Burns a vernacular tradition strong enough to prevent the polite English of the Enlightenment gaining absolute mastery. America was less fortunate. If it is true, as W. S. Howell and David Daiches have argued, that the form and style of Jefferson's Declaration of Independence and the American Constitution owe more than a little to the Scottish rhetoricians, then it is probably also true that the roots of the so-called 'genteel' tradition in American culture are to be found in American assimilation of the same Scottish rhetorical tradition.[19]

Throughout the nineteenth century the genteel tradition totally disregarded American vernacular English. The result was that the American vernacular was allowed expression only in the oral-based work of Southern and Western humorists, working in the American tall-tale tradition: the vernacular, that is, was acceptable only within a kind of literary sub-culture. Only with Mark Twain's emergence out of that tradition did American vernacular speech at last gain recognition as a viable mode of expression for American literature as a whole. And *Huckleberry Finn* did not appear until 1885: almost exactly 100 years after Blair and the other Scots began to take over the American college curriculum. As Ernest Hemingway famously remarked, the appearance of *Huckleberry Finn* meant a new beginning for American literature. But it in no way marked the end of the debate about correctness, decorum, and good taste in spoken and written English. The concerns of the Scottish Enlightenment with rhetoric and politeness are still in a variety of ways concerns very much with us in Scotland, America, and elsewhere today: consider, for example, the furore in the United States and Britain over African-American 'ebonics' in 1996. And I would like to end by agreeing with Adam Potkay that we should not be too quick to dismiss out of hand 'the ethos of politeness' in the context of language and culture; surely Potkay is right to argue that the ideal, if not the ideology, of polite intercourse does accord with America's 'own constitutional sense of civic equality'.[20] And for that matter with the nature of civil society everywhere.

Notes

1. R. W. Chapman, (ed.), *Johnson's Journey to the Western Islands of Scotland and Boswell's Journal of A Tour to the Hebrides With Samuel Johnson, LL.D.*, (London, New York, Toronto, 1951), pp. 419–20.
2. Gordon Turnbull, 'James Boswell: Biography and the Union', in Andrew

From Goosecreek to Gandercleugh

Hook (ed.), *The History of Scottish Literature, Volume 2, 1660–1800* (Aberdeen, 1987), p. 169.

3. See Thomas Somerville, *My Own Life and Times 1741–1814* (Edinburgh, 1861), p. 271.

4. See Douglas Duncan, 'Scholarship and Politeness in the Early Eighteenth Century' in Andrew Hook (ed.), *History of Scottish Literature, 1660–1800*, p. 58.

5. See Thomas P. Miller, 'Witherspoon, Blair and the Rhetoric of Civic Humanism', in Richard B. Sher and Jeffrey R. Smitten, (eds.), *Scotland and America in the Age of Enlightenment* (Edinburgh, 1990), p. 101.

6. The Ordinary Directors of the English Language Society included Hugh Blair, William Robertson, Adam Ferguson and John Adam. Extraordinary Directors included Lord Kames and Sir Alexander Dick. See *The Scots Magazine*, XXIII (1761), 389–90, 440–41.

7. See Miller, *op. cit.*, p. 104.

8. J. C. Bryce (ed.), *Adam Smith Lectures on Rhetoric and Belles Lettres* (Oxford, 1983), p. 198.

9. Hugh Blair, *Lectures on Rhetoric and Belles Lettres* (London, 1824), p. 433.

10. See David Daiches, 'Hugh Blair and the Rhetoric of American Independence' in Sher and Smitten, (eds.), *Scotland and America*, pp. 225–6.

11. Blair, *Lectures on Rhetoric and Belles Lettres*, p. 435.

12. See Thomas D. Kennedy, 'William Leechman, Pulpit Eloquence and the Glasgow Enlightenment' in Andrew Hook and Richard Sher (eds.), *The Glasgow Enlightenment* (East Linton, 1995), p. 63.

13. See Varnum Lansing Collins, *President Witherspoon. A Biography* (Princeton, 1925), II, 229.

14. For further details of the American impact of Blair's *Lectures on Rhetoric*, and the other Scottish rhetoricians, see my *Scotland and America 1750–1835* (Glasgow and London, 1975), pp. 75–76, 81, 88–89.

15. See G. W. Corner (ed.), *The Autobiography of Benjamin Ruch* (Princeton, 1948), p. 51.

16. Samuel Miller, *A Brief Retrospect of the Eighteenth Century* (New York, 1803), II, 377.

17. *Port Folio*, 4th Series, XIX (1825), 77.

18. Blair, *Lectures on Rhetoric and Belles Lettres*, p. 506.

19. See, W. S. Howell, 'The Declaration of Independence and Eighteenth-Century Logic', *William and Mary Quarterly* 18 (1961), 463–84. And David Daiches, 'Hugh Blair and the Rhetoric of American Independence', in Sher and Smitten (eds.), *Scotland and America*, 209–26. Howell argues that a crucial influence on the rhetorical structure of Jefferson's draft of the Declaration of Independence was William Duncan's *Elements of Logick* (1748). Jefferson would have studied Duncan's work at the College of William and Mary with William Small, himself, as already noted, a pupil of Duncan at Marischal College, Aberdeen in the 1730s. Daiches argues that both the American Con-

stitution and Jefferson's original draft of the Declaration are much indebted to Blair's ideas on style.

20. Adam Potkay, *The Fate of Eloquence in the Age of Hume*, (Ithaca and London, 1994),p. 19.

CHAPTER FOUR

Samuel Miller's *A Brief Retrospect of the Eighteenth Century* and its Scottish Context

*Samuel Miller's **Brief Retrospect of the Eighteenth Century** has a particular resonance at the end of the 1990s. It was conceived, written and published very much as a commemoration and celebration of the ending of one century and the beginning of another. But Miller's retrospect, however brief, aims to be all-seeing and all-inclusive; like Francis Bacon, he is prepared to take all knowledge to be his province. As far as I am aware no one, a hundred years on, attempted to survey the entire nineteenth century, while, now at the end of the twentieth, a single work covering the intellectual achievements of this century is about as likely to appear as one taking on the entire millennium. But the world of Enlightenment to which Miller belonged still believed in the universality of human knowledge; its character-istic encyclopaedias made general information available to all. Miller certainly believed that the effort at comprehensiveness could still be made–at least for one more time.*

*Samuel Miller was an American, and his book belongs to American cultural history. But in my view his work cannot be fully understood or accounted for within an exclusively Amer-ican context. Rather Miller's **Brief Retrospect** perfectly illus-trates how the specifically Scottish contribution to American academic and intellectual life often lies just out of sight beneath the surface of conventional American cultural history.*

Newsreel 1 of *The 42nd Parallel*, the first volume in John Dos Passos' *USA* trilogy, contains these newspaper headlines:

Samuel Miller's A Brief Retrospect

CAPITAL CITY'S CENTURY CLOSED

NOISE GREETS NEW CENTURY

LABOR GREETS NEW CENTURY

CHURCHES GREET NEW CENTURY

NATION GREETS CENTURY'S DAWN

One hundred years earlier the ending of the eighteenth century, and the opening of the nineteenth, had been greeted, not by newspaper headlines, but by 'century-sermons' delivered by Presbyterian, Congregational, and Unitarian ministers throughout America. Such sermons, normally preached on the last Sunday of the eighteenth century, most commonly aimed, according to Henry May, 'to distinguish between true and false progress in the age that was coming to an end, and to balance the threat of infidelity against the gains of revival'.[1] One such sermon, preached in New York City on the first of January, 1801, proved to be less ephemeral than the rest, occasioning what was to become a significant landmark in American cultural and literary history. In the Preface to his *Brief Retrospect of the Eighteenth Century*, Samuel Miller lets us know that his book owed its origin to his own design for a century sermon. Preaching on the the first New Year's Day of the new century, i.e. January 1, 1801, he tells us that

> instead of choosing the topics of address most usual at the commencement of a *new year*, it occurred to him as more proper, in entering on a *new century*, to attempt a review of the preceding age, and to deduce from the prominent features of that period such moral and religious reflections as might be suited to the occasion.[2]

The sermon's design of attempting 'a review of the preceding age' in due course grew into Miller's ambitious project to write and publish a multi-volume retrospect of the eighteenth century. Inevitably however, the new century had moved on before publication could be achieved. Nonetheless, *A Brief Retrospect of the Eighteenth Century* was published in New York in January, 1804, and in London in 1805. What then appeared, however, was only 'Part the First' of a still grander design. 'Part the First' containing in three volumes 'A Sketch of the Revolutions and Improvements in Science, Arts, and Literature' during the eighteenth century, was intended to be followed by three further parts covering eighteenth-century developments in the areas of Theology, Morals, and Politics. In the event none of these projected volumes ever appeared.

That Samuel Miller was never able to complete the subsequent sections of his *Brief Retrospect* produces mixed feelings in the modern reader. The work as it stands is genuinely important because it is 'the first American intellectual history'.[3] It impresses by the sheer range and quantity of the material it incorporates. Miller admits he felt it only right to draw attention to specifically American contributions to eighteenth-century cultural history–the author, he writes, 'was desirous of collecting and exhibiting as much information on the subject of American literature as the nature of his undertaking admitted' (p. xii)–but his work is entirely devoid of any kind of chauvinistic special pleading on behalf of America. Much more striking is the inclusion of large bodies of information about eighteenth-century intellectual life in a wide range of European countries including Great Britain, France, Germany, Italy, Sweden and Russia. Simply as a survey or compilation of an immense body of existing knowledge, the *Brief Retrospect* is certainly impressive. Yet it has to be admitted it is a long way short of a compelling read. Henry May describes it as 'monumentally dull reading' and it is difficult to disagree.[4] Whether three more three-volume sections would have done anything to alter this judgment seems unlikely. The trouble is the sheer volume of information the reader is expected to absorb. Often the *Brief Retrospect* begins to appear as little more than a gazetteer or a series of encyclopaedia entries. In fact I am not inclined to rule out Edinburgh's *Encyclopaedia Britannica*, first published in 1773, as a peripheral part of the Scottish context of Miller's work. However, dull or not, the *Brief Retrospect* is a highly illuminating work. Even if it is short on sustained analysis of the material it incorporates, it does provide us with a kind of snapshot of the intellectual life of its period. The extraordinary range of Miller's material, as well as his concern with the interaction of science, philosophy, and religion in the eighteenth century, open up what were clearly the major intellectual pre-occupations of his time. Guiding Miller's approach to such topics, and thus underpinning his whole view of the eighteenth century and its importance, are distinctively Scottish intellectual traditions. It is these traditions, rooted in the Scottish Enlight-enment, that provide the ultimate Scottish context of the *Brief Retrospect*, and it is to specific elements within that context that I now wish to turn.

II

Having decided to go forward and write his *Brief Retrospect*, Samuel Miller's next problem was how precisely to proceed.[5] When he was considering the structure of the work–the range of material that should be included, and the sources of information he should use–one man provided him with what he clearly regarded as authoritative advice. That man was Charles Nisbet, the Scottish president of Dickinson College in Carlisle, Penn-sylvania.

In most accounts of the Scottish influence on American education in the eighteenth century Nisbet tends to receive much less attention than his fellow-countrymen William Smith, president of the College of Philadelphia (later the University of Pennsylvania) and John Witherspoon, president of the College of New Jersey (later Princeton University). In the sense that Dickinson College failed to attain the kind of eminence achieved by the institutions headed by Smith and Witherspoon such discrimination is perhaps fair. But in his own person Nisbet did bring to America aspects of the Scottish intellectual tradition somewhat different from those represented by either Smith or Witherspoon.

The Scottish tradition that Nisbet embodied is hinted at by the soubriquet he had earned in Scotland while he was still a clergyman in Montrose: 'a walking library'.[6] And we need to remember that Nisbet's scholarly credentials were certainly good enough to persuade Witherspoon to put his name forward for the presidency of the College of New Jersey at a time when Witherspoon himself was deciding to decline the opportunity to move to Princeton. When in due course Benjamin Rush offered Nisbet the presidency of Dickinson College factors other than his scholarly reputation also played a significant role. From the time of the outbreak of the dispute between Britain and the American colonies through to the end of the Revolution, Nisbet remained one of the few publicly-announced Scottish friends of America. When Miller came to write Nisbet's biography he underlined this point:

> . . . in principle and feeling, [Nisbet] sided with the Colonies. His friend, Dr Witherspoon, had, in 1768, removed to America, and was known there as the active, uncompromising patron of the Colonial claims and feelings. Mr Nisbet, it is believed, substantially agreed with him in his general sentiments . . . In short, Mr Nisbet was a decided and warm friend of America in the contest in which she was engaged; and manifested his friendship as far as he was allowed by his situation.[7]

Such friendly manifestations included the encouragement of Scottish emigration to America and the preaching of anti-government sermons. One of these was so distasteful to the more conservative opinions of Montrose Town Council that its members rose in a body and walked out of the church. Nisbet even received the doubtful accolade of a letter from the Earl of Buchan expressing his surprise that a 'Scotch clergyman' should hold so high a place 'among the friends of liberty'.[8] Nisbet thus assumed the presidency of Dickinson College with both scholarly and patriotic credentials that clearly matched those of his old friend–John Witherspoon of Princeton.

Unsurprisingly, Charles Nisbet, like Witherspoon, figures prominently in the pages of the *Brief Retrospect of the Eighteenth Century*. Miller insists that Nisbet was an important acquisition not only for the future standing of Dickinson College, but for America's literary culture in general:

Soon after the charter for this college was obtained, the rev. Dr Charles Nisbet, of Montrose, in Scotland, was called to be its president. He accepted the invitation, and in the year 1784 arrived in America. It is scarcely necessary to say, that the eminent talents, and profound and general learning of this gentleman, were considered as an important acquisition to the literary interests of that country, and that he soon contributed to raise the character of the institution. From this period to the close of the century he continued to preside over it with usefulness and honour. (III, 252)

Samuel Miller was of course an American, not a Scot. His grandfather John Miller, however, had emigrated from Scotland to Boston in 1710. Nor did the young Miller receive his early education at either of the Scots-led institutions, Dickinson or Princeton. However Miller did attend the University of Pennsylvania in the late 1780s at a time when the Aberdeen graduate William Smith had been succeeded as provost by John Ewing, an honorary graduate of the University of Edinburgh and recipient of the freedoms of Glasgow, Dundee, Perth and Montrose.

After graduating from Pennsylvania in 1789–at the commencement exercises he delivered the Salutatory Oration in Latin and digressed in English to remonstrate against the neglect of female education–Miller was licensed by the Delaware Presbytery in 1791. However it was what followed that represented the crucial intellectual experience of Miller's life: the autumn and winter of 1791–92 were spent in Carlisle, Pennsylvania with Charles Nisbet at Dickinson College. The very fact that Miller went on to become Nisbet's biographer indicates in the clearest possible terms the depth of the impression Nisbet produced upon him. Miller was clearly bowled over by the range and universality of Nisbet's knowledge–and by the sociability which accompanied it. At the College of Philadelphia one of William Smith's principal aims had been to ensure that a liberal education combined knowledge and learning with politeness and ease of manners. Samuel Miller's experience in Philadelphia had been in keeping with such an aim. As John De Witt subsequently explained:

[Miller's] native social gifts had been cultivated . . . in the admirable circle of society to which he was admitted while living in Philadelphia, at the house of his sister, as a student in the University.[9]

What Miller found in Nisbet was another example of immense erudition combined with sociability. As he put it in his *Life of Nisbet*:

Probably no man on this side of the Atlantic ever brought into the social circle such diversified and ample stores of erudition;–such an extraordinary knowledge of men and books, and opinions . . .[10]

Through both his inheritance of the Smith tradition at the University of Pennsylvania and his daily contact over an extended period with Charles Nisbet at Dickinson College, Miller absorbed the aspect of the Scottish Enlightenment that had always been concerned to link progressive knowledge and enlightenment with improvement in taste and manners.

John De Witt believed that it was above all his experience with Nisbet that subsequently allowed Miller to move so easily into the intellectual and cultural society of New York City:

My belief is, that to this easy and habitual companionship with his teacher is largely due the ease with which Mr Miller soon after threw himself into the learned society of New York, the ease also at which he put every one of his students, and the happiness they always found in conference with him, in his own study.[11]

What De Witt describes here as 'the learned society of New York' can be identified more specifically as the Friendly Society of New York City, an organisation which Miller joined in 1793. Henry May describes the Friendly Society as 'perhaps the most brilliant of all the organisations of earnest and enlightened young men' of its time and place.[12] The society was led by Elihu Hubbard Smith and its membership included the novelist Charles Brockden Brown and the playwright William Dunlap.

Samuel Miller's A Brief Retrospect

Members of the Society read the works of leading exponents of the radical Enlightenment: Condorcet, Volney, William Godwin, and Mary Wollstonecraft. In theology their attitudes tended to be Deistical, and in politics they were Federalists. On neither count was Miller–an active Presbyterian clergyman, and a Jeffersonian republican–a typical member. The astonishing thing is that he was a member at all. No doubt he was attracted by the Society's combining of conviviality with strong intellectual interests, but it is hard not to think that Nisbet's example as role-model was also involved. Miller's readiness to preach a sermon to the Independence Day meeting of the Tammany Society in New York in 1793, in which he still found much to praise in the French Revolution's overthrow of tyranny, suggests an obvious parallel with Nisbet's political radicalism at the time of the American War. That by the 1790s Nisbet's own radicalism was decidedly on the wane does not necessarily mean that his protégé might not have found himself in sympathy with his mentor's earlier stance. Certainly as the eighteenth century came to its close, Miller remained radical in his politics. He supported Jefferson in the 1800 presidential election despite being perfectly aware of the charges of Deism levelled against him. 'I think myself perfectly consistent', he wrote, 'in saying that I had much rather have Mr Jefferson President of the United States than an aristocratic Christian'.[13]

When Miller expressed this opinion the writing of the *Brief Retrospect* was only a year to two ahead. And something of its tone occurs in the Preface to that work when Miller explains why he has felt obliged to include 'distinguished abettors of heresy or of infidelity' in his survey:

> A man who is a bad Christian may be a very excellent mathematician, astronomer, or chemist; and one who denies or blasphemes the Saviour, may write profoundly and instructively on some branches of science highly interesting to mankind. (p. xiii)

But Miller's equal concern over the diffusion of heresy and infidelity is clearly present in the text of the *Brief Retrospect*, and in the years that followed his doubts in this area continued to grow. Like Nisbet before him, Miller in time became an increasingly conservative Presbyterian. The defining symbolic moment was the founding of the Princeton Theological Seminary in 1812. Miller played a crucial role in this undertaking whose principal object was the defence and maintenance of a traditional Presbyterian Calvinism against revivalism and other forms of evangelical Protestantism. It is no surprise then that by 1830 Miller was prepared to denounce Jefferson as 'a selfish, insidious, hollow hearted infidel'.[14]

The Samuel Miller of 1801, however, who was contemplating writing *A Brief Retrospect of the Eighteenth Century*, was, whatever the future might hold, a liberal Presbyterian clergyman, strongly influenced by Charles Nisbet and the Scottish intellectual tradition he represented. It is hardly surprising, then, that in looking for help and advice with his grand project, it was to his mentor Nisbet that he turned. Nisbet's response survives in a letter dated Carlisle, 13 March 1801.[15]

Nisbet tells Miller he must pay attention to the organisation of his material: '. . . you must take time to collect and methodise your Materials'. He is alert to the lost opportunity that failure to produce the work at the very outset of the nineteenth century represents:

> If you had formed your Design a year sooner, you might have had them [your Materials] all in order, to be published immediately on the Decease of the late Century, which would have made a stronger Impression.

But given that such a publicity bonus is no longer available, Miller should not rush into print:

> . . . you must take some time before you think of publishing an Account of the Vastness and Variety of the matter that belongs to your Subject.

In the course of this long and somewhat rambling letter Nisbet attacks Franklin as a plagiarist of the discoveries of others, and writes at length on the eighteenth century's responsibility for the spread of atheism, Jacobinism, Socinianism, Platonism, and materialism. Protestant Christianity seems in Nisbet's view to have come under sustained attack throughout the eighteenth century. Indeed he shares John Robison's belief in the existence of an European-wide conspiracy 'whose Object was the gradual Abolition of Christianity and Civil Society'. Unless Providence interposes 'in an extraordinary manner', Europe will continue to suffer the effects of this group's 'infernal labours'. 'The Society of the Illuminati', Nisbet tells Miller, 'the German Union, the French Encyclopedie, and the French Revolution, are only Branches of a great Scheme, the Object of which was to write down all received Opinions in Philosophy, Religion, and Government, and to bring about a total Revolution in human Affairs'. The situation is no better in Britain where Socinianism flourishes and all its adherents are Jacobins in their politics. Dr Paley, with ideas borrowed from Hume, is one of this group, while Priestley's works, with their 'pretended Answer to Dr Oswald, Dr Reid and Dr Beattie' 'may be reckoned the Encyclopedie of the English Socinians'.

Amid these sweeping denunciations of eighteenth-century backsliding, Nisbet, as we have noted, occasionally remembers to offer Miller more practical advice. At one point Miller is reminded that

> Among the Novelties of the late century, you ought not only to take notice of Novels, which I believe are peculiar to it, but of the Multiplication and Influence of Reviews and Literary Journals.

And at the end of his letter, Nisbet feels obliged to tell Miller that he has 'a great Deal to do' and that to record 'the Transactions of 100 Years is no easy Task'. Samuel Miller may well have not needed these particular reminders, but the text of the *Brief Retrospect* demonstrates that he took notice of much of what Nisbet had to say. Nisbet's voice frequently echoes in the *Brief Retrospect of the Eighteenth Century*, even if at the end of the day Miller could not wholly share his mentor's darkly apocalyptic view of the period.[16]

III

The *Brief Retrospect* begins with a dedication to Jonathan Dickinson, dated November 25, 1803. In its course Miller establishes a polarity which runs through his whole account of the eighteenth century. Dickinson, he is confident, will endorse his recognition of 'the perfect harmony between the Religion of Christ and genuine Philosophy' while sharing his 'unfavourable judgment pronounced on those theories, falsely called philosophy, which pervert reason, contradict Revelation, and blaspheme its divine Author'. (pp. iv–v) Throughout his text, Miller is constrained to concede that the eighteenth century contains large measures of both 'genuine' and 'false' philosophy. Thus his overall stance towards the period he is portraying is one of simultaneous approval and disapproval. Miller is constantly moving between praise and blame; he sees progress and enlightenment on the one side, sinfulness and error on the other. Thus in the Introduction that follows the Dedication and the Preface, he firmly denies any notion of the inevitable progressiveness of history: new ideas are often less new than they seem, and originality is rare–but on the other hand new knowledge *is* possible. Any over-rating of the importance of the present should be avoided: it should be made to appear neither 'more awfully *degenerate*, or more extensively *enlightened*' than in fact it is. Miller remains certain, however, of the progressiveness of the eighteenth century:

> it will probably be acknowledged, that the century of which we have just taken leave has produced an unusual number of revolutions, and at least some improvements,–In *Literature* and *Science*–in *Political Principles* and *Establishments*–in the *Moral World*–and in the *Christian Church*. (p. 7)

Despite the fact that it is only the fields of 'Literature and Science' that are covered in the published version of *Brief Retrospect*, Miller's conclusions in his 'Recapitulation' are very much in line with the posture adopted in the Introduction. The eighteenth century is clearly identified as the Age of Enlightenment: an 'Age of Free Inquiry' as Miller calls it. But its

68

Samuel Miller's *A Brief Retrospect*

freedom has been carried too far: 'the most sacred principles of virtue and happiness have been rejected or forgotten'. (III, 288) Such central doctrines of the Enlightenment as the *supremacy of reason* and the *perfectibility of man* are eloquently attacked by Miller. In the nineteenth century, science and knowledge will go on developing; but the benefits will be as qualified as in the past. Miller's advice to the intellectual leaders of the future is to 'mark the mistakes of those deluded and presumptuous spirits who have misled and corrupted their species, and learn caution and wisdom from their errors'. (III, 323)

Miller's *Brief Retrospect* is unquestionably a celebration of the progress and achievements of the eighteenth century, but it is a celebration regularly coupled with warnings about declining standards, resulting from the popularisation of knowledge and the spread of superficial learning, and above all, about dangers resulting from the diffusion of morally and religiously subversive ideas. Such qualified approval of the Age of Enlightenment is generally characteristic of the Scots *literati*; Reid, for example, believed neither in human perfectibility nor the supremacy of reason. In other words, Miller stands squarely in the tradition of what May has called the Didactic Enlightenment in America, deriving essentially from the Scottish school of common sense philosophers. Given his educational background in Philadelphia and Dickinson, and his place in the Presbyterian intellectual tradition, such a stance was well-nigh inevitable. What the Scottish school offered America was an intellectual context that was modern, progressive, liberal, yet in no way revolutionary or subversive. Scottish common sense reinforced rather than undermined orthodox religion and morality. This was precisely its attraction for Miller and for so many other Americans. In the *Brief Retrospect* Miller celebrates the eighteenth-century advances in almost every area of science; but true philosophy has no problem reconciling such scientific advances with religion. Only scepticism and materialism pose a threat–and the doctrines of Reid and his school refute such errors. Miller's *Brief Retrospect* is in the end a major illustration of a dominant Scottish-American intellectual tradition.

From Goosecreek to Gandercleugh

IV

Samuel Miller begins the first chapter of the *Brief Retrospect* with an allusion to Hume's *Essays* arguing that the literary and scientific taste of one age differs from that of another far more widely than do the civil affairs of wars and politics in different ages. Is such a ready resort to Scottish texts characteristic of the work as a whole? Not really. The eighteenth-century Scottish Enlightenment and its luminaries appear in the *Brief Retrospect* only to a degree that confirms the well-established American receptiveness to Scottish thinkers and writers in this period. While exhibiting no sign of a pro-Scottish bias, Miller does regularly acknowledge the contribution in a variety of intellectual fields of the Scottish *literati*. But the manner of his doing so does have a particular significance. Here at the very beginning of the nineteenth century we can see the emergence of a problem that will go on clouding and obscuring the study of Scottish-American cultural links right down to the present. Miller is not sure how to refer to the Scots. He uses the terms Scotland, North Britain, and Great Britain apparently interchangeably. Scots are natives of Scotland or of North Britain or of Great Britain. Scottish cultural identity, that is, is problematic. For example, having rejected Humean scepticism, Miller expresses a preference for 'the principles and reasonings of certain modern metaphysicians of North Britain' which 'certainly form the most important accession which the philosophy of mind has received since the time of Mr Locke'. (II, 177–8). On occasion he even accepts the logical need to refer to England as South Britain. Discussing the pre-eminent models of English style, Addison, Swift, and Dr Johnson, he adds:

> To the above names might be added those of Dr Beattie, Dr Blair, and several others both in North and South Britain, either still living or lately deceased, who have contributed to form and extend a taste for elegant writing. (II, 30)

As the nineteenth century goes on the notion of South Britain will soon disappear, but the assimilation of Scottish cultural identity into an English, or British, context will become increasingly common.[17]

70

Samuel Miller's A Brief Retrospect

The Scottishness of eighteenth-century Scottish writers is not then a theme given much prominence in the *Brief Retrospect*. Nonetheless the range of Scottish writers included does indicate, at the opening of the nineteenth century, just how positive the American response was to Scotland's literary achievements. Thus Miller readily identifies Hume and Robertson as model historians: 'the former excels in ease, spirit, and interest, the latter in purity, dignity, strength, and elegance'. (II, 301). Scottish poetry is consistently praised: Blair's *The Grave*, Beattie's *The Minstrel*, Thomson's *Seasons*, Macpherson's *Ossian*, and the poems of Burns, all receive Miller's commendation. Ramsay's *The Gentle Shepherd*, and John Home's *Douglas* are also admired. Miller's general welcome for the literary achievements of the eighteenth century, Scottish or otherwise, does not however extend to its newest literary form. Miller, presumably with Nisbet's views much in his mind, denounced the growing popularity of the novel in the eighteenth century with an evangelical Presbyterian zeal. The vast majority of novels, we are told, are harmful and dangerous; novels 'dissipate the mind', they 'beget a dislike to more solid and instructive reading' and 'excite a greater fondness for the productions of imagination and fancy, than for the sober reasoning, and the practical investigation of wisdom'. (II, 393) Even worse, novels are 'seductive and corrupting in their tendency', often no more than vehicles for showing 'the religious and moral institutions of the world, as narrow, liberal and unjust'. (II, 394) (Miller presumably has in mind here the kind of Jacobin novels that Friendly Club members read with such enthusiasm.) His conclusion is that ideally he would '*wholly* prohibit the reading of novels'. (II, 399)

Such a general prohibition would benefit one group of readers in particular: women. Miller believes that '. . . far too great a portion of the reading of females is directed to *Novels*'. (III, 142) Yet it is noteworthy that this observation occurs in the context of a discussion of the 'remarkable revolution' in education happening in the eighteenth century which wins Miller's warmest approval. Women's education in particular has much expanded in the course of the century–and this process, he argues at length, should continue. Typically, however, this long-term supporter of the cause of women's education draws back from any endorsement of complete educational equality. Women may have rights, but they are still strictly limited. Mary Wollstonecraft's *Vindication of the Rights of Women*, for example, is denounced as a subversive work, and Miller's final vision of the consequences of equality between the sexes is as apocalyptic as anything in Nisbet's account of eighteenth-century religious scepticism: if all jobs were equally available to men and women the result would be to 'convert society into hordes of seducers and prostitutes'. (III, 142)

Given his views on the dangers of novel-reading for women and other readers, one wonders what Miller made in subsequent years of the overwhelming popular success of Scott and Cooper? The triumph of these two novelists, closely related to each other, might have suggested a link between Scottish and American literature that is not recognised in the *Brief Retrospect*. In a section headed 'Nations lately become Literary' Miller does include a general account of the literary culture of the United States. He makes much of the transformation in the country that has occurred between the opening and the closing of the eighteenth century. Expansion has been remarkable in all the crucial areas of the country's cultural life: more colleges and academies, more graduates, more libraries, more publications, more booksellers and printers. So far America's literary achievement has been modest, but Miller is in no doubt abut the brightness of the future:

> when the time shall arrive that they can give to their votaries of literature the same leisure and the same stimulants to exertion with which they are favoured in Europe, it may be confidently predicted, that letters will flourish as much in America as in any part of the world, and that they will be able to make some return to their transatlantic brethren, for the rich store of useful knowledge which they have been pouring upon them for nearly two centuries. (III, 285)

However, the countries with which Miller chooses to compare America are Russia and Germany–not Scotland. Yet the development of the Scottish Enlightenment was widely seen as representing for Scotland exactly the kind of eighteenth-century transformation that Miller did recognise in America. And in the early nineteenth century the example of eighteenth-century Scotland would be seen by some Americans at least as indicating precisely how a new, national literary culture could be created.[18] Once again one suspects that it was Miller's awareness of the range of Scotland's contribution to the Enlightenment, in European or international terms, that made him less conscious of what that contribution had meant in terms of changing the general perception of Scotland's own cultural identity.

V

Miller's *Brief Retrospect of the Eighteenth Century* is clearly a pioneering work in America's literary and cultural history. Even though Miller's original aims were grander than his actual achievement, to write such a wide-ranging intellectual history of the eighteenth century was a bold, even imaginative enterprise. Why, then, at the end of the day is the work less than exciting? Perhaps it is its Scottish context that is partly to blame. Miller, like Nisbet before him, may be seen as coming at the end of a Scottish intellectual tradition that has its roots as far back as the seventeenth century: the tradition of the Virtuoso. The Virtuoso tradition, represented by such men as Sir Robert Sibbald, Archibald Pitcairne, and Professors James and David Gregory, contributed much to the origins of the Scottish Enlightenment; and even if the kind of learning it represented was replaced by the more structured and disciplined approach of the Enlightenment proper, a reflection of the Virtuoso tradition can still be seen later in the eighteenth century in the diverse interests of some of the Scottish *literati*. The Virtuosi were patriotic, dedicated to the advancement of learning in all its branches, which they saw as upholding an ideal of virtue.[19] Miller's *Brief Retrospect*, particularly in its aim of providing a universal account of the eighteenth century, may be seen as reflecting

73

just such a tradition. But Miller's virtuosity is in the end shaped and controlled by something else: his commitment to the conservative Scottish common sense philosophy of the human mind. It is this second, more modern Scottish intellectual tradition that ultimately determines the flavour of the *Brief Retrospect of the Eighteenth Century*. Simultaneously approving and disapproving of the period he is reviewing, accepting a notion of progress, but denying any form of perfectibility, recognising developments in science, but warning against decline in religion and morality, Miller offers nineteenth-century America a vision of intellectual culture in which progress and benevolence could be gloriously linked. It is a vision that will prove wholly acceptable to the mainstream, conservative Protestant culture of America for much of the nineteenth century. Thus Miller's *Brief Retrospect of the Eighteenth Century* is a classic illustration of how a Scottish model made modern, progressive, and scientific thinking safely available to the dominant religious, educational and cultural power structures of the United States.

Notes

1. Henry F. May, *The Enlightenment in America* (New York, 1976), p. 338.
2. Samuel Miller, *A Brief Retrospect of the Eighteenth Century. Part the First; in Three Volumes: Containing a Sketch of the Revolutions and Improvements in Science, Arts, and Literature, During that Period* (London, 1805), p. vii. All subsequent references are to this edition.
3. May, *The Enlightenment in America*, p. 339.
4. *Ibid.*, p. 339.
5. In his *Early American Literature. A Comparatist Approach* (Princeton, 1982), p. 202. A. Owen Aldridge proposes the twice-yearly 'retrospects' in the London *Monthly Magazine* as a probable source for Miller's method of classifying the various literary genres and his categories of the major European literatures.
6. It is in Miller's biography of Nisbet that we learn that the clergyman from Montrose had acquired this nickname: 'He seemed to have read every book, and to have studied every subject which the best informed person at any time in his company could ever mention. He, perhaps, more fully deserved the title that was given him before he left Scotland–*a walking library* than any other man in the United States'. See, Samuel Miller, *Memoir of the Rev. Charles Nisbet, D. D.* (New York, 1840), p. 332.
7. Miller, *Memoir of the Rev. Charles Nisbet*, pp. 74–5.
8. *Ibid.*, pp. 93–4. The fuller context of the Earl of Buchan's comments is of

special interest in illuminating the way in which the pro-American party in the United Kingdom saw itself as defending traditional *English* liberties from a new Scoto-British tyranny: 'I find it *very singular* for a Scotch Clergyman to hold so high a place as you do among the friends of liberty, and the English Constitution of government. I wish I could call it *British*'.

9. John De Witt, 'The Intellectual Life of Samuel Miller, The Opening Address of the Session 1905–06 at Princeton Theological Seminary', *The Princeton Theological Review*, (April, 1906), 176.

10. Miller, *Memoir of the Rev. Charles Nisbet*, p. 211.

11. De Witt, 'The Intellectual Life of Samuel Miller', p. 173.

12. May, *The Enlightenment in America*, p. 233.

13. Samuel Miller, *The Life of Samuel Miller, D.D., LL.D.* (Philadelphia, 1869), I, 131.

14. *Ibid.*, p. 132.

15. Nisbet's letter is preserved in the Samuel Miller Papers in Princeton University Library. At its conclusion Nisbet promises to go on writing 'till I have given you all the Information in my Power'. However, no subsequent letters from Nisbet to Miller survive.

16. In the course of his letter to Miller, Nisbet asks 'Have you read the Pursuits of Literature'? And goes on, 'The Notes on this Work may be of great Use to you in your intended Publication'. *The Pursuits of Literature*, by Thomas James Mathias, originally published in 1794, and repeatedly republished into the early years of the nineteenth century, is a substantial satirical poem addressing almost every area of later eighteenth-century society, letters, and politics. However, the main bulk of the publication is made up of the vast and voluminous notes which document its various attacks. The work clearly appealed to Nisbet because of its deeply conservative stance in the context of the heady 'war of ideas' in the 1790s. Mathias writes that the skills of the satirist 'must be instruments of war, able to break down the strongholds of anarchy, impiety, and rebellion, and mighty to vindicate the powers of legitimate authority'. See [Thomas J. Mathias], *The Pursuits of Literature, A Satirical Poem*, (London, 1797), p. 42.

17. Gilbert Chinard's 1953 essay in Miller's *Brief Retrospect*–which seems to be the only extended modern account–provides an illustration of the point. Discussing Miller's lack of national prejudice, and his status as a good 'European', Chinard comments, 'For reasons which need no elaboration, Miller knew more about England than about any other country'. See Gilbert Chinard, 'Progress and Perfectibility in Samuel Miller's Intellectual History' in George Boas *et al* (eds.), *Studies in Intellectual History*, 1953, p. 100.

18. See, for example, Rufus Choate, 'The Romance of New England History', an address delivered in Salem in 1833 and published in *Old South Leaflets*, V, (Boston, 1902). For a fuller discussion of American awareness of the Scottish model for a national literature, see Andrew Hook, *Scotland and America 1750–1835* (Glasgow and

London, 1975) pp. 160–163, and Waldemar Zacharasiewicz, 'The Rise of Cultural Nationalism in the New World: The Scottish Element and Example', in Horst W. Drescher, Hermann Volkel (eds.) *Nationalism in Literature–Literarischer Nationalismus, Literature, Language and National identity,* Peter Lang, 1989, pp. 315–34.

19. For an account of the Virtuoso tradition in Scotland see Hugh Ouston, 'Cultural Life from the Restoration to the Union' in Andrew Hook, ed., *The History of Scottish Literature, Vol. 2 1660–1800,* (Aberdeen, 1987), pp. 11–30.

CHAPTER FIVE

Americans in Scotland
in the Eighteenth and
Early Nineteenth Centuries

*Immigration studies have always been a significant presence in
American historiography. There can hardly be a European
country whose contribution to the making of America has
not been recorded in a more or less scholarly volume. However,
such works are inclined to focus on the achievements of the
individual national immigrant and all too often are highly filio-
pietistic in nature. In fact the exact contribution of such incoming national groups to the development of American culture is
distinctly problematic. It may be true that in the early days of
American Studies too much emphasis tended to be placed on the
distinctive, 'nativist' dimension of American culture, but equally
it is easy to over-value the significance of any one immigrant
group. Assimilation may have been more or less to the taste of
different incoming groups, but neither the preserving nor the
abandoning of traditional customs and values necessarily produces a significant impression on the surrounding culture.
Immigrant Scots–apart from the Gaelic-speaking Highlan-
ders–in the eighteenth and nineteenth centuries seem usually
to have opted for quick assimilation into American culture and
society. Hence Scottish emigrants (unlike their sojourning fellow-countrymen in the colonial period who played such crucial
roles in the economic, religious, educational and political life of
America) do not invariably appear to have been the bearers of a
major Scottish influence upon America's cultural life.*

*The case of visitors from one country temporarily living in the
society of another is not at all identical to that of immigrants.
The original impulse to make such a visit implies the recognition
of a certain kind of interest or opportunity. Living in an*

77

unfamiliar society, which for some reason attracts them, such visitors, even if relatively few in number, are clearly in an almost ideal position to establish enduring social and cultural links between the societies in question; consequently they are much more likely to become the bearers of intellectual and cultural influence than the great majority of ordinary immigrants. A measure of cultural concern is built in to the very fact of being a visitor from one country living in another.

For these reasons the presence of Americans in Scotland in the eighteenth and early nineteenth centuries is a subject worth attending to. Who they were, why they came, where they went, and what they thought of what they did and saw–all of these throw interesting historical light on the cultural history of both Scotland and America.

Americans began arriving in Scotland about the middle of the eighteenth century. The first important point to be stressed is that these visitors were in no sense what a later age would call tourists. Their reasons for being in Scotland had little to do with the pursuit of pleasure, since education in one form or another was their primary goal. Hence the case of the most distinguished of these early American visitors was somewhat exceptional. It *was* the pursuit of pleasure of a kind that drew Benjamin Franklin to Scotland on two occasions–the first in 1759, the second in 1771; but the pleasures that Franklin pursued were at least as much of the mind as of the body. Franklin's visits to Scotland have been alluded to in an earlier chapter, however, hence it is unnecessary at this point to provide a detailed account of their significance; let me simply repeat that it is difficult to over-emphasise the enduring importance, for the Scottish-American intellectual exchange, of America's most distinguished eighteenth-century intellectual having formed close, personal ties with the leaders of the Scottish Enlightenment.[1]

If Franklin's actual presence in Scotland may be seen as symbolising the expanding network of intellectual relationships between eighteenth-century Scotland and America, American students attending the Scottish universities played an important part in maintaining and extending such ties. Franklin's particular role in ensuring that Edinburgh became the mecca of American medical students has been noted, but of course not all American students in Scotland were students of medicine. William L. Sachse has found that all told as many as 100 American students studied at Edinburgh before the American Revolution–twice as many as studied at Oxford and Cambridge. Glasgow attracted about 20 Americans, while King's College and Marischal College at Aberdeen enrolled between them another sixteen.[2] After the Revolution the numbers of students arriving at Edinburgh at least continued to grow. According to an Edinburgh man writing to a friend in Philadelphia in 1790 there were then 24 Americans in attendance at the university, the majority from the Southern states. In the winter of 1805–6, Benjamin Silliman, soon to become professor of chemistry at Yale, noted the presence of 25 American medical students alone; and in 1818 another American correspondent in Edinburgh reported there were 25 Americans among the matriculated students.[3] It would seem reasonable to deduce that something in the region of 25 American students were present at the University of Edinburgh in any year between 1790 and 1820 or thereabouts.

Those American students in Scotland–both the large number at Edinburgh and the smaller number at Glasgow and Aberdeen–are to be seen as highly significant bearers of Scottish cultural influence to America. The Medical Schools at Philadelphia and New York are the outward signs of that influence; but it is impossible to believe that many of these students re-crossed the Atlantic unaffected by their Scottish experience. These American students in Scotland had a reputation for hard work, a determination to make the most of their years of study abroad. But many of them nonetheless participated more widely in Scottish intellectual and cultural life. In Edinburgh some were admitted to the Speculative Society; others came in contact with the Scottish *literati*. Benjamin Rush, for example, as we learn from his *Autobiography*, knew Sir Alexander Dick and met David Hume and William Robertson. Studying under Drs Cullen, Monro secundus, Russell, Black and Gregory, he also joined the Edinburgh Medical Society and probably the Edinburgh Philosophical Society. He was friendly with the blind poet Dr Blacklock–Blacklock seems to have supplemented his income by letting rooms to American medical students. Like most eighteenth-century visitors, Rush was of course appalled by the filth and squalor of Edinburgh. But he never doubted the importance of the years he spent in the city: 'The two years I spent in Edinburgh', he wrote in 1800, 'I consider as the most important in their influence upon my character and conduct of any period of my life'.[4] His son James Rush was later to follow him at the University of Edinburgh.

Rush's comments admittedly amount to no more than a personal statement. But for the American from Carolina, Virginia, Pennsylvania–or even from Philadelphia or New York–study in Edinburgh must inevitably have been a stimulating experience. Leaving out of the question possible encounters with any of the group of brilliant individuals who had brought Edinburgh an international reputation, simply the contact in classes and student society with so many other young collegians from Scotland, England, Ireland, Wales, most of the countries of Europe, the West Indies and America, must have meant for the great majority a significant widening of intellectual and cultural horizons.

II

The Americans in Scotland in the eighteenth and early nineteenth centuries I have been describing were students, enrolled at the Scottish universities, and frequently proceeding to a degree: though of course it should be remembered that for most of this period the taking of a degree was still not thought of as an essential part of a university education. Early in the nineteenth century, however, a new breed of American began to arrive in Scotland. His interest was still essentially educational and intellectual, and, much like Franklin, he came to Scotland because he wished to experience something of the vigour and excitement of Scottish intellectual life. Frequently his own higher education in America had already subjected him to Scottish influence: by 1800 the pattern of education in American colleges–curriculum, textbooks, courses–had already been profoundly influenced by aspects of the Scottish Enlightenment. For these American intellectuals in Scotland, Edinburgh of course remained the centre of attraction. By the opening of the nineteenth century the city was firmly established as one of the pre-eminent cultural capitals of Europe; thus, with access to continental Europe made difficult by the Napoleonic wars, Edinburgh was inevitably attractive to Americans with intellectual and cultural interests.

However, it was not only the fact of Edinburgh's intellectual distinction that attracted American visitors. Many Americans seem to have come to recognise in the city the existence of a kind of democracy of the intellect. From early in the eighteenth century the intellectual and cultural life of Edinburgh, like that of Glasgow and Aberdeen, had never been divorced from its polite society. The club or society in all of these cities had traditionally been the focus of intellectual debate and exchange; of good eating and better drinking; but also of individual self-improvement in civic virtue. By the early nineteenth century the patterns of intellectual and social life had probably become rather more formalised. But there can be no doubt that in Scotland intellectual and cultural endeavour continued to be associated with desirable social status. Polite society and in-tellectual society still had a great deal in common. To the American, often uneasy in the complex social world of Europe, and of course customarily debarred from the aristocratic levels of European society, the intermingling of Edinburgh's polite, social and intellectual life was particularly appealing. George Ticknor's view was not untypical of his fellow-countrymen:

> It is a great thing too, to have so much influence granted to talent as there is in Edinburgh, for it breaks down the artificial distinctions of society, and makes its terms easy to all who ought to enter it, and have any right to be there.

81

And Ticknor is convinced that it is precisely this recognition of intellectual ability that is 'the secret of the fascination of society at Edinburgh'. He continues:

And it is a still greater thing to have this talent come familiarly into the fashion of the times, sustained by that knowledge which must give it a prevalent authority, and at once receive and impart a polish and a tone which give a charm to each alike, and without which neither can become what it ought to be to itself or the world.[5]

Ticknor's views make it clear that the existence of the democratic intellect in Scotland had been recognised and appreciated by visiting Americans in the early nineteenth century. Other related factors reinforced Scotland's appeal. One was that as the years of the new century passed, so Scottish memories of the depth of American hostility to the 'Scotch' in the Revolutionary period seem to have faded, and the older sense of Scottish-American friendship and solidarity in the Colonial period was renewed. Certainly American visitors in the early nineteenth century inclined to the view that the Scots as a whole responded more hospitably to Americans than did the English. And the evidence does suggest that few Americans had reason to complain of their Scottish reception. Even thorough-going Tories, such as Professor John Wilson or Mrs Anne Grant of Laggan, whose home, as we shall see, became familiar to many visiting Americans, seem to have been able to set aside their prejudices against republican America when meeting and entertaining individual Americans. Benjamin Silliman, for example, like so many American travellers before and after him, was much struck by the low opinion and ignorance of America he encountered in Great Britain:

A few, (I am sorry to say that as far as my observation extends they are very few) possess correct information and make that rational and candid estimate of the United States, which an unprejudiced American can hear without displeasure. People of this description are less numerous in England than in

82

Scotland, where there is much more kindness towards us, and some share of real knowledge, concerning the American republics.[6]

Even though Silliman immediately qualifies this statement by saying that even in Scotland such enlightened individuals are relatively rare, his opinion is clearly of some significance. Silliman's statement helps to explain why, in the early nineteenth century, no Scottish literary or intellectual circle was necessarily closed to the properly-introduced visiting American.

There is one further point to be made in trying to explain what it was that brought culturally interested Americans to Scotland in this period. As the nineteenth century went on, Scotland's appeal was ceasing to be intellectual only. Scottish writers had provided their country with a powerful and appealing romantic glamour. It was Scotland's writers, her poets and novelists, who had converted her hills, moors, and glens into what would soon be often described as a new 'classic ground'. Edinburgh itself was the perfect symbol of Scotland's increasingly dual appeal for the American visitor in the early nineteenth century: city of acknowledged intellectual distinction, of a famous university, of Francis Jeffrey and the *Edinburgh Review*, but city too of romantic history and beauty; and city above all of Sir Walter Scott. I shall come back to the significance of the emergence of this dual image.

But first, to give some impression of the kind of experience enjoyed by my second major category of American visitors to Scotland, I shall describe the visits of the two American intellectuals whose Scottish experience has already been referred to: Benjamin Silliman and George Ticknor.

Silliman's *A Journal of Travels in England, Holland and Scotland* was published in New York in 1810, and soon established itself as a minor classic. It came to serve as a model and guide for subsequent Americans who wished to keep and publish European journals. Silliman arrived in Edinburgh on November 22, 1805, and soon joined two fellow-countrymen in lodgings in the city. He remained in Edinburgh until April, 1806 when he left for Glasgow on his way back to the United States. Although he was not matriculated as a student in the university, the greatest part of Silliman's time seems to have been taken up by study: presumably in preparation for his assumption of the newly-created Chair in chemistry at Yale University to which he had been appointed. Clearly he did not take part in Edinburgh's winter social season. However his journal indicates that he made many friends among the university faculty: he was later to provide subsequent American visitors like John Griscom, another chemistry professor, with letters of introduction to them. With his two American friends he attended a party given by Dugald Stewart–and was surprised by the informality of the occasion. Attempting to raise the subject of American literature, he was disappointed by the lack of knowledge of the subject displayed by Stewart and his other guests. Silliman encountered several Scots who remembered Benjamin Rush, and other American students of an earlier generation; and on at least one other occasion he discussed American literature with a 'literary man'–almost certainly the literary historian Robert Anderson who, through his connection with the Lowell family in Boston, became a key figure in Edinburgh's Scottish-American society. Once again Silliman was disappointed by his interlocutor's lack of enthusiasm for American writers.

As compared with the American students who preceded him, and the tourists who came after him, Silliman emerges as a rather intermediary figure. Clearly his social experience of Edinburgh was wider and more varied than that of the students of an earlier generation. But in an important sense Silliman remained a student in Edinburgh: his attendance at university classes and lectures by Professors Gregory, Hope and Stewart clearly was the controlling factor during his stay. It was still very much the Scotland of the Scottish Enlightenment that had drawn Silliman to the northern half of the United Kingdom. Of his Edinburgh experience he subsequently wrote: 'No five months of my life were ever spent more profitably; and this residence laid the top stones of my early professional education'.[7]

The second American, whose Scottish experience I wish to

describe, was destined to become one of America's outstanding nineteenth-century scholars. George Ticknor sailed for Europe in 1815, in the company of Edward Everett, later to be an editor of the *North American Review*. For the next four years he travelled and studied in Europe before returning to Boston to occupy the new Smith professorship of French and Spanish at Harvard. His travels brought him into contact with some of Europe's most distinguished thinkers and writers including Goethe, Chateaubriand and the Schlegel brothers; and before his arrival in Scotland in February, 1819, he had already got to know several distinguished Scottish figures. At his home in Sydenham he had met Thomas Campbell; and at Holland House in London he had been introduced to Sir James Mackintosh, Sydney Smith, and Henry Brougham. Inevitably then, Ticknor arrived in Edinburgh with a background that ensured his immediate admission to the city's social and intellectual world.

Like so many of his countrymen, Ticknor was much impressed by Edinburgh's appearance; it is certainly, he wrote, 'one of the beautiful cities of Europe'. But his early days in the Scottish capital were unhappy ones. He entered no capital of Europe, he says, 'with a lighter heart and more confident expectations of enjoyment . . . And yet it was there I was destined to meet the severest suffering my life had yet known'.[8] The day after his arrival he received letters announcing the death of his mother. After this event his first call in the city was on Mrs Anne Grant of Laggan. This extraordinary lady had come to play a significant part in the social relations between Scotland and America in the early part of the nineteenth century. Anne MacVicar, as she originally was, the daughter of an officer in the British army, had spent most of her childhood in pre-Revolutionary America where she had become a protégé of Margarita Schuyler of Albany, a member of one of the most influential families in the province of New York. The Schuyler home in Albany had become the centre of the social life of the northern frontier. Back in Scotland, Anne MacVicar married a Highland minister, and became Mrs Grant of Laggan. However, her husband died in 1801 and it was to writing that Mrs Grant turned to sustain herself and her large family. She published a successful book of poems, and subsequent works described her life in the Scottish Highlands, and her childhood in America. In 1810 she moved to Edinburgh, and by then her ties with America had been renewed. Through the agency of Charles Lowell, a student in Edinburgh from 1802–4, of the famous Boston family, her book *Letters from the Mountains* was republished in Boston in 1806; an edition of *Memoirs of an American Lady* followed in New York in 1809. For the rest of her long life Mrs Grant remained on the most intimate terms with the Lowell family. Inevitably, visiting Bostonians in Scotland arrived bearing letters of introduction to her, and they in turn wrote similar letters on behalf of other Americans. In this way Mrs Grant's home became a remarkable rendezvous for American visitors to Scotland. And of course an introduction to Mrs Grant meant an easy entry to most of Edinburgh's social and literary circles. Herself a High Tory her house was nonetheless frequented by a wide range of the Edinburgh *literati*, not excluding Jeffrey and the other Whigs associated with the *Edinburgh Review*. What is sufficiently clear is that year after year Mrs Grant came to expect to receive American visitors to Scotland. In 1819 she wrote to a friend: 'You must know that, in the summer . . . many tourists come from London, from America, and from Ireland with letters of introduction to me'.[9] This, therefore, was the lady on whom Ticknor paid his first Edinburgh call. Later he wrote in his journal: 'I went quite . . . often to Mrs Grant's where an American, I imagine, finds himself at home more easily than anywhere else in Edinburgh'.[10] At Mrs Grant's Ticknor met Robert Own, then engaged in his New Lanark venture, John Wilson of *Blackwoods Magazine* whom he described as 'a pretending young man, but with a great deal of talent', and James Hogg, whose manner must have offended the Bostonian's fastidiousness: Hogg is described as 'vulgar as his name'.[11]

If Mrs Grant had made a favourable impression on Ticknor, Ticknor had equally impressed his hostess. A letter of June, 1819, indicates Mrs Grant's high opinion of Ticknor, and also highlights the extent to which her house had become a meeting-place for visiting Americans:

> The American character has been much raised among our literary people here, by a constellation of persons of brilliant talents and polished manners, by whom we were dazzled and delighted last winter. A Mr Preston from Virginia, and his friend from Carolina, whose name I cannot spell, for it is French [Hugh S. Legaré], Mr Ticknor, and Mr Cogswell, were the most distinguished representations of your new world.[12]

– and the letter goes on to mention 'a handsome and high-bred Mr Ralston from Philadelphia'.

Ticknor also paid frequent visits to the home of another of Edinburgh's distinguished hostesses: Mrs Archibald Fletcher. Ticknor describes Mrs Fletcher as an outstanding conversationalist and '*the* lady in Edinburgh by way of eminence'.[13] Mrs Fletcher had a Whig coterie to match Mrs Grant's Tory one. Like Mrs Grant, Mrs Fletcher reciprocated Ticknor's admiration. In a letter she described Ticknor and Cogswell as 'among the most cultivated and agreeable Americans we had ever known' and subsequently she maintained an occasional correspondence with Ticknor.[14]

Ticknor's contacts with Edinburgh's intellectual society were not limited to these visits to the salons of the city's leading literary ladies. He spent two or three afternoons with Playfair, and was impressed by the old professor's elegance of both mind and manner. One morning he breakfasted with the venerable Henry Mackenzie at Lady Cumming's. He met and visited John Pillans, headmaster of the city's famous High School. He also met Robert Anderson, the philosopher Thomas Brown, George Thomson, editor and song-collector, Archibald Alison, author of the *Essay on Taste*, and of course Jeffrey 'who was everywhere, in all parties, dances, and routs, and yet found time for his great business . . .'[15]

Despite all these gratifying encounters Ticknor was not entirely satisfied with Edinburgh society. In a letter to his father, March 1, 1819, he complained that the society of men of letters in the city was not quite what he had hoped it would be. Conversations at dinner, and on other occasions, tended to consist of a series of speeches; the Edinburgh *literati* only lived up to his expectations when talked to individually. Of course Ticknor does not seem to have been much interested in conversation of a purely social nature. Like Silliman, indeed, he had not come to Edinburgh solely for entertainment, intellectual or otherwise. He told his father he had come with the desire 'to learn something of Scottish literature and literary history, and pick up my library in this department and in English'.[16] To satisfy his first aim he went instantly to Dr Robert Anderson whom he described as 'the person . . . who best knows English literary history, to say nothing of Scotch, which was, as it were, born with him'.[17] Subsequently he writes that he had received assistance in this field, not only from Anderson, but from Jamieson, Thomson, and Walter Scott.

Meetings with Scott, for Ticknor as for so many other American victors to Scotland, became the high-point of his Scottish experience. Ticknor's impression of the great man was entirely favourable. 'He is, indeed', he wrote, 'the lord of the ascendant now in Edinburgh, and well deserves to be, for I look upon him to be quite as remarkable in intercourse and conversation, as he is in any of his writings, even in his novels'.[18]

Ticknor dined with Scott on more than one occasion. One morning Scott took him on a tour of the city pointing out the houses of Hume, Blair, Robertson and the rest of the intellectual leaders of the previous generation. Impressed as he was by Scott it is not surprising that Ticknor's one trip away from Edinburgh should have been to Abbotsford. With his friend Cogswell, he spent two entertaining days with Scott at his Border home, before continuing south to the Lake District to visit Southey and Wordsworth.

Ticknor had come to Scotland in 1819 for essentially intellectual reasons. His intellectual sophistication, however, is clearly much more marked than that of Silliman. If he recognised that in Edinburgh, as elsewhere in Europe, there were opportunities available to him that he would not find in Boston or New York, still he did not grasp them in the spirit of the provincial outsider. If he shared with his student predecessors in the pre-Revolutionary period their determination to learn, that determination co-existed with a new sense of intellectual equality. For Ticknor there is no question of simply bowing down before the shrine of European culture. Ticknor may of course be seen as a special case; but I am inclined to think that his attitude to some degree represents a developing sense of intellectual self-confidence on the part of the American intellectual world.

III

Earlier I made brief reference to the view that in the early nineteenth century Scotland's appeal for Americans ceased to be purely or exclusively an intellectual one. A major consequence of the popular successes of Scottish literary romanticism throughout the Western world, culminating in the amazing triumph of Scott and the Waverley Novels, was the conversion of Scotland itself into a kind of archetypal land of romance. Scotland's heroic and bloody history, its wild, sublime, and pastoral landscapes, its popular folk culture of ballad and song, its traditionally valorous and zealous people—all of these contributed to the creation of a view of Scotland as a country in which the basic ideologies of romanticism could be seen to be enacted or embodied. Of course there was nothing necessarily contradictory or mutually exclusive about Scotland's intellectual and romantic appeals. In so far as the country's romantic appeal, in these early years at least, depended upon a close and detailed knowledge of Scottish writing, its basis too was in a sense intellectual. In the case of the individual visitor a powerful attraction could be found in both appeals—frequently they supported rather than contradicted each other. But the balance between the two kinds of attraction did not remain a stable one: the pattern is rather that of a gradual weakening of the intellectual appeal, a gradual strengthening of the romantic one. Early in the nineteenth century, the American visitor—like Silliman—did not venture far beyond the cities of Edinburgh and Glasgow. By the end of the 1820s Americans still came to

Edinburgh but the source of its attraction was now mainly the city's beauty and its romantic associations. In other words, in this period a third and final type of American visitor is beginning to appear in Scotland: one who may be accurately described as a *tourist*.

The main object of the American tourist in Scotland was of course to travel over as much as possible of Scotland's famous 'classic ground'. But in the first place the tourist was irresistibly drawn to Edinburgh. To reach the city, easily the most popular route was the east coast one through the northern counties of England entering Scotland at Berwick-upon-Tweed. Other possibilities were the west route through Carlisle, or the sea-passage from London direct to Edinburgh. Once in Edinburgh the tourist hurried to see Holyrood Palace and the Castle; the palace, given its multiple associations with Mary Queen of Scots, the miracle of Rizzio's blood and the rest, excited the deeper emotions. In 1776, George Logan, an American Quaker from Pennsylvania, had been a medical student in Edinburgh. He had visited Holyrood and described it as 'miserably situated'; like Franklin before him, he had gone on to list the palace's associations with Mary without any particular emotion.[19] Such restraint was hardly characteristic of those American visitors arriving a generation or two later. But Edinburgh had much more to offer the tourist: the elegance of the New Town, the beautiful and varied prospects of the city gained from Arthur's Seat or Calton Hill, and of course there was hardly a close or wynd of Old Edinburgh lacking in some literary, historical, or romantic association.

After spending a week or so in Edinburgh, most tourists set off on their Scottish tour by sailing up the Forth to Stirling. The next stage was by coach to Callander and across the *Lady of the Lake* country to Loch Katrine, and on by foot to Loch Lomond. A boat trip round the loch, and down the River Leven, was followed by another boat trip up the Clyde to Glasgow. This short route–it could be covered in two days–was easily the most popular one. Some Americans, however, chose to make a more extended Highland tour: from Stirling north to Perth and on to

Inverness. Then down the Caledonian Canal by boat, either disembarking at Ballachulish and proceeding overland through Glencoe to Loch Lomond and the Scott country again, or sailing on out to visit Iona and Staffa before returning to the Clyde. Occasionally a route was followed east from Inverness along the Moray Firth to Aberdeen, then down the east coast to Edinburgh. From Glasgow the popular routes led south to Ayrshire and the Burns country, and so back to England by way of Dumfries, or, more popular, the southerly route back to Edinburgh via the Clyde valley, taking on visits to the different Falls of Clyde and Robert Owen's model industrial village at New Lanark.

Exactly how many American tourists followed one or other of the tourist routes I have described, in the early nineteenth century, is difficult to estimate. The number is high at least in the sense that Americans who visited Europe in the early decades of the nineteenth century seem automatically to have included a trip to Scotland in their itinerary. In this period more than a dozen American travellers published journals which include extended accounts of their Scottish visit. Some of these were originally published in the form of a series of articles appearing in a multiplicity of American newspapers and magazines. Since the great majority of these accounts describe identical areas of Scotland, one must consider that the American reading-public had a perennial appetite for descriptions of a romantically-conceived Scotland.

But what is most significant about the phenomenon of the emergence of the American tourist in Scotland in the early decades of the nineteenth century is its literary origins. The tour of Scotland that the traveller undertakes, and which he lovingly recreates for the readers back home, is essentially a literary pilgrimage: it is the Scott country, the Burns country, the *Ossian* country, that he and his readers visit. It is the pages of Scottish literature, combined with a knowledge of romantic Scottish history–itself largely deriving from literary sources–which direct the tourists steps. Hence the rapt attention paid to those areas, scenes, and buildings associated either with the key figures in Scotland's romantic history–Wallace, Bruce, Mary Queen of Scots, Prince Charles Stuart and the Jacobite cause, Rob Roy etc.–or with the scenes and settings of the key works in the history of Scottish literary romanticism: Home's *Douglas*, Macpherson's *Ossian*, the poems of Burns and, pre-eminently, the poems and novels of Scott. This is the Scotland which had come to be seen as a new 'classic ground' to be approached with the same emotions of reverence and excitement once reserved for the classical landscapes of Greece and Italy. To turn the pages of the published journals of American travellers in Scotland is to turn the romantic pages of Scottish literature and history.[20]

What emerges from this account of the presence of Americans in Scotland–from the industrious medical student in the mid-eighteenth century to the enraptured tourist at Abbotsford in the 1830s–is a particular insight into the pattern of Scottish cultural history in this crucial period. What Scotland means to the foreign visitor changes dramatically. In the eighteenth century Scotland attracts Americans because it is a centre of progress and enlightenment. What is on offer to the American visitor is intellectual self-improvement. In the early years of the nineteenth century, the Scotland of the Scottish Enlightenment continues to attract. But slowly another pattern begins to emerge. As the rational world of the Enlightenment comes under increasing pressure from the romantic sensibility, the romantic image of Scotland, like the eye of the Ancient Mariner, glitters and fascinates with ever greater power. In the end it is the spell cast by romantic Scotland that is binding–on America just as on the rest of the outside world. The story of American visitors to Scotland in the eighteenth and early nineteenth centuries is part of the wider story which is the changing cultural history of Scotland itself.

Notes

1. See Chapter Two, 'Philadelphia, Edinburgh and the Scottish Enlightenment' pp. 00 for a fuller discussion of Franklin's Scottish visits.
2. See William L. Sachse, *The Colonial American in Britain* (Madison, 1956), pp. 34–5.
3. Andrew Hook, *Scotland and America, 1750–1835* (Glasgow and London), 1975, p. 219 (note 2).

4. George W. Corner (ed.), *The Autobiography of Benjamin Rush* (Princeton, 1948), p. 43.
5. George S. Hillard (ed.), *Life, Letters, and Journals of George Ticknor* (Boston, 1876), I, 227.
6. Benjamin Silliman, *A Journal of Travels in England, Holland, and Scotland* (New York, 1810), II, 348–9.
7. See, George P. Fisher, *Life of Benjamin Silliman* (London, 1866), I, 168.
8. *Life, Letters, and Journals of George Ticknor*, I, pp. 276–7, 275.
9. J. P. Grant (ed.), *Memoir and Correspondence of Mrs Grant of Laggan* (London, 1845), II, 224.
10. *Life, Letters, and Journals of George Ticknor*, I, pp. 278.
11. *Ibid*.
12. *Memoir and Correspondence*, II, 211.
13. *Life, Letters, and Journals of George Ticknor*, I, p. 279.
14. Mrs Eliza Fletcher, *Autobiography* (Boston, 1876), p. 140.
15. *Life, Letters, and Journals of George Ticknor*, I, p. 280.
16. *Ibid*., p. 274.
17. *Ibid*.
18. *Ibid*., p. 280.
19. See Frederick B. Tolles, *George Logan of Philadelphia* (New York, 1953), p. 29.
20. Shirley Foster's pamphlet, *American Women Travellers to Europe* (Keele University Press, 1994) indicates continuing American responsiveness to the romantic image of Scotland throughout the nineteenth century. For Sophia Hawthorne Scotland is a 'peculiarly enchanted' realm, with the grandeur of its Highland scenery and its constant echoes of Scott. For Harriet Beecher Stowe, Scotland, already 'dear' to her from her acquaintance with Scottish ballads, the songs of Burns, and 'the enchantments of Scott', is a site of 'wild, poetic beauty'. For Margaret Fuller, despite her horror at the poverty and misery evident in the streets of Glasgow and Edinburgh, Scotland's classic ground retains its romantic sublimity and literary suggestiveness.

CHAPTER SIX

Scott and America

It is often difficult to determine whether the popular success of a foreign author is best explained by the 'universal' dimension of his or her work, transcending or eliding cultural difference, or rather by local factors within the foreign audience that happen to make it especially responsive to the author's writing. At the general level of plot, character and theme, Walter Scott was perfectly alert to the tension between an emphasis on the universal on the one hand, the local and particular on the other. In the opening chapter of his own first novel, **Waverley,** *he explains to the reader that he has chosen to throw the force of his narrative upon the characters and passions of the actors:*

> *those passions common to men in all stages of society, and which have alike agitated the human heart, whether it throbbed under the steel corslet of the fifteenth century, the brocaded coat of the eighteenth, or the blue frock and white dimity waistcoat of the present day.*

Having made the universal, essentialist case, however, he immediately qualifies it: 'Upon these passions it is no doubt true that the state of manners and laws casts a necessary colouring. . . .' And a little later in Chapter Five, he expands upon the author's need to attend to the influences brought to bear by the local specifics:

> *I beg pardon, once and for all, of those readers who take up novels merely for amusement, for plaguing them so long with old-fashioned politics, and Whig and Tory, and Hanoverians and Jacobites. The truth is, I cannot promise them that this story shall be intelligible, not to say probable, without it. My plan requires that I should explain the motives on which its*

action proceeded; and these motives necessarily arose from the feelings, prejudices, and parties of the times.

Scott, that is, wants to have it both ways: his novels will explore the great, unchanging universals of human nature and human feeling, but will simultaneously demonstrate that human motives and behaviour are conditioned by the particular historical circumstances of their day and age. The essay that follows argues that Scott's amazing appeal to his original American readers may have had much in common with his appeal to readers world-wide; but perhaps there were special factors, too, which made Scott's American audience an unusually receptive one.

Sir James Mackintosh, that life-long friend and admirer of America, remembered how as a schoolboy in the days of the American War he had set up an impromptu House of Commons composed of fellow scholars, and delivered the speeches of Burke and Fox attacking the policies of Lord North's administration. Had Walter Scott been a member of Mackintosh's House of Commons we know of one schoolboy at least who would have risen to the defence of North and his policies. From Scott's *Memoirs* of his early life we learn that as a boy he took a lively interest in the progress of the war in America, and that his sympathies were not in the least engaged by the patriotic struggle of the colonists to free themselves from the control of a Hanoverian king. On the contrary. Scott records that he waited hopefully to hear of Washington's defeat 'as if I had had some deep and personal cause of antipathy to him'. General Washington was not able to oblige the youthful Scott's expectations in this matter, but Scott's revenge, as it were, was nonetheless complete. Where the might of British arms failed, Scott's pen triumphed. The United States established in successful defiance of the British Crown was in turn conquered by Walter Scott. And nowhere in the world was Scott's conquest so complete and enduring. Scott's pen was indeed mightier than the sword.

If there is more than a little amusement in the picture of the youthful Scott waiting hopefully for news of the defeat of the country that was subsequently to idolise him, there is something positively ironic about Scott's initial reception as a writer in America. That Scott was to find in America one of his largest and most enthusiastic audiences has of course always been recognised; much less well-known is the story of Scott's inauspicious introduction to the American literary scene. A girl called Joanna Graham was a childhood friend of Scott in Edinburgh. In 1780 her mother, Isabella Graham, a widow, had set up a private school in the city and among her friends and patrons was Mrs Walter Scott, the mother of the writer. Presumably it was this friendship that led to Joanna Graham and Walter Scott coming to know each other. In any event Joanna left Edinburgh for New York with her mother in 1789. Mrs Graham's decision to return to America, where she had briefly resided previously while her husband was alive, was arrived at partly through the influence of John Witherspoon, that most distinguished of Scottish-Americans, president of the College of New Jersey at Princeton, whom she had met in Edinburgh in 1784. In New York Mrs Graham opened a school for young ladies which was one of the earliest of such establishments to be set up in America. In due course Joanna Graham married another exiled Scot in New York and became Mrs Divie Bethune, her husband being a successful merchant and philanthropist. Whether or not Scott maintained any kind of contact with the Graham family after their removal to New York I am unable to say; the chances are no doubt that he did not. But he does not seem to have forgotten Joanna completely.

When Scott's first major poetic work–the *Lay of the last Minstrel* appeared in 1805, among those who received a presentation copy of the poem was Mrs Divie Bethune of New York. Through this happy circumstance a number of the New York *literati* were thus enabled to read the poem at a time when its author's reputation was yet to be made. As was of course the normal procedure with any new work that had been deemed worthy of publication in Britain, the question was raised whether the poem merited republication in New York. After due deliberation the coterie of critics decided that the answer was no. The poem, they decided, was 'too local in its nature' to have universal appeal. One can fairly assume that this opinion was one that this particular group of Knickerbocker literary *savants* would subsequently have dearly liked to forget. As it was, not all American publishers were impressed by their decision; David Longworth printed the first, introductory section of the poem in the *Belles-Lettres Repository* of 1805; the whole poem appeared in Philadelphia later in the same year; New York fell into line in the following year, and 1806 also saw publication of the poem at Charleston, South Carolina; publication followed at Philadelphia again in 1807 and 1810; at Boston in 1807 and 1810; at New York in 1811; at Baltimore in 1811 and 1812; and at Savannah, Georgia, in 1811. The pattern established here with the *Lay of the Last Minstrel* was of course repeated with each of the narrative poems that followed it: extensive and repeated American republication followed hard on the heels of the appearance of a new Scott poem in Britain. And collected editions of Scott's poems were soon making their appearance in America. Hence three years before the publication of *Waverley*, Scott's popularity in America was already so great that a writer in the *American Review* could remark that,

> no poetical works, not excepting even those of Cowper and Burns, have been more widely circulated or read with more avidity in this country, than those of Walter Scott, who is now as a poet, on the highest pinnacle of fame and popularity. The 'Lay of the Last Minstrel' belongs to every private library, and is familiar to the memory of almost every man among us, who has the most inconsiderable pretensions to literature.[1]

The writer goes on to state that five thousand copies of the *Lay of the Last Minstrel* had been sold, and already, only a year after its initial publication, four thousand copies of the *Lady of the Lake* (four thousand was later to be the circulation figure of the

From Goosecreek to Gandercleugh

North American Review, the most influential and powerful of the early American literary periodicals). Even if these figures do not strike us as particularly impressive–they do make it clear that Scott's narrative poems, however local their nature, did enjoy a substantial vogue in America.

The Lay of the Last Minstrel itself in fact won immediate and widespread critical approval on its appearance in America. It was first praised in the *Literary Magazine*, a periodical then edited by Charles Brockden Brown. In 1805 a contributor to the magazine wrote of the *Lay*: 'there has just fallen into my hands a poem, which has given me so much pleasure that I cannot forbear calling the attention of your readers to it'. It is 'a very beautiful and entertaining poem, in a style which may be justly deemed original, and which affords evidence of the genius of the author'.[2] In fact these sentiments are not all entirely what they seem: the second part of the quotation is evidence of a direct crib from the *Edinburgh Review*'s notice of the poem which had appeared shortly before. The *Port Folio*, probably the most respected of the American literary periodicals at the opening of the nineteenth century, proceeded more straightforwardly: it simply reprinted in its columns a large part of the *Edinburgh*'s article. As early as 1807, then, the *Port Folio* was able to refer to Scott's 'honourable name' as 'now perfectly familiar to every lover of poetical description'. And finally, in the following year, 1808, in the course of a laudatory notice of *Marmion*, Scott is recognised in the *Port Folio* as the newest in a long line of distinguished Scottish poets:

> Scotland has long been eminently distinguished for the splendour of her poetical reputation. Drummond of Hawthornden, Hamilton of Balfour [Bangour], Thomson, Beattie and Burns have glorified their country by the most brilliant colours of imagination. To these *time honoured* names we may now add that of Walter Scott, who in every respect is most certainly their compeer.[3]

Substantial and widespread as it clearly was, Scott's vogue as a highly-praised poet, in America as elsewhere, was soon

98

eclipsed in its scale by the amazing response to Scott the novelist. Exact figures for the numbers of copies of the Waverley Novels produced in America are of course impossible to arrive at. In 1823, in a speech entitled *Discourse concerning the Influence of America on the Mind*, C. J. Ingersoll asserted that 'nearly 200,000 copies of the Waverley novels, comprising 500,000 volumes, have issued from the American press in the last nine years'.[4] Two years later, in 1825, John Neal, the Baltimore novelist and critic, subsequently author of a series of articles on American literature in *Blackwood's Magazine*, wrote that 'half a million of the great Scotch novels, we dare say, have re-issued from the American press. They are read by everybody–every-where–all over the States'.[5] Even if these estimates are little more than informed guesses it is perfectly clear that Scott's novels had reached a reading-public most of which had no 'pretensions to literature' at all. During his travels in North America between 1828 and 1831 James Stuart, grandson of the philosopher Dugald Stewart, noted that copies of Scott's works were to be found 'even more frequently than Mr Cooper's novels, wherever we go in this country'.

The immense popularity of the Waverley Novels with the American reading-public was echoed by a chorus of critical praise. Dissenting voices were few and far between. For a brief period the *Port Folio* went through an anti-Scott phase, arguing that *Waverley* was too poor a work to be attributed to Scott. But within a few years it fell into line with the rest of the American periodicals, expressing a boundless enthusiasm for each succes-sive new work by Scott. Everywhere the pattern of review was the same: a few introductory pages, mostly of praise, then many pages of extracts from the work in question. Phrases such as 'the wealth of his imagination', 'the reach and majesty of his power' are typical of the American critical reaction to Scott: he 'stands upon an eminence, to which approaches have been made, but no one has placed himself by his side'. If anyone at all shared Scott's lofty eminence, it could only be Shakespeare: 'the novels of Scott, have become in fact, a literature of themselves', an-nounced the *Southern Review*, 'and we know not if his writings were expunged, what deeper injury could be inflicted on English literature, except sentence of oblivion were passed on Shakespeare himself'.[6]

This enthusiasm for Scott in America inevitably had many ramifications. The American public apparently had an inexhaustible appetite for anything connected with the author of the Waverley Novels. A favourite area of investigation and explanation was the background material which Scott had drawn on for individual novels. Articles about the 'Originals' of characters and settings appearing in the novels clearly had a wide appeal. In 1818 the editor of the *Analectic Magazine*, introducing an article called the 'Original of the Black Dwarf', commented on this enthusiasm for everything connected with the Waverley Novels:

> The public feeling is alive to all that issues from the prolific genius of the author of Rob Roy, etc. and connects with whatever is illustrative of his works, the eagerness of curiosity and the attention of interest. Under this impression we give place to the following account of The Black Dwarf . . .[7]

Americans displayed 'the eagerness of curiosity and the attention of interest' in relation to another aspect of Scott: the cloak of anonymity under which *Waverley* and its successors was produced. Once again American interest in the question was almost obsessional. Among the many suggestions made on the problem of the true authorship of the Waverley Novels more than one linked the novels with a North American author. In 1819 the *Analectic Magazine* pronounced all such suggestions worthless: 'With respect to the disputed parentage of these novels, we are positively informed, that the many stories of their transatlantic origin, so confidently circulated in the United States, are destitute of all foundation'.[8] Only a year before, in discussing *Rob Roy*, the same magazine, largely on the flimsy evidence of the use of the word 'wig-wam', and in earlier writings of the term 'the plantations', had cheerfully attributed the authorship of the novels to a Dr Greenfield who had visited America some years before.[9] A much more popular attribution was to Walter Scott's brother, Thomas Scott, who lived in Montreal. Professor John Griscom, an American chemist who travelled in Britain and Europe in the period 1818–1819, and who studied for some months in Edinburgh, mentions the canvassing of this idea, and a comment in the Philadelphia *Literary Gazette* a year or two later in 1821 confirms the popularity of the suggestion:

> The Quarterly Review, a few years ago hinted, that the merit of authorship belonged to a *brother* of Walter Scott, living beyond the Atlantic, and the same idea has been more than once expressed in our newspapers. We understand that at Montreal, the place of residence of Mr Thomas Scott, the fact is universally believed . . .'[10]

In his book of reminiscences called *Old New York*, written about the middle of the nineteenth century, J. W. Francis, for long a member of the literary circles of New York, recalls hearing arguments in favour of the view that the true author of the Waverley Novels was Scott's brother in Canada. According to Francis, Charles Mathews, the English comic actor, in the course of a visit to New York, was the first person 'who gave a pretty decisive opinion that Scott was the author of the Waverley Novels'. Mathew's decisive opinion was given five years before Scott's own public admission at the Ballantyne dinner in 1827, at a time when, again according to Francis, 'we in New York were digesting the argument of Coleman, of the Evening Post, and his correspondents, who attempted to prove that such could not be the truth, and that a Major or Col. Scott, of Canada, was the actual author'.[11] Quite clearly the idea that Thomas Scott could be the author of the Waverley Novels was taken perfectly seriously. Indeed the notion seems to have been widely enough debated for one to suspect that the prospect of at least a transatlantic residence for the author of the sensationally successful Waverley Novels exercised a substantial and fascinating appeal.

Before turning to the question of why Scott was so much to the American taste I wish to mention one other area of evidence, rather different in its nature from what has gone before, which reveals the power and pervasiveness of Scott's impact upon America. This is the effect Scott had on the American view of Scotland. Scott consummated a literary and cultural tradition which converted Scotland into the most romantic country in Europe. Nowhere was this development registered more clearly than in America; for many Americans Scott endorsed, confirmed, and authenticated what they had long suspected–that Scotland was beyond compare as the land of romance. As such, Scotland exercised a peculiar fascination, and American travellers in Europe almost invariably at some point in their European journey visited the northern half of the United Kingdom. What they saw, where they went, how they responded, all reflected their enthusiasm for Scott above all else. Walter Scottland was indeed the main object of their visit; Walter Scottland was no less than a new classic ground. The point is made over and over again by different American visitors. Calvin Colton, an American journalist and economist, between 1831 and 1835 served as European correspondent of the *New York Observer*. Of Scotland Colton wrote:

> The genius of a single man has consecrated those wide regions, as modern classic ground, and the history of that country as a classic legend. Italy and Greece have at this moment, if possible, less interest in the eye of travellers for their classic associations, than the land which gave birth to Walter Scott.[12]

Orville Dewey, an American cleric who travelled through part of the Scottish Highlands in the summer of 1833, reiterates the theme. In Glasgow on July 20, he described the tour he had just completed:

> From Edinburgh, I have come round through the Highlands to this place. Every step of the way has been on classic ground; the beautiful windings of the Forth with the Grampian Hills on the north; Stirling Castle; the wild grandeur of the Trossachs; Ben Nevis and Ben Venue; and the haunted waters of

Loch Katrine, every rock and headland garlanded with romance; the haunts of Rob Roy, the Lennox country, and the soft scenery of the Leven.[13]

But it was not only Americans who were writing and thinking about their own firsthand experience of travel in Scotland who tended to conceive of Scott and his influence in precisely these terms. American critics and commentators too were peculiarly alive to this particular dimension of Scott's achievement. A writer in the *North American Review* in 1831 noted both the transformation wrought by Scott on the face of Scotland and the impetus his writings had given quite literally to travels in the Scottish Highlands: 'a hundred years ago, the Highlands of Scotland were as little known as the Rocky Mountains', but Scott's pen 'has thrown them open as completely as a thousand military roads, and travellers will wander over them in all generations to come'.[14] The tone of such comments is almost religious in its reverence. And indeed some commentators did make explicit use of religious imagery: Scotland is a new holy land, and Scott's admirers visit his homeland as literary pilgrims. Almost two generations earlier, in the Revolutionary period, many colonial Americans had identified Scotland and the Scots– much more than England and the English–with the British government's policies of absolute tyranny and oppression. The romantically poetic image of Scotland seems almost magically to wipe away that less than appealing past.

II

The Scott's reception in America was consistently enthusiastic and that his impact was correspondingly deep and wide are evident enough. Less obvious is any satisfactory explanation of Scott's success. Of course a large part of Scott's appeal in America must have been identical with the appeal felt by readers in Scotland, England and throughout all of Europe. The universality of Scott's success clearly indicates that there was much in his work that appealed to contemporary readers whatever their place of origin. What precisely it was has never been definitively identified. Scott's romanticism obviously played a major part, and the Waverley Novels do exhibit central characteristics of the whole romantic movement: an interest in the past, particularly the heroic and colourful past; an interest in societies remote from the civilised present, with manners and customs more striking and dramatic than those typical of the conventional modern world; an interest in the world of passionate feeling and commitment, again out of step with the moderate rationalism of the present. But such grounds are not enough on which to convict Scott of uninhibited romanticism, and hence in turn, to identify his romanticism as the source of his triumph. Scott's romanticism, as we all now recognise, is in fact hedged around with reservations, ambivalences, limitations, uncertainties. It is almost as likely that these inhibitions about the world of romance were the secret of his success as that it was his romanticism alone that explained it. The period 1814 to 1832–the period that spanned the writing of the Waverley Novels–was a period of social and political counter-revolution in both Europe and America. On the face of it the writer to be idolised in such a period is hardly likely to have been an exponent of revolutionary romanticism. On the whole it seems much more probable that Scott succeeded precisely because his romanticism, with its undoubted popular appeal, was in the end unthreatening because removed to the safety of the past.

But still one is not entirely satisfied. To appeal to the social and political history of Europe and America to explain the Scott phenomenon, seems to leave *literary* history itself too much out of account. Perhaps it is dangerously easy to dissolve literary movements into broader socio-political terms. Existing explanations of the Scott phenomenon in America exhibit such dangers all too clearly. The most popular account of the reasons behind Scott's American success derives ultimately from some remarks by Mark Twain, in chapter 46 of *Life on the Mississippi*, to the effect that Scott was responsible for the American Civil War. Scott's romantic nationalism, his celebration of bogus aristocratic values, his advocacy of medieval notions of chivalry and nobility, had, according to Twain, inspired the

South with a set of misguided notions about its self-identity, what it believed in, and what it represented.

Subsequent commentators have offered somewhat modified versions of Twain's thesis. The recurring suggestion is that Scott's American success owed most to the fact either that conservative Southern society shared the aristocratic principles and virtues his work was seen as celebrating, or that at least these were the values the South most admired. In other words Scott's appeal in America is best understood in terms of the nature of Southern society. Now it is perfectly true that some of the more extreme manifestations of the Scott vogue in America occurred in the Southern states. It was in the South, for example, that quasi-medieval tournaments, modelled on that described at Ashby in *Ivanhoe*, became a common form of popular entertainment. Southern plantations and Southern children did frequently owe their names to Scott's novels. But in the end the sociology of the South is hardly adequate as an explanation of Scott's appeal in America. How does one explain the fact that it was not only in the South that Scott was enthusiastically received in America? There is no hard evidence that Scott was read in Charleston or New Orleans with any significantly greater enthusiasm than in Boston or New York. Perhaps the South did respond to certain aspects of Scott's work with peculiar fervour; perhaps it is even true that the reading of Scott encouraged the South towards certain notions of its own social and cultural identity which had previously remained less well-defined. But it is equally clear that Scott appealed in parts of America which in no way shared the social structure of the South.

What best explains Scott's American appeal is something much less glamorous than Twain's socio-political account. It is instead literary history in a remarkably traditional sense. The basic weakness in Twain's case, and in that of the modern commentators who have either tried to disprove his contention or in a modified form agree with it, is its lack of a truly historical perspective. Almost without exception all of these commentators treat Scott in America as a wholly isolated phenomenon; as

105

if Scott had arrived in America like some meteor from outer space. The American reading public one gathers, responded ecstatically overnight to what was literally a Great Unknown. But was Scott in fact a kind of literary bolt from the blue as far as America was concerned? Is it true that Scott emerged from no literary context, that no preparation had been made, no trail been blazed? The answer of course is that it is not true. And I mean a great deal more than that the success of the narrative poems smoothed the way for the Waverley Novels. The first half-dozen or so Waverley Novels, all of them concerned with periods in the Scottish past, rocketed Scott to a position of unparalleled fame and admiration in America not because they represented something unfamiliar and unknown, but because they represented the consummation of a Scottish literary tradition which had long been welcomed and admired in America. The Waverley Novels were an instantaneous success in America because there was much about them that was familiar, instantly recognisable.

Americans had long been eager readers of Scottish literature, both in its Anglo-Scottish and, perhaps more surprisingly, in its Scottish vernacular manifestations. The origins of American interest go back to the mid-eighteenth century but its range and intensity increase in the later eighteenth and early nineteenth centuries, until of course it reaches a climax with Scott himself. For example, two key works in what might be called the Anglo-Scottish dimension in the Scottish literary tradition, had long been widely-known and highly popular in America: John Home's play *Douglas*, and James Macpherson's *Ossian*. *Douglas* was first performed in Britain in 1756. Three years later it was being acted in Philadelphia; for at least the next sixty or seventy years the play held its place on the American stage. In fact it is clear that demand for the play increased as the eighteenth century went on. The first edition of *Douglas* did not appear until 1790, but numerous editions followed in Philadelphia, New York, Baltimore and Boston until as late as the 1820s. In 1825 the *New York Literary Gazette* was prepared to describe the play as 'one of the best modern tragedies'.[15]

Scott and America

How is one to account for this continuing and even growing American interest in a basically sentimental eighteenth-century play? The likeliest explanation is related to the appearance in the 1760s of what James Macpherson claimed were translations of the ancient Gaelic bard Ossian. Macpherson's poems created an immense sensation throughout Europe and America. No single works did more than the *Fragments of Ancient Poetry, Fingal,* and *Temora,* to create, define, and advance European romanticism. Macpherson's work is full of the appeal of the heroic past, of landscapes grandly sublime, of lofty and noble action, all suffused with a hint of elegiac melancholy. Everywhere people of sensibility were moved to enthusiasm by Macpherson's work. *Ossian's* importance in the development of romanticism has always been generally recognised; but the *Ossianic* poems were important in another direction. They were immensely significant in the cultural history of Scotland. Culloden represented the final defeat, in political terms, of the traditional Gaelic culture of the northern and western section of Scotland by the dynamic Anglo-Saxon culture of the south, the victory of the expanding commercial civilisation of Lowland Scotland, and the new intellectual and philosophical movements that were developing with it, over an older Celtic civilisation, with its own oral, literary, and intellectual traditions. George Pratt Insh was right to argue, half a century ago, that what the *Ossianic* poems represented, despite the support they gained from most of the *literati* of the Scottish Enlightenment, was a counter-attack launched with the pen rather than the sword: an attempt to impose upon Scotland, as her truest and most traditional self, a romantic image created out of the wild grandeur of her highland scenery, and the heroic simplicity of a poetic Highland past. In terms of that mythopoetic image John Home's play took on a new lease of life. The central characters of *Douglas*–Randolph and in particular Young Norval–seem to pre-figure the grand, heroic protagonists of the *Ossianic* poems. It was the ease with which the play could be romanticised in this way, could be assimilated into the developing romantic image of Scotland, which best accounts for its enduring American popularity.

From Goosecreek to Gandercleugh

Of course this account of *Douglas* assumes that Macpherson's *Ossianic* poems were enthusiastically received and read in America. Assuredly they were. Thomas Jefferson, for example, having decided that the rude bard of the North was 'the greatest Poet that has ever existed' wrote, like the true man of the Enlightenment he was, to a friend in Edinburgh in 1773 demanding that he be sent a dictionary and a grammar that he might learn the language of the originals. Jefferson's feelings were broadly shared by the American reading public, even if few of them would have been prepared to go so far as to see Ossian as the greatest poet of all time. Imitations and versifications of Macpherson's work were common; theatrical productions based on *Ossian* were produced; and numerous American editions of the poems were printed. But once again it is notable that attention seems to be at its height around the opening of the nineteenth century. The implications of this situation are that by that period American readers were becoming generally familiar with romantic images of Scotland, focusing on the heroic Scottish past, Scotland's landscapes, and her chivalrous, warlike people.

But it is not only the major products of the Anglo-Scottish literary tradition that were read in America. The vernacular tradition too, despite the obvious difficulties presented by its language, was far from unknown in America. Allan Ramsay's pioneering work *The Gentle Shepherd*, for example, originally published in 1725, was highly popular in America. It was printed at Philadelphia in 1750 and very frequently thereafter; Ramsay's poems too were also republished in America. But once again the kind of praise that Ramsay received in America around the end of the eighteenth century makes it clear that it was the romantic aspects of his work that had special appeal. But by the end of the eighteenth century Ramsay's fame was nothing as compared with that of a later Scottish poet–Robert Burns. Two years after the Kilmarnock edition of 1786, Burns's poems were published in America. From this point on a series of editions of Burns's poetry issued from the American press–eight editions in Philadelphia alone between 1801 and 1823. Indeed as the nineteenth century went on, the Burns cult in America came to rival that in Scotland. Boston, for example, boasted a Burns Club in 1850, and it celebrated the poet's centenary in 1859 with a gala extravaganza in the Parker House Hotel, the guests including Emerson, Longfellow, Lowell, Holmes and N. P. Willis, while letters were read out from J. G. Whittier and Edward Everett.[16]

There is little evidence that Burns's vernacular was any barrier to American appreciation, though it is true that anthologies tended to reprint some of his more popular English language poems. What has to be remembered in this connection is that Burns's American audience was in a position no different from that of his English one. And some American commentators were even ready to go so far as to suggest that the Scottish vernacular was more acceptable to American ears than to English ones: 'the dialect of [Scotland] is more familiar and more grateful to us than to the inhabitants of [the] sister kingdom', wrote Robert Walsh in the *American Review* in 1811.[17] What Walsh has in mind here it is difficult to say: perhaps simply the presence of many Scots and Ulster-Scots immigrants in America. But he may also have been aware of the existence of an off-shoot of the Scottish vernacular tradition in verse 3,000 miles away in America. Between 1790 and 1820 there was quite a vogue for the writing of poems in the Scottish vernacular, mainly of course in imitation of Burns, in America. Produced mainly in New England, New Jersey, and Pennsylvania, most of this verse is of course of little or no literary value, but the fact that it could be written at all is of some interest. It suggests sustained interest in Burns and perhaps other Scottish vernacular poets; and it certainly implies the existence of an American audience to some degree receptive towards Scottish vernacular poetry.[18]

Burns's success in America had one other significance at least. The received American critical perspective on Burns was that which derived from Henry Mackenzie's notion of him as the 'heaven-taught ploughman'. Seen as representative of the type of natural genius, unconstrained by the rules of art, the product of a simple, rural, unsophisticated society, Burns's example did much to popularise the romantic notion of the Scottish peasant as possessor of a natural heritage of poetry and song. The taste for Scots songs existed in America before Burns began to write; but the Burns vogue did much to develop and extend that taste. If *Douglas* and *Ossian* provided an enduring romantic gloss for the Scottish Highlands and the Highlander, Ramsay, Burns and other vernacular poets came to be seen as performing a very similar function for the Scottish Lowlands and the Lowland peasantry.

The likeliest explanation of Scott's immediate and enduring success in America should now be obvious. The Waverley Novels, and in particular that crucial early group concerned with Scotland and the Scottish past, draw their strength from both the main traditions of Scottish writing familiar from the early eighteenth century onwards: the vernacular and Anglo-Scottish traditions. These writings, which came increasingly into prominence as the romantic sensibility developed in Europe and elsewhere, were as well-known in America as in England and Scotland. What Scott did was to build on these existing literary traditions; his achievement was to bring them to a brilliant consummation. The magic of the Wizard of the North was not a question of the boldly new, the startlingly original. When Scott began to write Scottish literature was clearly very much a going concern; what Scott was able to do was to take advantage of an existing situation and elevate it to new and unparalleled heights. *Douglas, Ossian*, Burns, Ramsay, the whole tradition of Scottish ballad and Scottish song, all these prepared the way for Scott, helped to make Scott possible. Therein lies the probable key to his success–in America and perhaps elsewhere.

III

What finally of Scott's influence on American literature? His influence was in fact, as we might guess from his immense popularity, considerable–both on individual American writers and on the general context of America's literary culture. In connection with this second area Scott did much to help the creation of a situation in which American literature could finally come into existence. Since the end of the Revolution Americans had been calling for the establishment of a national literature; Scott did as much or more than anyone else in showing America how to do just that. Once again it is Scott's Scottishness, and his relation to Scots writing in general, that is in question here. At the beginning of the eighteenth century Scotland was seen as a poor, backward, culturally dependent nation; by the time of Scott she was the proud possessor of a national literature, enthusiastically read and admired throughout most of Europe and America. Her writers had given her a cultural and national identity and self-definition. How had it been done? Scottish writers had turned back to their own land, its history, traditions, legends; they had written about their own countryside, its mountains, rivers and glens; they had written of the customs and manners of their own people. And in all these areas Scott's own contribution was of course pre-eminent. The message for America was obvious; and it was recognised. For a period in the 1820s and 1830s there was what one scholar described as a 'romance ferment' in America. What Scott had done for Scotland through the Waverley Novels, American authors by writing about American manners, American scenes, American history, should do for America. Scott was repeatedly offered as both example and model.

The appearance of James Fenimore Cooper's novel *The Spy* in 1821 was the signal for a flood of American romances cast in the mould of the Waverley Novels. Cooper's novel was praised precisely because it seemed to have much in common with Scott's historical romances. As John Neal put it in 1825, *The Spy* 'was , at least, an approach to what we desire–a plain, real, hearty, North American story; a story, which, if we could have our way, should be altogether American–peculiarly and exclusively so, throughout: as much American to say all, in a word, as the Scotch novels are Scotch'.[19] The vast majority of these American romances of the 1820s and '30s now remain unread. Doubts about the availability in America of suitable material for historical romances, which had been commonly expressed before the appearance of the Waverley Novels, soon began to be expressed again. The romance ferment itself began before long to die down. But there cannot be the slightest doubt that Scott, and the Scottish writers who had preceded him, did much to point the way forward for the development of a genuinely national American literature.[20]

As far as individual American authors go Scott's influence is abundantly evident on that first strikingly successful and original American novelist whose name has already been mentioned: James Fenimore Cooper. Throughout his career, and much to his own chagrin, Cooper was widely known as 'the American Scott'. And the nick-name, offensive or not to its bearer, was not without its justification. The Scottishness of Scott has much in common with the Americanness of Cooper: the choice of settings and themes, the concern for manners and modes of life uncharacteristic of the civilised present and its social structures. But the influence of Scott on Cooper is probably even more specific. In Cooper's handling of the major theme of his Leatherstocking novel series, the clash between primitivism and civilisation, between frontier and society, between settlers and native Americans, there is an obvious link with Scott's exploration of the contrast between the way of life, the customs and manners of the Scottish Highlander, and those of progressive, modern Scotland and England. The Highland line becomes Cooper's frontier. And in Cooper too there is much of Scott's ambivalence over precisely where the author's sympathies lie; perhaps one senses in the end in both authors a major collision between head and heart. Like Scott, Cooper is intellectually a conservative, an upholder of the traditional values of civilised society–law and order, enlightenment, rational moderation and tolerance and the rest; but like Scott again he is emotionally drawn to another world, in this case a freer, more individual, independent world, not anarchic, but without the constraints inevitably imposed by civilised society. Cooper saw Scott as a rival, if possible to be outdone; at the same time it is clear that Scott helped Cooper tremendously to see more clearly what his true subjects were.

In the eighteenth century the Scottish Highlander had frequently been compared to the natives of America: Dr Johnson for example, in his *Tour of the Western Isles*, makes use of the comparison more than once, and Hugh Blair, in his *Critical Dissertation on the Poems of Ossian*, makes the connection between the eloquence of the *Ossianic* figures and that of the American Indian. In the 1820s in America the situation was exactly reversed. American commentators and authors believed that the existence of the Native Americans gave them the chance to duplicate Scott's success with the Scottish Highlander. The example of Cooper shows that the notion was not entirely without foundation. At his best Cooper can suggest that the Native American, despite his obvious primitive savagery, does embody an heroic tradition now fading and passing away–though here perhaps it is Macpherson's *Ossian*, rather than Scott, that lies behind Cooper's treatment. In his handling of the language of the Native American and particularly in the exalted rhetorical eloquence attributed to the chieftains, Cooper was once again deeply indebted to the example of Scott and Macpherson's *Ossian*: Scottish Highlander and American chief often declaim in a remarkably similar sonorous style.[21]

Of course Scott's influence on the nineteenth-century novel–Scottish, English, European, American–was pervasive. But let me end by linking Scott with an American novelist whose work has apparently little in common with his own. Apart from his treatment of history and the past, Hawthorne's subjects and themes–his psychological exploration of individual guilt and evil, of flawed idealism, of the ambiguous status of the artist, seem remote from the world of the Waverley Novels. Nor is there much connection between Hawthorne's delicately polished style, his preference for quasi-poetic modes of symbolism and allegory, and Scott's more humdrum English usage. But in one area at least Hawthorne seems to have learned from Scott: the device which Alexander Welsh calls 'tentative statement' in Scott's case, seems to pass from him to Hawthorne. In Scott's hands, tentative statement becomes a way of presenting exotic or romantic or supernatural material without accepting full authorial responsibility for its existence. The author pretends simply to report what others or tradition or legend has said. In a very similar manner, Hawthorne, too, frequently gives only tentative assent to events or interpretations of events which his author/narrator is describing. Hawthorne may carry this mode of writing further than Scott into a questioning of the ambiguous nature of reality itself, but the origin of the technique clearly lies in the example of Scott.[22]

Henry James clearly thought of Scott as essentially a provider of classy light entertainment. But reviewing Nassau Senior's *Essays on Fiction* in 1864 he paid tribute to Scott as 'the inventor of a new style' of fiction, and the possessor of an imagination 'vast and rich'; and the popularity which Nassau Senior had celebrated forty years earlier, he wrote, 'has in no measure subsided'. These youthful Jamesian judgements, I suspect, are ones with which most nineteenth-century American readers and writers would have agreed.

Notes

1. *American Review*, I (1811), 166.
2. *Literary Magazine*, IV (1805), 99.
3. For these references see, *Port Folio*, V (1805), 306–8, 313–15; *Port Folio*, New Series, IV (1807), 134; and *Port Folio*, New Series, VI (1808), 302.
4. *North American Review*, XVIII (1824), 162.
5. See F. L. Pattee (ed.), *American Writers, A series of Papers Contributed to Blackwood's Magazine (1824–1825)*, (Durham, 1937), p. 196.
6. *Southern Review*, IV (1829), 499.
7. *Analectic Magazine*, XI (1818), 332.
8. *Analectic Magazine*, XIII (1819), 123.
9. *Analectic Magazine*, XI (1818), 309.
10. *Literary Gazette*, I (1821), 129.
11. J. W. Francis, *Old New York, or, Reminiscences of the Past Sixty Years* (New York, 1858), p. 242.
12. Calvin Colton, *Four Years in Great Britain, 1831–35* (New York, 1835), II, 11.
13. Orville Dewey, *The Old World and the New; or, a Journal of Reflection and Observations made on a Tour of Europe* (New York, 1836), I, 64–5.
14. *North American Review*, XXXII (1831), 392.
15. *The New York Literary Gazette*, I (1825), 91.
16. See [Robert Burns] *Celebration of the Hundredth Anniversary of the Birth of Robert Burns, by the Boston Burns Club*. January 25th, 1859. (Boston, 1859). (The National Library of Scotland has a copy of this item.) James M. Montgomery in 'How Robert Burns captured America,'

Studies in Scottish Literature, 30 (1998), 235–48, states that by 1859 there were fifteen Burns clubs in America, and that the centenary itself was celebrated in some sixty locations across the United States (p. 238).

17. *The American Review*, I (1811), 166.
18. For a fuller discussion of this off-shoot of the Scottish vernacular tradition in America, see my *Scotland and America* (Glasgow and London, 1975) pp. 133–41.
19. See Pattee, *American Writers*, pp. 209–10.
20. For further illustrations of this point, see *Scotland and America*, pp. 160–63, and Waldemar Zacharasiewicz, 'The Rise of Cultural Nationalism in the New World: The Scottish Element and Example', in Horst W. Drescher, Hermann Volkel (eds.) *Nationalism in Literature–Literarischer Nationalismus, Literature, Language and National Identity*, Peter Lang, 1989, pp. 315–34.
21. Susan Manning in her article 'Ossian, Scott and Nineteenth Century Literary Nationalism,' *Studies in Scottish Literature*, 17 (1982), 39–54, recognizes the link between Macpherson and Cooper while emphasising the contribution of both Macpherson and Scott to the creation of Scottish literary nationalism.
22. In 'Scott and Hawthorne: The Making of a National Literary Tradition' Susan Manning finds other parallels in the writing modes of the two. See J. H. Alexander and D. Hewitt (eds.), *Scott and His Influence* (Aberdeen, 1983), pp. 421–31.

CHAPTER SEVEN

Hogg, Melville
and the Scottish Enlightenment

Filio-pietism, or an exaggerated respect and admiration for one's ancestors, is a danger inherent in all forms of ethnic and immigration studies; and accounts of the Scottish influence in America have not always succeeded in avoiding it. An unsuspecting reader might sometimes quite reasonably assume that he or she is being asked to believe that everything good in the American way of life–like every good American–somehow possesses a Scottish ancestry. Needless to say the modern academic study of Scotland's connection with America avoids any such sentimental assumption; yet even in academic research the emphasis still largely falls (understandably enough) on the positive aspects of Scotland's contribution to America. Scottish philosophy and rhetoric, Scottish science and medicine, Scottish literature and criticism, Scottish education and teachers, the Scottish universities and their graduates, Scottish economic and commercial know-how: all of these are seen as contributing to the formation and development of the United States. And rightly so.

Nonetheless, there is another, more negative perspective that needs to be recognised. America had to pay a price for the Scottish exports it welcomed so warmly. I have already argued that American emulation of the Scottish rhetorical model contributed to a long-enduring hostility towards the use of the American vernacular in the country's serious literature; and in a later essay I shall argue that there was and is a sinister legacy to American enthusiasm for Scottish romanticism. In the essay that follows I suggest that two major writers, one Scottish, one American, subtly articulate in similar fashion a profound distrust of the central values of the Scottish Enlightenment as they had come to be reflected in the social economies of Scotland and America in the nineteenth century.

Modern criticism of *The Private Memoirs and Confessions of a Justified Sinner* has successfully rescued Hogg's novel from the oblivion into which it descended almost from the moment of its publication. The imaginative power and extraordinary insight of the book are now generally recognised and it has become a critical commonplace to see it as Hogg's major achievement. Even made into an opera, the work is at last perhaps reaching the kind of audience that Hogg originally had in view. However, ever since André Gide's pioneering introduction to the Cresset Press edition of 1947, it is fair to say that it is the psychological dimension of the book's subject that has remained the main focus of critical attention. It is in Hogg's penetrating presentation of religious fanaticism, his study of Robert Wringhim's terrifying antinomianism and its moral and psychological consequences, that the heart of his imaginative achievement is seen to lie. Few readers, I believe, would wish wholly to dissent from such a view. Nonetheless, it is possible to argue that it is a mistake to see the book as in any way exclusively concerned with the subject of religious fanaticism. 'The Private Memoirs and Confessions' of Robert Wringhim, after all, take up not a great deal more than half the book. In other words, it is the form of Hogg's novel that points towards its wider meanings.[1]

The most striking feature of the form of *The Justified Sinner* is a narrative procedure that is either extraordinarily clumsy or extremely sophisticated. Hogg employs two narrators: the editor, who provides the first account of the novel's central action and also supplies the concluding pages, and Wringhim, whose personal narrative is framed by the editor's two sections. By appearing in his own person in the concluding section, Hogg, among other things, seems to insist on the fictional independence of both Wringhim and the editor; both are imaginative creations and neither necessarily speaks for the author. The technique–and the use of an editor in particular Hogg presumably derived from Scott. In the Waverley Novels Scott very frequently interposes a whole series of formal and stylistic distancing devices between himself as author and the fictional world he creates. In Scott's case the impulse to achieve as anonymous a relationship as possible between himself and the fictions he devises seems to have a great deal to do with the doubts and uncertainties of a moral nature which he, like so many of his contemporaries, experienced in relation to the status of fiction in general, and fiction of a more 'Gothic' nature in particular. Hogg's editor is equally concerned to make the lurid and sensational story he relates as acceptable as possible to the civilised, enlightened, and impeccably moral, modern reader. And an important dimension of this effort is the attempt, traditional among novelists since Defoe at least, to persuade us of the undoubted authenticity, the 'truth', of the tale he is telling. But, as I hope to show, Hogg in the end employs his editor not so much to conciliate and persuade modern society as subtly to undermine and subvert it.

By employing two narrators Hogg is able to achieve a variety of contrasting effects. The broad similarity in content of the two sections is misleading; in terms of style and tone the two are sharply differentiated. The impression that the editor is constantly concerned to create is very much that implied by his title: as an editor he is detached, neutral, uncommitted. Robert Wringhim's 'Memoirs and Confessions' have simply chanced to come into his possession; as an editor he is making the document available to the public with whatever additional information about the people and events Wringhim describes he has been able to find. Hence he invites the reader to see his account as a factual one to be set against Wringhim's fascinating but obviously unreliable personal history. It is no accident that the editor is an Edinburgh man, university trained, able to count J. G. Lockhart, Scott's son-in-law and biographer, among his friends. His voice is that of enlightened, secular, literary Edinburgh; he is the man of common sense, eager to clarify and explain; and he constantly invites the reader's assent because he assumes that the reader is just such a modern, civilised fellow as himself.

Consider the carefully created tone of the opening paragraph of the Editor's Narrative:

It appears from tradition, as well as some parish registers still extant, that the lands of Dalcastle (or Dalchastel, as it is often spelled) were possessed by a family of the name of Colwan, about one hundred and fifty years ago, and for at least a century previous to that period. That family was supposed to have been a branch of the ancient family of Colquhoun, and it is certain that from it spring the Cowans that spread towards the Border. I find, that in the year 1687, George Colwan succeeded his uncle of the same name, in the lands of Dalchastel and Balgrennan; and this being all I can gather of the family from history, to tradition I must appeal for the remainder of the motley adventures of that house. But of the matter furnished by the latter of these powerful monitors, I have no reason to complain: It has been handed down to the world in unlimited abundance; and I am certain, that in recording the hideous events which follow, I am only relating to the greater part of the inhabitants of at least four counties of Scotland, matters of which they were before perfectly well informed.[2]

Throughout this passage, the editor's stance is very much that of the disinterested, scholarly researcher. The quibble over the spelling of 'Dalcastle', for example, is very much in keeping with the tone of the whole paragraph. We are being invited to believe that there is no question of the editor's doing more than passing along to us the fruits of his diligent enquiries and researches. Like a true scholar he is reluctant to commit himself further than his facts allow: hence the tentativeness of many of his statements, his unwillingness to take full editorial responsibility for the information he is offering us. 'It appears from tradition . . .'; 'that family was supposed to have been . . .'; 'to tradition I must appeal'–such phrases establish the characteristic tentative note. Nevertheless, there is to be no questioning of the authenticity of the tale itself; its truth is attested to by the fact that it is common knowledge, already well known to a considerable section of the Scottish people. The editor's task is simply to 'record' the 'hideous events' which follow, so there can be no question of his deliberately exploiting sensational materials. The editor's strategy here—and of course it is Hogg's strategy too—has two main ends in view. First, to win the reader over to an acceptance of the editor as an entirely neutral and reliable narrator; and secondly, to convince us both of the authenticity of the tale and of the moral propriety of telling it.

The persona of the editor, established by this opening paragraph, is sustained throughout his entire narrative. He emerges as a man of the modern world, more than willing to investigate the mysteries of an earlier, less sophisticated age, in a spirit of cool, detached, scientific enquiry. Like a truly enlightened modern man he believes that 'the better all the works of nature are understood, the more they will be ever admired (p. 40)'. When he reports the investigation of Wringhim's supposed grave, it is entirely appropriate that he records every detail with the meticulousness expected of a scientific monograph. Hogg, I believe, finally allows us to see his editor as a figure wholly representative of the cultural milieu of the Edinburgh of his time; or, to put it in today's historical terminology, the editor, in his attitudes, values and assumptions, is a characteristic product of the Scottish Enlightenment.

Robert Wringhim, on the other hand, is the product of a very different Scottish tradition. Wringhim represents everything that is alien to the editor's enlightened world; his narrative is characterised by precisely those qualities of passion, fervour, and conviction which the secular rationalism of the Enlightenment disdains and fears. The contrast in tone between the two narrators could not be more striking, and it is evident even at the level of diction and vocabulary. Where the editor's language is simple, prosaic, unadorned, Wringhim's is elaborate, colourful, poetic. Wringhim speaks throughout in the complex rhetoric of the religious tradition to which he belongs. Where the editor employs the language of scholarly, sceptical, scientific enquiry,

120

Wringhim speaks out in the language of religious conviction and commitment.

Consider, in turn, Wringhim's opening paragraph:

My life has been a life of trouble and turmoil; of change and vicissitude; of anger and exultation; of sorrow and of vengeance. My sorrows have all been for a slighted gospel, and my vengeance has been wreaked on its adversaries. Therefore, in the might of heaven I will sit down and write: I will let the wicked of this world know what I have done in the faith of the promises, and justification by grace, that they may read and tremble, and bless their gods of silver and of gold, that the minister of heaven was removed from their sphere before their blood was mingled with their sacrifices.

The contrast between this and the opening of the Editor's Narrative is simple and obvious. We have moved out of one world into another. The editor's neutral, disengaged, colourless tone, has been replaced by Wringhim's immediacy, intensity, and deeply-engaged, emotional, personal commitment. Direct statement has given way to a formal rhetoric couched in a specific religious vocabulary. A heightened oratorical conviction has been substituted for the cool lucidity of the enlightened editor. Language and style make it brilliantly evident that Wringhim inhabits a world, envisions a reality, wholly alien to the understanding of the editor. Producing this contrast, Hogg is consciously extending the meaning of his book.

At the simplest level, the Editor's Narrative does enable us to see how Wringhim's subjective fanaticism produces distortions of the truth. Nonetheless, there are probably few readers who are entirely willing to see the two narratives as simply presenting on the one hand the truth, on the other the crazy distortions of a religious fanatic. If this were indeed the whole story, then the novel is after all no more than a study of psychological aberration in a religious context, and the Editor's Narrative serves no very essential purpose: the reader might well have been left to make out the unreliability of Wringhim's subjective narrative for himself. Rejecting such a view, one is insisting that neither narrative is conclusive; the capacity to see and understand, to grasp the reality behind appearance, is allowed to neither narrator; both operate within the limitations imposed by their social and cultural contexts. Part at least of the novel's meaning then becomes that truth is an elusive concept, not necessarily to be arrived at either by an impassioned subjectivity or a cool objectivity.

It is not my contention, however, that Hogg extends the meaning of his book only by allowing us to recognise in his dual narrative structure a dramatisation of even a variety of possible metaphysical oppositions and contrasts. What is striking is how firmly he embeds both his narrators in specific Scottish social and cultural worlds. How the personality of both narrators is suggested by the tone and gesture of their respective rhetorics has already been noted. But as we have seen, the editor is also provided with a social existence: his college background, his friends in Edinburgh's literary world, his assumption of a shared set of values with the enlightened, modern reader. When we look carefully at Robert Wringhim we see that he too exists at levels beyond that of the eccentric individual. It is to underline this point that Hogg provides Wringhim's life and actions with a firmly defined historical, social, and political context.

Much of the action of the novel takes place in the period immediately preceding the Treaty of Union between England and Scotland in 1707. We learn that whereas Wringhim's supposed brother and father belong to the High Church, Episcopalian, Jacobite party, the Wringhims, father and son, are adherents of the Whig, Presbyterian, faction. The social implication of this difference in allegiance is also made clear; the 'court' party, to which the Colwans belong, is identified as drawing most of its strength from the aristocracy, the noblemen and young gentlemen of the day; the 'country' Whig party, while not without some aristocratic support, is seen to draw much of its strength from its popular, Presbyterian base. Wringhim senior, Hogg tells us, was sometimes '*of real use,*' (p. 20) to the leaders of the Whig party, and as such admitted to their

counsels. What is clear, then, is that the Wringhims are identified with one of the parties which, in the early eighteenth
century, divided Scotland in religious, political, and perhaps
class terms. The point of this identification is precisely to make
us recognise that Robert Wringhim's religious attitudes and
ideas are not ones cut off from the mainstream of Scottish life
and culture in the eighteenth century. Of course Hogg is careful
not to equate Wringhim's antinomianism with official Presbyterianism; but the two are allowed to have a great deal in
common. Wringhim's language, his emotional fervour, his
conviction of his own recitude, as well as many of his basic
theological beliefs–all of these would be very much at home in
the world of orthodox Calvinism. When, therefore, the modern
editor introduces Wringhim's 'Memoirs' as evidence only of 'the
rage of fanaticism in former days' (p. 93) and concludes in the
novel's final sentences that Wringhim himself must have been
either 'the greatest fool' and 'the greatest wretch' that ever lived,
or 'a religious maniac', (p. 254) what we are hearing is the voice
of the Scottish Enlightenment when it is confronted by that
dimension of traditional Scottish culture which above all else it
was concerned to eradicate. In other words, in the two narratives of his novel, Hogg represents the two key voices in eighteenth-century Scottish culture: the voice of enlightened reason
and moderation on the one hand, the voice of religious passion
and commitment on the other. As a man of letters in early
nineteenth-century Edinburgh it is in a world that represents the
triumph of that first voice that Hogg moves; but as a peasant-
farmer in the Scottish Borders he is familiar with that second
voice and understands its continuing importance in, if not the
official, then nonetheless the popular culture of his day.

Of course I am not suggesting that Hogg approves of Wringhim: the sinner's pride, self-deceptions, and moral obliquities–
and the way in which the particular cast of his religious beliefs
helps to create these vices–are all made abundantly evident. But
that is not at all to say that Hogg stands behind the bland
superiority of the editor. Rather what Hogg is doing is opening
up areas of human emotion and experience which neither

Humean scepticism nor the common sense philosophy of the Scottish Enlightenment can begin to comprehend. The assumptions of enlightenment are subtly subverted by their juxtaposition with a darker, more passionate, more determinist and irrational world. Twice in the Editor's Narrative we are reminded that we have nothing on earth but our senses to depend on (pp. 80, 84–5). But, in the given case, such absolute reliance on the empirical data of the senses hardly begins to help us understand what is going on, still less to comprehend Wringhim's character and behaviour. What Hogg dramatises then in the narrative form of his novel is the gulf of incomprehension between the modern, civilised world of enlightened Scotland, and another equally historical Scotland, whose values and assumptions at every point come into conflict with the secular rationalism of the Scottish Enlightenment. Hogg endorses the values of neither of his narrators; Wringhim's extremism is made self-evident, but the editor's naive rationalism is equally, if more subtly, subverted.

II

Through the formal structure of *The Private Memoirs and Confessions of a Justified Sinner* Hogg articulates his deepest intuitions about the condition of Scottish culture in the eighteenth and early nineteenth centuries. But why, it may be objected, only through the form of his novel? Why not more directly, more explicitly? The answers to such questions are to be found in Hogg's complex relationship with the social and literary world in which he had acquired his identity as a writer.

Throughout his literary career, Hogg occupied a decidedly anomalous position in cultured Edinburgh society. After all, as we all know, his title as 'The Ettrick Shepherd' was no mere compliment to a 'pastoral' poet: Hogg indeed was a shepherd and sheep farmer. By any normal standard, his origins totally unfitted him for admission to polite society in Edinburgh or anywhere else. It is of course perfectly true that, to an unusual degree, entry to genteel society in Edinburgh in the later eighteenth and early nineteenth centuries had become almost as much a question of literary or intellectual distinction as of rank or birth. Visitors to the city in this period remark on this point again and again; in Edinburgh, fashionable society and the *literati* are hardly to be distinguished. Nonetheless, to this democracy of the intellect–if that is what it was–there were limits. And the person of James Hogg defines these limits quite clearly. Of course in one sense Hogg was accepted by the literary world of Edinburgh; he was largely its own creation, living testimony to that whole dimension of romantic ideology, much favoured by the Edinburgh critics, that saw the poet as the unsophisticated child of nature. Combining pastoral beauty with wilder and more sublime landscapes, the Border country of Hogg's origins was seen as an ideal home for the romantic muse; in the poetry of the Ettrick Shepherd that ideal was made real. But Hogg the man was a very different figure from Hogg the poet and 'Ettrick Shepherd'. In 1819, George Ticknor, a visitor from Boston, met Hogg at the home of Mrs Grant of Laggan; subsequently Ticknor summed up the encounter in a single phrase: to the Bostonian, Hogg seemed as 'vulgar as his name'.[3] Precisely the same view was taken by the Edinburgh *literati* as a whole. Few there were who could resist a jest or two on the appropriateness of Hogg's name. In other words, it was Hogg's fate to be simultaneously taken up and rejected by the polite world of literary Edinburgh: he was at once inside and outside that world, cultivated and exploited by it at one and the same time.[4] Thus R. P. Gillies records that Hogg 'became a very notable personage, whom a certain class considered it an honour to have at their convivial parties; and in other circles (though this required more time) it was deemed laudable (or at least excusable) to parade him as a curiosity'.[5]

Of course Hogg's own behaviour contributed in different ways to his 'curiosity' value. He played the role of the pea-sant-poet, for example, with considerable panache: insisting that he had inherited Burns's role as a ploughman-poet, and visiting London wearing his shepherd's plaid. His fondness for Glenlivet also became something of a legend. But it is in relation to

Blackwood's Magazine that the ambivalent position he occupied in enlightened Edinburgh becomes most evident. Despite his own early contribution to the success of the new magazine, he soon began to feature less and less as an author and more and more as the butt of John Wilson's humour. In August, 1821, Wilson published the most cruel of all his descriptions of his supposed friend and colleague:

> Only picture to yourself a stout country lout, with a bushel of hair on his shoulders that had not been raked for months, enveloped in a coarse plaid impregnated with tobacco, with a prodigious mouthful of unmeasurable tusks, and a dialect that set all conjecture at defiance, lumbering suddenly in upon the elegant retirement of Mr Miller's backshop, or the dim seclusion of Mr John Ogle! . . . What would he himself have thought, if a large surly brown bear, or a huge baboon, had burst open his door when he was at breakfast, and helped himself to a chair and a mouthful of parritch? . . .[6]

Such a portrait inevitably infuriated Hogg, but on this as on other occasions his feelings of anger and outrage do not seem to have been of long duration. In his *Memoirs of the Author's Life* he does get to the stage of writing that 'after twenty years of feelings hardly suppressed' his treatment by Blackwood had driven him 'beyond the bounds of human patience' and he goes on to threaten legal action.[7] But such bluster issued in no action. In the end, as Douglas Mack has put it, 'Hogg generally accepted his role as the butt of the Blackwood wits as the price to be paid for the enjoyment of what he called in one of his letters "their too much loved society".'[8]

The *Memoirs of the Author's Life* may not always be a strictly accurate and truthful account of Hogg's career; but at least it is an index of Hogg's feelings about his life as a literary man. From this point of view it provides strong evidence of Hogg's awareness of the problematic position he occupied in the literary society of Edinburgh. Discussing some of the difficulties he had met with in his relationship with Blackwood, he writes:

Hogg, Melville and the Scottish Enlightenment

For my own part, I know that I have always been looked on by the learned part of the community as an intruder in the paths of literature, and every opprobrium has been thrown on me from that quarter. The truth is, that I am so. The walks of learning are occupied by a powerful aristocracy, who deem that province their own peculiar right; else, what would avail all their dear-bought collegiate honours and degrees? No wonder that they should view an intruder, from the humble and despised ranks of the community, with a jealous and indignant eye, and impede his progress by every means in their power.[9]

Even if one discounts the not untypical suggestion of paranoia here, Hogg could hardly have expressed his sense of alienation from a socially conscious literary establishment more directly. In a passage in the *Familiar Anecdotes of Sir Walter Scott* he repeats the notion of his victimisation by the aristocracy of letters:

At that period the whole of the aristocracy and literature of our country were set against me and determined to keep me down nay to crush me to a nonentity . . .[10]

Such passages as these make it clear that Hogg was perfectly well aware of the precariousness of his position in the genteel world of polite letters in Edinburgh. As a poet and novelist he depended upon that world which he also knew was quite ready to use and abuse him. Perhaps he could not afford to attack it openly, but as a lover of hoax, parody, and similar devices, there were other possibilities open to him. In writing *The Justified Sinner* he found a way of getting back at the John Wilsons of the Edinburgh literary world; by portraying the enlightened editor as boringly pedantic and unimaginative, and by showing how 'James Hogg' turns his back on him and refuses to cooperate in the grave-opening expedition, Hogg hints at his rejection of literary Edinburgh and its values. Perhaps when he began Hogg had nothing more in mind than a few sly digs at his tormentors, but the end result goes a great deal further. In its final form *The*

127

Justified Sinner is an acute and penetrating analysis of the major divisions within Scottish culture. Thus it is only in the context of Hogg's relationship with the Scottish literary world of his day, and the relationship in turn of that world to the totality of Scottish cultural life in the eighteenth and early nineteenth centuries, that the form of the novel is to be finally understood. So understood, it becomes both the agent and the vehicle of a profoundly subversive effect.

III

To impute a connection between James Hogg and the Scottish Enlightenment is unexceptionable; to discuss Herman Melville within the same context will strike many readers as decidedly eccentric. What is in question? Melville's Scottish ancestry, perhaps, as Hugh MacDiarmid identified it in *A Drunk Man Looks at the Thistle*:

> Melville (a Scot) kent weel how Christ's
> Corrupted into creeds malign
> Begotten strife's pernicious blood
> That claims for patron Him Divine . . .

–or Hogg's unquestionably large and enthusiastic readership in America. Clearly the Calvinism common to Scotland and New England formed an important part of the background of both writers, and it is equally clear that *The Justified Sinner*, both in its form and content, would have been a book very much to Melville's taste. But the case is not one of literary influence. As I have indicated, America's taste for the poets and novelists of romantic Scotland in the early nineteenth century was quite catholic enough to include Hogg. The great majority of Hogg's works, prose and poetry, were reprinted; and transatlantic critics and reviewers of the day were disposed to find much to admire in them. *The Justified Sinner*, however, is an exception.[11] Just as the book seems to have been largely ignored by the literary establishment in England and Scotland, so it was not deemed worthy of reprinting in America. This degree of neglect of Hogg's novel has yet to be satisfactorily explained. Was it a

128

consequence of Hogg's decision to publish the work anon-
ymously? Was it that such a novel was not the kind of thing
that the Ettrick Shepherd was expected to write? Or was it that
for the Britain and America of the 1820s the book contained just
too many examples of Hogg's offensive bad taste: the explicit-
ness of his references to prostitution, for example? In any event
it appears that *The Justified Sinner* would not have been readily
available in America, and in all probability by the 1840s and
'50s, it had been largely forgotten. Thus there is little chance that
Melville had read it.[12]

Comparative literary study is not however solely concerned
with the question of literary influences. To set Melville beside
Hogg is to suggest how a particular literary form may be
explained not in terms of any alleged debt or influence, but
rather as the way in which two different authors, working in
distinct but not wholly unrelated contexts, articulate their sense
of the complex relationship between themselves and their society. Thus the narrative structure of *The Justified Sinner*, and its
implied meaning, provide an interesting parallel with the formal
structure of several of Melville's fictions. Like Hogg, Melville is
well aware of the potential for ironic, satiric, and other effects,
inherent in the employment of a narrator figure in a fictional
work, and he exploits that potential on several occasions.
However it is to 'Benito Cereno' that I wish to direct particular
attention. To compare this much debated story with the much
less exhaustively studied *Justified Sinner* is to clarify the significance of the form of each.

Such critical dispute as exists over the form of 'Benito Cereno'
has focused on the relationship between the story narrated by
Amaso Delano and the legal deposition that follows. It has
frequently been noted that in including the deposition Melville
sticks quite closely to the text of the original legal document. It is
this observation that has led to the suggestion that Melville has
failed to 'work up' his material sufficiently in aesthetic terms.[13]
But in refusing to rewrite this material Melville may well have
been acting quite deliberately; if his intention was to juxtapose
Delano's subjective narrative with the facts of the case as these

were subsequently legally recorded, then he had little reason to alter the original legal deposition in any extensive way.

What Melville has done is to provide the reader with what is really a dual narrative structure quite similar to that of *The Justified Sinner*. In both works a limited subjective consciousness is set against an apparently factual, objective account. But in neither case does the intention seem to be to allow one account to correct the other. Set beside Delano's personal narrative, the legal statement of the case in Melville's story reveals its own limitations. Allen Guttmann seems to me to see the matter correctly when he writes that 'Melville *wanted* the prose official and dreary because the official and attested view of the matter . . . is *the very thing which Melville is subverting*'.[14] Here in 'Benito Cereno', as elsewhere in his work, Melville is suggesting that his society and culture accept as the 'truth' what is at best only part of the truth. Among the meanings of the so-called cetological chapters in *Moby-Dick* is the suggestion that as avenues to absolute truth or reality a whole range of rational, analytical, scientifically-documented methodologies are totally inadequate. Precisely the same point is made in the course of 'Benito Cereno'. A Spanish sailor on board the *San Dominick* tries to communicate wordlessly with Amaso Delano by way of a complicated knot he is making. For the sailor it is clear that the point of the knot is its meaning; he intends it to indicate symbolically to Delano that he is in the presence of a mystery that needs to be unravelled–'undo it, cut it, quick', these are almost the only words the sailor is able to mutter. But the naive Delano fails to understand; what he can recognise is no more than a baffling combination of 'double-bowline-knot, treble-crown-knot, back-handed-well-knot, knot-in-and-out-knot, and jamming-knot'.[15] This analysis of its constituent parts may or may not be accurate; but the ironic point is the gap between this description of the old sailor's knot and what really matters–what the knot is intended to convey.

Delano's limitations are revealed as the limitations of his consciousness, his habits of mind, his assumption that things are what they seem to his senses to be. The reader who believes that the legal deposition really provides him with a key to unlock the mystery of 'Benito Cereno' simply repeats in large measure Delano's mistake. Similarly, to believe with the lawyer-narrator in the coda to 'Bartleby' that the little nugget of biographical information he has come upon satisfactorily explains all that has gone before, is once again to repeat the same fundamental error. In all these cases Melville's point is that it is only through an act of the creative imagination that one can begin to comprehend the complex nature of any reality; like science in *Moby-Dick*, the law in 'Benito Cereno' arrogates to itself an authority of definition which in fact it does not possess.

Even more consciously than Hogg, Melville is concerned as an artist to undermine and subvert his audience's assumptions and habits of mind. Again and again he is driven to challenge the complacent optimism of mid-nineteenth-century American society. I have argued that in *The Justified Sinner* it is not only Calvinist extremism but also the complacencies of the Scottish Enlightenment that are the objects of Hogg's satire. Melville's anguished obsession with the Calvinist deity is generally recognised; much less well understood is the fact that it was under the defensive walls of the Scottish Enlightenment that his most powerful satiric charges were laid. The official philosophy of that confident and complacent ante-bellum American society which it was Melville's primary aim to undermine and subvert was neither more nor less than a 'naturalised' form of the common sense philosophy of the Scottish Enlightenment. It was in the ideas of Thomas Reid, Dugald Stewart, and James Beattie, as these were disseminated throughout the whole of America by way of the writings, teaching, and preaching of countless American professors, college-presidents, and clergymen, that the society found its best protection from other, more dangerously radical, ideas and philosophies. The Scottish Enlightenment in its reactionary, post-Humean phase, with its 'metaphysics of actuality', its commitment to the actual as the test of the real, its devaluation of the imagination, its confident assertion of man's control over his destiny, and its religious orthodoxy, sanctioned and sustained all those aspects of American society that most outraged Melville. Hence it is this philosophy, and the entire range of intellectual, religious, and social values it underpinned, that Melville is largely concerned to attack. Perhaps because, like Hogg, he needed to write for a society whose values repelled him, his attack has often to be covert rather than direct. It is then through the form of 'Benito Cereno' no less than through the character of Amaso Delano, that Melville indicates the limitations of the common sense philosophy of mid-nineteenth-century American society when it is confronted by a dark and ambiguous reality.

I have suggested that James Hogg's scepticism about the enlightened society of early nineteenth-century Scotland stemmed at least in part from the anomalous position he occupied in the social and literary worlds of Edinburgh. Melville's impulse towards a radical criticism of the sustaining philosophy, Scottish in origin, of his own society, may also be linked to the problematic position he came to occupy in the social and literary world of his day. Brought up in an atmosphere of family comfort and financial security, Melville was deeply and permanently affected by his father's bankruptcy in 1830. Much of the rest of his life was taken up by an unavailing struggle to achieve economic independence either through his writing or by some other means. Of course where Hogg's origins were of the humblest, Melville's were, in American terms, aristocratic. But that background made it all the more difficult for Melville to accept his society's reluctance to accord him the kind of position he felt was his due. Both these writers, then, experienced some degree of alienation from the society for which they were writing; that alienation may go some way towards explaining how it is that remarkably similar patterns of formal structure and expression may be detected within their fictions.

Notes

1. A useful discussion of the novel's form can be found in Robert Kiely's *The Romantic Novel in England* (Cambridge, Mass., 1972), pp. 208–32.
2. James Hogg, *The Private Memoirs and Confessions of a Justified Sinner*,

ed. John Carey (Oxford, 1969), p. 1. All subsequent references are to this edition.

3. *Life, Letters and Journals of George Ticknor*, ed. by G. S. Hillard, (Boston, 1877), I. p. 278.

4. I am broadly in agreement with Douglas Gifford's view of Hogg's position in the literary society of Edinburgh as expressed in his Introduction to the Scottish Academic Press edition of Hogg's *The Three Perils of Man*. However, Professor Gifford does not see the significance of the form of *The Justified Sinner* in terms at all similar to mine.

5. R. P. Gillies, 'Some Recollections of James Hogg' in *Fraser's Magazine*, October 1839, quoted by A. L. Strout, *The Life and Letters of James Hogg* (Lubbock, Texas, 1946), I. 70.

6. Strout. op.cit., p. 223.

7. James Hogg, *Memoirs of the Author's Life and Familiar Anecdotes of Sir Walter Scott*, edited by Douglas S. Mack (Edinburgh and London, 1972), p. 59.

8. *Ibid.*, p. ix.

9. *Ibid.*, p. 46.

10. *Ibid.*, p. 105.

11. For a discussion of Hogg's American reputation see my *Scotland and America 1750–1835* (Glasgow, 1975), pp. 152–3.

12. The *National Union Catalogue* astonishingly lists no American edition of *The Justified Sinner* earlier than T. Earle Welby's 1925 New York edition. Such a publishing history, if it is accurate, certainly reinforces the suggestion that the book was not well known in nineteenth-century America. Of course some American libraries, and no doubt individuals as well, may well have owned copies of the first (1824) or later British printings of the novel: the 1828 printing, *The Suicide's Grave*, or the altered version entitled *Confessions of a Fanatic* in *Tales and Sketches by the Ettrick Shepherd*, 6 vols. (Glasgow, 1837 and London 1852); or the versions appearing in *Works*, ed. T. Thomson, 2 vols. (Glasgow, 1865–6), and *Tales*, 2 vols. (Glasgow, 1880, 1884). Harvard University Library, for example, possesses the first edition and both the Glasgow, 1837, edition and that edited by T. Thomson. Nonetheless, given Hogg's undoubted appeal for the American reading-public–in 'Some Recollections of James Hogg' (*Fraser's Magazine*, October, 1839). R. P. Gillies recalls Hogg declining an invitation to dinner because he was 'engaged wi' two grand American gentlemen that's travelled a' the way from Philadelphy *just to see mei* . . .'–the absence of an American edition of *The Justified Sinner* is certainly significant.

Hawthorne is another American novelist who might well have found Hogg's novel of particular interest, and one can readily imagine Melville and Hawthorne finding much to say to each other about it. But although Hawthorne certainly knew and read some of Hogg's early work, there is no evidence that he knew *The Justified Sinner*. Interestingly, the Harvard University Library's copy of the first edition of the novel is inscribed to William Dean Howells. So presumably at least one major

American author of the second half of the nineteenth century had read it. Again, old Judge McKelva, in Eudora Welty's novel *The Optimist's Daughter*, owns a copy, which apparently he and his wife used to read aloud to each other, in their Mississippi home. On the whole, however, the evidence so far available suggests that the general American enthusiasm for Hogg in the nineteenth century did not extend so far as to include *The Justified Sinner*.

13. See 'Benito Cereno' by Richard Harter Fogle in Richard Chase ed., *Melville, A Collection of Critical Essays* (Englewood Cliffs, N.J. 1962), p. 117.
14. Allen Guttmann, 'In Defence of Babo' in *A Benito Cereno Handbook*, ed. Seymour L. Gross (Belmont, California, 1965), p. 144.
15. Herman Melville, *Billy Budd and The Piazza Tales* (New York, 1961), p. 189.

CHAPTER EIGHT

Carlyle and America

Reading and responding to an author in his or her own lifetime may well be a quite different experience from reading the work of an author whose career is over. The first category of reader responds to the works as they appear: the future direction, the final destination, remain unknown, while changes in manner or meaning are unforeseeable. What matters is what has already been written–and read. Carlyle is a case in point. For readers everywhere in the 1820s, '30s, and '40s, Carlyle often seemed to be the most exciting, the most challenging, the most radical writer of his time; for us, all too aware of the late Carlyle's irascible anti-democratic outpourings, it is difficult to recapture that original enthusiasm. We are second-category readers, our views coloured by what we know will happen to Carlyle, by the direction in which he will move. Carlyle's original American readers had no such awareness until the 1850s, and their responses, detailed in the essay that follows, lets us see with particular vividness just how compelling his original impact could be.

The example of Carlyle also lets us see something else: the difficulty in defining and recognising 'Scottishness'. In 1826, in a move many have seen as signalling the end of the period of Scotland's greatest intellectual achievements, the Scotsman Carlyle chose to leave Edinburgh to pursue his career in London. Thereafter is he to be designated a Scottish or an English writer? In America at least, the case of Carlyle seems to confirm the view that awareness of Scotland's separate cultural identity tended to decline as the nineteenth century went on.

Few things are more surprising in Carlyle's life than that he succeeded in never setting foot in America. Certainly the pos-

135

sibility of a transatlantic visit was something he frequently considered, though probably never with great seriousness. In his very first letter to Emerson, dated 12 August 1834, initiating on his side a correspondence that was to extend over almost forty years, Carlyle remarked:

> Surely we shall see you in London one day. Or who knows but Mahomet may go to the Mountain? It occasionally rises like a mad prophetic dream in me that I might end in the Western Woods![1]

Emerson in reply was more than willing to take up the point:

> Now as to the welcome hint that you might come to America, it shall be to me a joyful hope. Come and found a new Academy that shall be church and school and parnassus, as a true Poet's house should be . . . If you cared to read literary lectures, our people have vast curiosity and the apparatus is very easy to set agoing. (Slater, p. 110)

In his next letter, written in February 1835, Carlyle refers with gracious indirectness to Emerson's invitation as that of 'a brave friend . . . who opens the door of a new western world . . .' and then goes on: 'As for America and Lecturing, it is a thing I do sometimes turn over, but never yet with any seriousness'. (Slater, p. 117). Emerson proceeded to work indefatigably to persuade Carlyle to consider the matter with due seriousness. In a letter written from Concord on 30 April 1835 he set out at length the various possibilities which were open to Carlyle should he undertake the Atlantic crossing; the financial rewards of lecturing are extensively detailed; the probability that he would be offered the editorship of a new journal to be called *The Transcendentalist* or *The Spiritual Inquirer* is mentioned; and the opportunity to reprint some of his writings in America is also alluded to. Emerson admits that Carlyle would not be universally welcomed; an opposition party does exist, but it will not prevail. Harvard University, and conservatives in literature and religion, will do their best to demolish Carlyle. But, writes Emerson, 'If we get a good tide with us, we shall sweep away the whole inertia, which is the whole force of these gentlemen . . .' (Slater, p. 127). Altogether the picture painted by Emerson is an extremely bright one; when it is linked with the basic factors which had produced it, to which I shall turn in a moment, it is hard not to believe that Carlyle must have felt tempted. However, his reply, dated 13 May 1835, reveals him as grateful but, in a literal sense, unmoved. Nothing but good news, he admits, comes to him from across the Atlantic: 'As if the "golden west", seen by Poets, were no longer a mere optical phenomenon, but growing a reality, and coining itself into solid blessings!' The idea 'may hover for the present among the gentlest of our day-dreams; mild-lustrous; an impossible possibility' (Slater, p. 128). In the years that followed Emerson frequently returned to the theme, but the 'impossible possibility' of 1835 never moved any closer towards realisation. In fact in the long run the movement was in the opposite direction until at last what had long remained an 'impossible possibility' dwindled to an outright and unequivocal impossibility.[2]

Our main concern with these exchanges between Carlyle and Emerson is not the literal subject: whether or not it was ever possible that Carlyle should go to America for a brief visit or an extended sojourn. Rather it is with the context in which such a question could even be raised. Why should anyone in America in the early 1830s even have been interested in Carlyle? Known who he was? Been interested in his writing? What is still more extraordinary, why should anyone in America in the early 1830s have been so keen to urge upon Carlyle the desirability of his crossing the Atlantic in person? How had it come about that Carlyle, at this relatively early stage of his career, could be so confidently assured of the warmth and enthusiasm of the American welcome that awaited him?

The answer to such questions is suggested by a comment made by Carlyle to Emerson to which allusion has already been made: 'good news, good new friends; nothing that is not good' comes to Carlyle from across the Atlantic; for Carlyle the 'golden west' of the poets is fast becoming a reality. What is the good news? Who are the good new friends? What other forms does this transatlantic goodness take? Emerson's letters once again supply many of the answers. Bur rather than quoting extensively at this point to indicate the nature of Emerson's feelings towards Carlyle, let me simply identify the tone of all the early letters as one of immense admiration and intense enthusiasm. And this, of course, is the great point. America is good news for Carlyle because in the early years, up to and including the publication of *Sartor Resartus*, it was *only* in America that he had found a receptive and even enthusiastic audience. In August 1834, Carlyle wrote to Emerson contrasting the reception in England of the serialised version of *Sartor Resartus*, then appearing in *Fraser's Magazine*, with Emerson's praise–Emerson had written: 'Evermore thanks for the brave stand you have made for Spiritualism in these writings'. Here is Carlyle's comment:

> You thank me for Teufelsdröckh: how much more ought I to thank you for your hearty, genuine tho' extravagant acknowledgement of it! Blessed is the voice that amid dispiritment stupidity and contradiction proclaims to us: *Euge*! Nothing ever was more ungenial than the soil this poor Teufelsdröckhish seedcorn has been thrown on here; none cries, Good speed to it; the sorriest nettle or hemlock seed, one would think, had been more welcome. For indeed our British periodical critics, and especially the public of Fraser's Magazine (which I believe I have now done with) exceed all speech; require not even contempt, only oblivion. (Slater, pp. 102–3).

That Carlyle should have been feeling so dispirited over the first unveiling of *Sartor Resartus*, so disappointed at the public response–or rather lack of it–to this, his first major work, makes it very understandable that news of any kind of favourable reception in America must have arrived as good news indeed.

But it may be objected that Emerson is not America; that Emerson's admiration and enthusiasm for Carlyle are peculiar to himself. In fact this is not the case. Emerson was far from being either the only or the earliest admirer of Carlyle in America. Nor did Carlyle's fame and influence in America arise solely after the appearance of *Sartor Resartus*. His early essays in the *Edinburgh Review* and other British periodicals were eagerly read in America. The mere fact that they appeared in the *Edinburgh*, for example, was enough to guarantee them considerable American respect. No periodical, probably not even the native *North American Review*, carried more weight in the American literary and intellectual world than the *Edinburgh Review*. Through his essays in the *Edinburgh*, Carlyle gained as it were immediate entrée into the cultural establishment of America. There was no problem over availability; the *Edinburgh Review* had been reprinted entire in America probably from as early as 1810 or 11.

There is abundant evidence of the impact in America of Carlyle's earliest essays. James Freeman Clarke, a Unitarian minister in Boston and friend of Emerson, gives this account of Carlyle's impact in the years before *Sartor Resartus*:

> It was about the year 1830 that readers of books in this vicinity became aware of a new power coming up in the literary republic . . . Especially to the younger men, this new writer came, opening up unknown worlds of beauty and wonder. A strange influence, unlike any other, attracted us to his writing. Before we knew his name, we knew *him*. We could recognize an article by our new author as soon as we opened the pages of the Foreign Review, Edinburgh, or Westminster, and read a few paragraphs. . . .

And Clarke goes on to note some particular examples of the interest Carlyle was already inspiring. He tells of a young man 'who used to walk from a neighbouring town to Boston every week, in order to read over again two articles by Carlyle in two numbers of the Foreign Review lying on a table in the reading room of the Athenaeum'. Clarke knew 'other young men and young women', he goes on, 'who taught themselves German in order to read for themselves the authors made so luminous by this writer'.[3]

James Russell Lowell, too, looking back on the same period, recalled the early influence of Carlyle's periodical essays: 'What contemporary', he wrote, 'will ever forget what was somewhat vaguely called the "Transcendental Movement" of thirty years ago? Apparently set astir by Carlyle's essays on the "Signs of the Times", and on "History", the final and more immediate impulse seemed to be given by *Sartor Resartus*'.[4] I shall return to the question of Carlyle's connection with the growth of the American transcendental movement, but Lowell's comments at least acknowledge the impact of the early essays.

In 1835, just over a year after *Sartor* had been appearing in *Fraser's*, Alexander Everett, the Boston editor of the *North American Review*, described Carlyle as 'the most profound and original of the living English philosophical writers. He is the person, to whom we look with the greatest confidence to give a new spring and direction to these studies in the mother country'.[5] Again, in April 1833, in his *Select Journal of Foreign Periodical Literature*, Andrews Norton, a Unitarian scholar hostile to Carlyle and what he understood Carlyle to represent, assailed the Scottish writer in a manner which revealed his thorough acquaintance with his opponent's work. Norton sees Carlyle as the head of a new–and disreputable–school of writers:

> They are priests of some one or other new revelation from nature to mankind, which, though it cannot yet be fully understood, is to effect wonderful things; and especially to sweep away all old notions of philosophy, morals, and religion.[6]

In 1839, an anonymous reviewer in a New York journal, summed up Carlyle's early impact upon America:

> The disquisitions upon Richter, German Literature, and Robert Burns, first attracted the attention of reading men in this country. These were followed by the essays on the 'Signs of the Times' and 'Characteristics',–productions of an order so remarkable and startling, that they created a prodigious sensation in the intellectual world; the before applausive murmurs of many were changed into groans and hisses, while others shouted out a louder cry of joy and hope.[7]

These various reports all provide evidence of the fact that Carlyle was a figure of some renown and considerable debate in America well before the publication of *Sartor Resartus* in book form. Particularly significant is the fact that Americans of a conservative stamp both in religion and literature already felt it necessary to enter the lists and rebut his opinions. The article by Andrews Norton, whom Carlyle described as the 'Unitarian Pope', is one such attempt, and another had appeared in the *North American Review* in 1831. This 1831 article discusses Carlyle's essays–in especial 'Signs of the Times'–at great length; and launches an all-out attack on the transcendental aspect of Carlyle's thought: 'Give us Locke's mechanism, and we will envy no man's Mysticism'.[8] But the point about such attacks is that they testify to the prevalence of Carlyle's ideas, and suggest that these ideas are receiving a ready welcome in some quarters at least. Such early American interest in Carlyle is also indicated by the history of the publication of Carlyle in America. The translation of *Wilhelm Meister*, published in Edinburgh in 1824, was published at Boston in 1829. And the *Life of Schiller*, which appeared in book form in England in 1825, was published at Boston in 1833, and again at New York in 1837.

There is one single fact, however, that puts the exceptional degree of American interest in Carlyle beyond dispute: the fact that the first publication in book form of *Sartor Resartus* occurred in America. Emerson had received several copies of the work in the form of off-prints from *Fraser's* stitched together. One of these he gave to the lady who was soon to become his second wife, and through her a recent Harvard graduate called Le Baron Russell had been able to read the work. Such was Russell's enthusiasm for what he read that he persuaded a Boston publisher to bring out a subscription edition in book form. *Sartor Resartus* thus appeared in its first edition in Boston in April 1836. The venture was a great success. The first edition of 500 copies was soon sold out. A second edition was issued– and some of these were ordered from England. On 13 September 1837 Emerson reported a total sale of 1166 copies.

This early success of *Sartor Resartus* was in the years that followed consolidated by American editions of most of Carlyle's writings. Emerson's work on Carlyle's behalf in this connection was outstanding. *The French Revolution*, the *Miscellanies, Heroes and Hero-Worship, Past and Present*, and the *Life and Letters of Cromwell*, all of these were published in America largely under Emerson's supervision. And thanks to that supervision, Carlyle, unlike the vast majority of his English contemporaries whose works were freely pirated in America, even derived considerable financial return from these American undertakings. Joseph Slater reckons Carlyle's payments up to 1847, when Emerson ceased to take an active interest, to have been £655. Such a sum was no doubt more than welcome to Carlyle; more important, perhaps, is that the American publication of his books gained him fame and admirers abroad at a time when success seemed to have eluded him at home.

We have already seen that from the time of the appearance of his earliest essays in the British periodicals, some opposition to Carlyle existed in America. But that opposition was in no way able to contain the tremendous impact produced by the American appearance of *Sartor Resartus*. It was *Sartor* above all that made Carlyle one of the dominant cultural influences upon America in the nineteenth century. Both in its matter and in its manner, *Sartor Resartus* was to prove of high significance in American culture for several decades after 1836. The subsequent books had their admirers and their detractors, but after *Sartor* there was no dispute in America over the fact of Carlyle's importance, his impact and his influence. In May 1838, Emerson wrote to Carlyle that 'Carlyleism is becoming so fashionable that the most austere Seniors are glad to qualify their reprobation by applauding this review'. (Slater, p. 183). (The allusion is to the essay on Scott.) W. E. Channing asserted that he had read *The French Revolution* five times, while Charles Godfrey Leland said that he had read *Sartor Resartus* 'forty times, ere I left College'.[9] A more extended tribute to *Sartor* is paid in his autobiography by William Henry Milburn, the blind author and preacher:

Carlyle and America

I much question if Christopher Columbus was more transported by the discovery of America than was I in entering the
new realm which this book *Sartor* opened to me . . . It became
a sort of touchstone with me. If a man had read *Sartor* and
enjoyed it, I was his friend: if not, we were strangers. I was as
familiar with the Everlasting No, the Center of Indifference,
and the Everlasting Yea as with the sidewalk in front of my
house.[10]

As early as October 1835 Emerson had written to Carlyle to say
that 'now that doctors of divinity and the solemn review itself
break silence to praise you, I lose my plume as your harbinger'.
(Slater, p. 140).[11] And Harriet Martineau's remarks, published
in 1837, may be taken as summing up the tremendous impact
that *Sartor Resartus* had made:

> Perhaps this is the first instance of the Americans having taken
> to their hearts an English book which came to them anon-
> ymous, unsanctioned by any recommendation and even ab-
> solutely neglected at home. The book is acting upon them
> with wonderful force. It has regenerated the preaching of
> more than one of the clergy; and, I have reason to believe, the
> minds and lives of several of the laity.[12]

Miss Martineau's point that Carlyle had been admired much
more in America than in his own country is one that was
frequently repeated. In an unfriendly review of *Cromwell's Letters*, for example, in the *North American Review*, C. C. Felton
spoke of Carlyle's 'ascendancy in this country . . . which he is far
from possessing in his own'.[13] But the essential point remains that
in the American context Carlyle, both before and increasingly
after the publication of *Sartor Resartus*, was a tremendously
enlivening and invigorating force. When James Russell Lowell
looked back on Carlyle's career in his highly measured essay
which formed part of *My Study Windows*, it was Carlyle's
inspiriting power that he was finally compelled to emphasise:

> Though not the safest of guides in politics or practical
> philosophy, his value as an inspirer and awakener cannot

be over-estimated. It is power which belongs only to the highest order of minds, for it is none but the divine fire that can so kindle and irradiate. The debt due him from those who listened to the teachings of his prime for revealing to them what sublime reserves of power even the humblest may find in manliness, sincerity, and self-reliance, can be paid with nothing short of reverential gratitude.[14]

Equally, Henry David Thoreau, in his much more enthusiastic account entitled *Thomas Carlyle and his Works*, published in 1847, places special emphasis on what he calls Carlyle's *vivacity*. In endeavouring to find something to quote 'as the fairest specimen of the man', Thoreau encounters a peculiar difficulty because, 'What we would quote is, in fact, his vivacity, and not any particular wisdom or sense'.[15] And it was to Carlyle's power of awakening, stimulating, and enlivening his readers that Emerson himself alluded when he wrote his preface to the Boston edition of the *Miscellanies*. Emerson reminded his American readers of 'pages which, in the scattered anonymous sheets of the British magazines, spoke to their youthful mind with an emphasis that hindered them from sleep' (Slater, p. 5). There cannot be the slightest doubt that from the late 1820s and through the 1830s and 1840s, Carlyle was a most potent force on the American intellectual and cultural scene. Both those for him and those against him agree on the point. Carlyle had become a force to be reckoned with in America.

I have so far made use of the Emerson-Carlyle correspondence simply to illustrate and document specific points. But at this point I should like to turn to the broader significance of the enduring friendship between the two men. The friendship is important on two counts; first, it helps to explain *how* Carlyle came so quickly to be established and admired in America; and second, it helps to bring us closer to the larger question of *why* Carlyle exerted such a powerful influence beyond the Atlantic.

The story of Emerson's first meeting with Carlyle is well-known. Emerson had arrived in Europe in 1833. Much impressed by his reading of Carlyle's periodical essays–at first, of course, Emerson did not know the identity of the person who had written them–he was determined to meet their author. Finally in August 1833 his ambition was realised. Having arrived at Craigenputtock he stayed for almost 24 hours–most of them taken up with walking and talking. The visit was an immense success. The two men talked of common acquaintances, of the leading literary figures of the day, of politics, and society and religion. That Carlyle's life at this point was an isolated and lonely one no doubt tremendously reinforced the significance of Emerson's visit. It was Jane Carlyle who expressed most forcibly the nature of the impression Emerson had made: 'It was like the visit of an angel; . . . and though he staid with us hardly twenty-four hours, yet when he left us I cried–I could not help it' (Slater, p. 14). Emerson and Carlyle were to meet again on other occasions–several times during Emerson's stay in England in 1847–48 and once more in 1872–but it was in their correspondence that the friendship truly subsisted. So much so that a critic as distinguished as Matthew Arnold suggested that it was in his correspondence with Emerson that Carlyle would finally survive:

> I should not wonder if really Carlyle lived, in the long run, by such an invaluable record as that correspondence between him and Emerson, of which we owe the publication to Mr Charles Norton–by this and not by his works, as Johnson lives in Boswell, not by his works.[16]

Arnold's opinion may well strike us as somewhat eccentric, but no one would wish to belittle the literary value of the Carlyle-Emerson correspondence. Certainly as far as Carlyle and America goes, the mere existence of this correspondence is powerful testimony to Carlyle's continuing impact upon America.

What has to be borne in mind in this connection is the position that Emerson was coming to occupy in American cultural and spiritual life just about the time of the opening of the correspondence with Carlyle. He had recently resigned his pulpit in the Unitarian church and was moving rapidly towards the embracing of those transcendental doctrines which were soon to be pre-eminently identified with his name. It is highly probable that Emerson's encounters with Carlyle's early essays, then with the man himself, then with *Sartor Resartus*, did much to encourage him to continue further along the path upon which he had already set out. Emersonian Transcendentalism might well have developed had Carlyle never existed; but it is abundantly clear that Emerson recognised in Carlyle a fellow-spirit and a powerful inspiration. There is much in Carlyle's thought that must have produced in Emerson a shock of recognition. Carlyle's attack on the materialism of the age, his emphasis on the supremacy of intuitive reason over mere understanding, his recognition of the visible universe as but a garment or symbol of the real; above all the passionate energy with which he insisted on the spiritual value of individual life—all of these were notions that Emerson himself was fast coming to share. It is hardly surprising then that he would have welcomed Carlyle's presence in America and, failing that, did everything in his power to ensure that Carlyle's works and his ideas should be rapidly and widely promulgated in America. And once again we have to remind ourselves of the degree of Emerson's own success and prestige. In the period between roughly 1835 and the Civil War Emersonianism undoubtedly dominated the intellectual climate of America; Transcendentalism in this period was in the ascendant. Emerson and his fellow-Transcendentalists set the tone of America's cultural and spiritual life. Thus it inevitably follows that Carlyle's close personal association with Emerson more or less guaranteed his American success. He could have found in America no champion more likely to gain him support, a following, and increasing influence. If Carlyle owed Emerson much for his financial efforts on his behalf with American publishers, he owed him even more in terms of his establishment in America as a prophet to be both attended to and honoured.

However, as has already been indicated, Carlyle and Emerson did not have everything their own way in America. From the earliest pre-*Sartor* days there had always been a party in America opposed to Carlyleism. Those who were stirred and enlivened by Carlyle's first essays were mainly the young—men like Emerson himself dissatisfied with the present state of society, disappointed by its materialism, its neglect of spiritual values, and coming to feel that the new religious orthodoxies of the Unitarian type–replacing the sterner Puritanism of New England–were too dry and moderate in tone to engage the deeper sources of religious and spiritual feeling. Such young men were attracted by the emotional appeal of Transcendentalism and it was above all the note of transcendental discontent in Carlyle's work that drew them to him. As Van Wyck Brooks suggests, Carlyle 'represented the romantic spirit on its ethical and religious side, where the New England mind was most at home'.[17] But precisely such ethical and religious romanticism was deeply offensive to men of a more conservative frame of mind. Transcendentalism itself was looked upon as a rather dangerous novelty by such men; so it is hardly surprising that they should have looked upon American Transcendentalism's Scottish ally with considerable disfavour.

The leading exponents of Transcendentalism in America were naturally and inevitably admirers of Carlyle–Emerson himself of course, Thoreau, Frederick Henry Hedge, W. H. Channing, Bronson Alcott, Orestes Brownson, George Ripley and Henry James, Sr. But by and large those who disapproved of the Transcendental movement tended also to disapprove of Carlyle. Thus the literary coteries of New York, always sceptical of New England Transcendentalism, tended to be hostile towards Carlyle. Lewis Gaylord Clark, for example, the influential editor of the *Knickerbocker Magazine*, said of *Sartor Resartus* that 'The writer walks beneath a German cloud more dense than a Scotch mist'.[18] Edgar Allan Poe was still more disparaging, referring to the author of *Sartor Resartus* as an 'ass',[19] while the *New York Sun* described *Sartor* as 'what old Dennis used to call "a heap of clotted nonsense"'.[20] J. H. Barrett, however, in the course of an unfavourable notice in *The American Whig Review*, was forced to acknowledge that 'we cannot speak of Thomas Carlyle with contempt or deny to *Sartor Resartus* a place among the writings that have given an impulse and a direction to the literature of the time'.[21] The most important of all the native literary periodicals–the *North American Review* of Boston–also tended to link its distrust of Transcendentalism with criticism of Carlyle. As we have seen it did in fact notice *Sartor Resartus* favourably, but subsequently it remained more critical.

Thus from the earliest period, Carlyle's connection with American Transcendentalism gained him considerable support and some hostility. Such hostility as existed was certainly not powerful enough to prevent the spread of his influence and the growth of his American reputation. As a writer in *The New Englander* put it in 1850: 'Macaulay and Dickens have had more readers, but neither of them has raised up a school'.[22] But in fact in the end Carlyle's reputation was to decline in America. The cause was Carlyle's increasingly hostile comments on American society, politics, and contemporary affairs.

From the earliest days Carlyle had believed he could see grave deficiencies in American society. In February 1835, when his possible visit to America was under discussion, he had written to Emerson that he fancied America to be 'mainly a new Commercial England, with a fuller pantry: little more or little less. The same unquenchable, almost frightfully unresting spirit of endeavour, directed (woe is me!) to the making of money . . .' 'So that you see when I set foot on American land it will be on no Utopia . . .' (Slater, p. 117). But the relatively good-natured quality of these criticisms was not to remain characteristic of Carlyle's opinions on America. In two works in particular he expressed views of America and American questions which were highly offensive to most Americans, including many of his erstwhile admirers: these were his 'Occasional Discourse on the Nigger Question', in *Fraser's Magazine* in 1849, and his *Latter Day Pamphlets* published in 1850. This latter work contains Carlyle's angriest and most extreme attack on the principles of democracy and America. America is dismissed because it has produced no 'great thought', no 'great noble thing'. All it has done is double its population every twenty years: 'They have begotten, with a rapidity beyond recorded example, Eighteen Millions of the greatest *bores* ever seen in this world before . . .' The 'Occasional Discourse' contained sentiments equally or even more offensive. Carlyle attacked the notion of racial equality and economic freedom from a neo-feudalist standpoint, apparently advocating a kind of new serfdom for all inferior races and classes. These were hardly the kinds of sentiment likely to find favour in Concord–or for that matter anywhere in America where the abolitionist cause was gaining momentum.

Inevitably the situation was different in the Southern states. Despite Poe's disparagement, alluded to above, the South from the earliest days had responded positively to Carlyle, with the result, as Michael O'Brien has shown, that he had helped to shape the nature of Southern romanticism.[23] Thus when outside pressures on the South and its institutions began to grow in the 1840s and '50s, it was hardly surprising that Southerners welcomed enthusiastically what they saw as support from one of the day's greatest writers. In 1848 the *Southern Quarterly Review* wrote:

> The spirit of Carlyle is abroad in the land. The strong thinker, the earnest soul, is making an impress wherever the Saxon tongue and Saxon blood prevail. Here, in our Western World, even more than in his own native Isle, is the advocate of faith and sincerity and work . . . beginning to be appreciated.

A few years later, in 1853, the same magazine argued that the only sensible comments on the subject of slavery came in England from the *Times* newspaper and Carlyle, 'the greatest, the wisest, and the bravest living author . . .' William Gilmore Simms, the popular Southern novelist, praised Carlyle in very similar terms as a lofty, bold and objective analyst of the institution of slavery. And leading Southern apologists for slavery, such as George Fitzhugh and Thomas Cobb, saw themselves as disciples of Carlyle sharing not only his views on slavery but all his criticisms of democracy and the modern world.[24]

Emerson however, who must surely have been aware of the solace and reassurance the South was finding in Carlyle's attitudes in the years leading up to the Civil War, seems not to have been specially disturbed by his outspoken and extremist views. Slater suggests that he perhaps felt that Carlyle was too remote from the actualities of American politics for his opinions to matter. Certainly the correspondence in this period declined in volume–and the delays in writing all occur on Emerson's side. Yet the relationship remained unbroken. And it was even to survive Carlyle's stance on the Civil War itself. In public Carlyle pretended to a position of neutrality on the war; in private his Southern sympathies were made all too clear. He admired the nature of Southern society; rule by a gallant, inflexible aristocracy, not interested in notions of human liberty and equality. His deepest feelings were clearly engaged on the Southern side. Emerson, despite his own total commitment to the righteousness and justice of the Northern cause, was able to tolerate Carlyle's unfriendly opinions. But such was hardly the position of Americans at large. There can be no doubt that Carlyle's views on the slavery question and on the Civil War did much to undermine his lofty American reputation. Not of course that by this time Carlyle cared very much. In *Shooting Niagara: and After*, published in 1867, he made it clear that his views on America and American affairs remained wholly unchanged:

> half a million . . . of excellent White men, full of gifts and faculty, have torn and slashed one another into horrid death, in a temporary humour, which will leave centuries of remembrance fierce enough: and three million absurd Blacks, men and brothers (of a sort), are completely 'emancipated'; launched into the career of improvement–likely to be 'improved off the face of the earth' in a generation or two.

Again, these were hardly the kinds of views likely to recommend themselves to Carlyle's former admirers.

In fact there is considerable evidence that numbers of Americans–among them, no doubt, many who had once responded so eagerly to Carlyle's transcendental enthusiasm–did feel that their mentor had betrayed them. One such wrote a letter to the *Atlantic Monthly* in October 1863. The writer identified himself as a former admirer, one who 'along there in the remote solitudes of Maine' had read *Sartor Resartus* 'afoot and on horseback, sleeping with it under my pillow and wearing it in my pocket till pocket and it were worn out . . .' Now Carlyle has chosen to identify himself with a cause that sanctions crimes and brutalities of the most flagrant nature. 'Yes, Thomas Carlyle', he writes, 'I hold you a party to these crimes . . . You approve the system; you volunteer your best varnish in its commendation . . .' (Slater, p. 47). One H. H. Furness went even further, sending Carlyle a photograph of a 'scourged black' with a note saying 'Please observe an instance of "hiring for life". [A reference to Carlyle's solution to the slavery question.] God forgive you for your cruel jest and your blindness'.[25] In 1867 James Freeman Clarke summed up what were no doubt the views of most of Carlyle's erstwhile American admirers: 'He is our "Lost Leader", but we have loved and honored him as few men were ever loved and honored We shall always be grateful to the real Carlyle, the real Carlyle of *Sartor*'.[26]

Had he expressed none of the views to which I have been referring Carlyle's reputation and influence in America would still have declined in the period after the Civil War. They would have declined as American Transcendentalism itself declined. And in the period of rapid economic development and industrial expansion, which followed the war, Transcendentalism soon ceased to set the tone of American intellectual life. The scientific philosophies of a new age quickly gained the ascendancy; the doctrines of Darwin and in particular of Herbert Spencer seemed much more in tune with the realities of American life. The age of Transcendentalism was over. But even so, Carlyle himself quite clearly did much to ensure, by the extremism of his views on America and American affairs, that he should lose that position of dominance in American intellectual and cultural life which for so long made it possible to believe that in no other part of the world was Carlyle so honoured and respected as he was in America.

From Goosecreek to Gandercleugh

II

What I have done so far is describe Carlyle's relationship with America. I have tried to document the frequent assertion that Carlyle was one of the most important external influences on nineteenth-century America. But except in suggesting that Carlyle's transcendentalism was what appealed to Emerson, and that this explains in turn why Emerson was so eager to encourage the spread of his ideas in America, I have hardly attempted to suggest *why* Carlyle made so great an impact upon America. Unsurprisingly, perhaps, my inclination is to argue that American receptiveness to Carlyle was much bound up with the Scottishness of Carlyle's work. Carlyle, that is, could appeal to an existing American responsiveness to Scottish intellectual traditions. Given Thoreau's 1847 allusions to an English Carlyle, this may appear a somewhat whimsical case to make. But in the early 1830s, when Americans were first becoming aware of Carlyle's existence as a writer, such a failure to recognise his Scottishness would have been much less likely to occur. For a variety of economic, political, religious and cultural reasons, the impact of what may broadly be called the Scottish Enlightenment had been extraordinarily marked on almost every aspect of the developing cultural life of America. American education, American medical studies, American science, American writing and literary criticism, and American philosophy, all of these had been receptive of Scottish influence to the degree that each took on a distinctively Scottish coloration. As evidence of this, let Emerson himself stand as a solitary example of how Scottish influences bore on Americans of his generation: at Harvard University he was required to read Reid's *Inquiry Into the Human Mind*, an he wrote an undergraduate prize essay on Dugald Stewart. But if Reid and Stewart formed part of Emerson's intellectual inheritance, they contributed even more to the development of Carlyle's thinking. Recent scholarship has insisted on the depth and pervasiveness of Carlyle's debt to the philosophers of the Scottish Enlightenment.[27]

What, however, is the significance of the situation I have indicated in relation to Carlyle and America? In the first place it suggests how much Carlyle and many of his early American readers had in common. They shared a similar intellectual and philosophical background even in the context of rejecting it. It was the modified empiricism of the Scottish common sense school of philosophy–and, perhaps, more importantly, the moderation in religion that went with it–against which young Americans of Emerson's generation, just like Carlyle himself, were in part reacting. As mentioned above, Carlyle was undeniably much influenced by the thought of the Scottish Enlightenment; but in important ways he was reacting against its spirit and tone. As Ralph Jessop has recently put it:

> The quest for knowledge and wisdom in some of Carlyle's early writings seeks escape from the constraints of what he seems to have felt was a dryasdust discursive reasoning, precision, the coldness of Scotch logic, sceptical self-questioning and uncertainty. Questing for knowledge and wisdom alone were not sufficient for him. In Carlyle's texts there is an artistic drive for a third dimension which alone could make possible the attainment of true knowledge and wisdom, defying the mechanistic and sceptical tendencies of the Scottish Enlightenment. . . .[28]

Many young Americans, educated, like Emerson, in the same tradition of the Scottish common sense school, seem to have felt exactly as Carlyle did. Hence the shared appeal of the new German idealistic philosophy, Goethe and the German romantic writers, and the rest. Some at least then of the pressures which were pushing Carlyle towards a new transcendentalism of vision were pressures experienced too by his early American readers.

But Carlyle and his American readers shared something else, something probably of even greater significance. They shared a Puritan or Calvinist consciousness. Perry Miller has demonstrated how American Transcendentalism, whatever its debts to German and other external influences, has its roots firmly embedded in the native Puritan tradition.[29] It is from the Puritan tradition, bypassing the cool rationality of Unitarianism, that

American Transcendentalism draws its emotional energy and inspirational enthusiasm. Is it not this note of energy, of enthusiasm for man's spiritual nature, that seems to have electrified Carlyle's earliest American readers? And is its source too, in turn, not to be found in Carlyle's perhaps intellectually discarded Calvinism? Once again in relation to Carlyle and his American readers it is a case of like speaking to like.

But what finally of the speech itself? His detractors both in England and America constantly reserved their sternest censures for Carlyle's language and style. In the early 1850s Evert Duyckinck, friend and patron of Herman Melville, rebuked Melville for writing in 'the run-a-muck style of Carlyle'.[30] Similarly a journalist who attended Brown University subsequently recalled how, in the early 1840s, 'our efforts to write like Carlyle drove the Professor of Rhetoric nearly frantic'.[31] 'Carlylese' became a recognised writing mode, and the staid American reviewers frequently spoke contemptuously of Carlyle's 'sect of silly imitators'. Obviously there was little in Carlyle's style to win the approval of those purists for whom the supreme virtues of style were classical elegance, correctness and good taste.

But Carlyle's style, however far it departed from established models, was itself the corollary of a conscious aesthetic stance. The poet-philosopher is of necessity a visionary or seer; his concern is with the greater reality that lies behind appearances. Everyday reality is then a symbol of the greater reality; the visible is but the symbol or garment of the invisible. Hence the literary mode of the poet-philosopher is necessarily a symbolic one. Only through his symbolism may the reader be brought to the apprehension of the truth. American Transcendentalism similarly embraced the symbolic mode and a symbolic aesthetic. 'Every natural fact is a symbol of some spiritual fact', wrote Emerson in *Nature*, and such a perspective became the basis for a symbolist aesthetic available to American writers whether or not they shared Emerson's view of the nature of the spiritual facts which the natural facts symbolise. What we may ask was the source of American Transcendentalism's symbolic vision? Whence had come the notion that the visible world is but a series of revelations of the invisible or spiritual? Once again the answer seems to lie in America's own past. The symbolising strain in American Transcendentalism represented the revitalisation of the old Calvinist way of seeing the hand of God in the most mundane aspects of everyday reality. As an American scholar has suggested, 'it is safe to assume that the effects of Puritan beliefs upon the American mind habituated it to the symbolic mode of vision, with the result that eventually, in Emerson and other men of his time, the revolt against the *jejune* rationalism into which the formal theology had developed expressed a sensibility more fundamentally Puritan that the theoretical positions it rejects'.[32]

I would argue, then, that American familiarity with a generally symbolic literary mode did much to gain Carlyle a sympathetic reading in America. No doubt *Sartor Resartus* in turn did much to encourage American Transcendentalism towards the reconstruction of that symbolic mode. But in any case the potential of such a way of writing had always remained present in the American context. One may even go a little further and suggest that the roots of Carlyle's symbolic style are to be found in precisely the same tradition that gave rise to the symbolic mode of American Transcendentalism: the Calvinist tradition that Carlyle shared with his American readers. Scottish Calvinism, like American Puritanism, had always tended towards a symbolic reading of the physical world. Let me refer to a single example. In his *Life of Henry Erskine*, Alexander Fergusson describes a Mrs Elizabeth Steuart, an old Scotch lady of the traditional type, a strict Presbyterian. According to Fergusson, Mrs Steuart 'saw analogies in everything, and delighted in working them out to the extreme end'. And he goes on to generalise:

> Much of the preaching in the Scotch church at that period was formed upon this habit of thought—one very easily carried to excess, especially as it was a peculiarity frequently displayed in Presbyterian eloquence, that every type which the preacher's ingenuity could detect was held to be intended by the Almighty.[33]

From Goosecreek to Gandercleugh

It seems to me entirely possible that this Scottish Presbyterian concern for types and analogies has a great deal to do with the development of Carlyle's symbolical vision, his concern for the realities which lie behind the garment of the universe. If I am right then we can understand all the more clearly why in the American context Carlyle's style should have proved less of a barrier than it did elsewhere. And perhaps we see, too, why Carlyle should have exerted a positive influence on American writing: *Moby-Dick*, itself, for example, is clearly influence by *Sartor Resartus*.[34] In fine, Carlyle is certainly to be recognised– as Thoreau explains so precisely–as one of the forces releasing American literature from the stylistic restrictiveness of the so-called genteel tradition in American letters largely deriving, ironically enough, from the study in America of the Scottish rhetoricians, Blair, Kames and Campbell.[35]

The link between the symbolic habit of mind in both Scottish Calvinism and American Puritanism is only part of a wider pattern of cultural relationship between Scotland and America in the early nineteenth century. Thus the American receptiveness to Carlyle is finally to be understood within the context of that pattern and, in particular, of a general American responsiveness to earlier and ongoing Scottish intellectual traditions. Just as American enthusiasm for Sir Walter Scott had been prepared for by an existing American vogue for earlier exponents of Scottish literary romanticism, so the positive response to Carlyle had been set up by a continuing American indebtedness to earlier Scottish philosophical and religious thought.

Notes

1. Joseph Slater, ed. *The Correspondence of Emerson and Carlyle* (New York and London, 1964), p. 105. All subsequent references are to this edition. Though Carlyle himself did not, several members of his family did end in 'the Western Woods'. His brother Alick, one of his sisters, and a half-brother all emigrated to Canada. Their story is told in *The Letters of Thomas Carlyle to His Brother Alexander, With Related Family Letters*, ed. Edwin W. Marrs (Cambridge, Mass., 1969).

Carlyle and America

2. In connection with these exchanges on the topic of a Carlylean descent upon America it is impossible not to quote Henry James's accurate and amusing comment (from an essay review on the Carlyle-Emerson correspondence in the *Century Magazine*, June 1883): 'The reader at this point of the correspondence feels a certain suspense: he knows that Carlyle never did come to America, but like a good novel the letters produce an illusion. He holds his breath, for the terrible Scotchman may after all have embarked, and there is something really almost heart-shaking in the thought of his transporting that tremendous imagination and those vessels of wrath and sarcasm to an innocent New England village'.

3. See William Silas Vance, 'Carlyle in America Before *Sartor Resartus*', *American Literature*, 7 (1935–36), p. 375.

4. *Ibid.*, p. 369.

5. *Ibid.*, p. 370.

6. *Ibid.*, p. 372.

7. *Ibid.*, p. 373.

8. *Ibid.*, p. 369.

9. See Frank Luther Mott, 'Carlyle's American Public', *Philological Quarterly*, 4 (1925). p. 248.

10. *Ibid.*, pp. 248–9.

11. Emerson is referring to Alexander Everett's friendly notice of *Sartor* in the *North American Review*, 41 (1835), pp. 454–82.

12. Mott, p. 247.

13. *Ibid.*, p. 255.

14. James Russell Lowell, *My Study Windows* (London, n.d.), pp. 190–1.

15. *The Writings of Henry David Thoreau* (Walden Edition, Boston 1906), IV, p. 350. Thoreau's 1847 essay represents the culminating point in American (and in particular New England) enthusiasm for Carlyle at a time just before the beginning of the decline in his American reputation. Thoreau expresses enormous and almost unbounded appreciation of Carlyle's energy, his language and style, and his point of view. 'When we remember', he write, 'how these volumes came over to us, with their encouragement and provocation from month to month, and what commotion they created in many private breasts, we wonder that the country did not ring, from short to shore, from the Atlantic to the Pacific, with its greeting. . . . Of all that the packets have brought over to us, has there been any richer cargo than this? What else has been English news for so long a season? What else, of late years, has been England to us–to us who read books, we mean? . . . Carlyle alone since the death of Coleridge, has kept the promise of England'. *Ibid.*, p. 320. Thoreau's use of 'English' and 'England' here–despite his initial identification of Carlyle as 'a Scotchman' speaking English with a 'broad Scotch accent'–is striking. Whether it indicates Carlyle's assimilation into the mainstream of English culture after his move to London, or, a more general decline in American awareness of any separate Scottish cultural identity, or both, is difficult to determine.

16. Matthew Arnold, *Discourses in America* (London, 1885), p. 167.

17. Van Wyck Brooks, *The Flowering of New England, 1815–1865* (London, 1936), p. 193.

18. Mott, p. 252.

19. *Ibid.*, p. 253.

20. *Ibid.*, p. 252.

21. *Ibid.*, p. 253.

22. *Ibid.*, p. 248.

23. Michael O'Brien, 'The Lineaments of Antebellum Southern Romanticism', *Journal of American Studies* 20 (August, 1986), 168–88. O'Brien identifies Carlyle as only one element in a wider Scottish contribution to the development of Southern romanticism. 'Indeed, in intellectual matters', he writes (p. 179), 'the South of 1820 is almost more Scottish than English'.

24. For these references, and a full discussion of Carlyle's Southern reputation, see Gerald M. Straka, 'The Spirit of Carlyle in the Old South', *The Historian* (1957), 39–57.

25. Mott, pp. 258–9.

26. *Ibid.*, p. 262.

27. See in particular Ralph Jessop, *Carlyle and Scottish Thought* (London and New York, 1997), *passim*.

28. Jessop, p. 202.

29. See Perry Miller, 'From Edwards to Emerson' in *Errand into the Wilderness* (Cambridge, Mass., 1956), pp. 184–203.

30. See Perry Miller, *The Raven and the Whale* (New York, 1956), p. 299.

31. Mott, p. 250.

32. John F. Lynen, *The Design of the Present* (New Haven and London, 1969), p. 44.

33. Alex. Fergusson, *Henry Erskine* (Edinburgh and London, 1882), p. 374.

34. Melville borrowed *Sartor Resartus* from his friend Evert Duyckinck in June or July 1850–that is, while he was immersed in the composition of *Moby-Dick*. The strong influence of Carlyle's book is apparent both in the novel's prose and its characterisation.

35. We believe', wrote Thoreau in 1847, 'that Carlyle has, after all, more readers, and is better known today for this very originality of style, and that posterity will have reason to thank him for emancipating the language, in some measure, from the fetters which a merely conservative, aimless, and pedantic literary class had imposed upon it, and setting an example of greater freedom and naturalness'. *The Writings of Henry David Thoreau*, IV, pp. 330–1. In this connection it is interesting to find Mark Twain, that major exponent of the freedom and naturalness of the vernacular tradition in American writing, asserting that he too was an enthusiastic reader of Carlyle: 'I have a reverent affection for Carlyle's books, and have read his *Revolution* eight times . . .' However, as the comment comes in a humorous sketch called 'My First Lie and How I got Out of It', in which Carlyle is accused of lying about a lie not living, perhaps we should remain sceptical. Twain's explanation of Carlyle's

remark is that 'he said it in a moment of excitement, when chasing Americans out of his back-yard with brickbats. They used to go there and worship. At bottom he was probably fond of them, but he was always able to conceal it . . .' See *The Man That Corrupted Hadleyburg and Other Stories and Essays*, Shelley Fisher Fishkin (ed.), Oxford University Press, 1996, p. 177.

CHAPTER NINE

Macaulay and America

The inclusion of an account of the reception in America of the nineteenth century's most popular historian–in a book concerned with Scottish-American literary connections requires some explanation. Zachary Macaulay, the historian's father, was a Highland Scot, born in Inveraray and descended from a Gaelic-speaking, Presbyterian, Western Isles family. But Macaulay's putative 'Scottishness' is not just a question of ancestry; his historical writing, too, is of Scottish descent, as modern historians have recognised. In 1967, in his famous and seminal essay on the Scottish Enlightenment, Hugh Trevor-Roper refers to Macaulay as one of the 'great Scottish Whig historians', while in his **Subverting Scotland's Past,** *published in 1993, Colin Kidd describes Macaulay as 'a second-generation Anglo-Scot whose education in the works of Millar and Robertson significantly influenced his historical and political thought'.[1]*

In the essay that follows, I do not argue that Macaulay's Scottish ancestry, in the literal, family sense, had much to do with his American popularity–though his father, as we shall see, was a familiar figure in some American circles–but his position in the Scottish Whig historical tradition is another matter. The central thesis of Colin Kidd's own original and provocative study is that the Scottish historians of the eighteenth century passed a largely negative verdict on the history of their own country. The history of Scotland had little to offer the new nation emerging from the Treaty of Union in 1707; it was the history of England that provided a usable model for a modern, civilised country. Now when the American republic was created in 1776, a major emphasis in the nation's emerging culture centred on the notion that it was only the United States' **newness** *that counted: the USA was a country with a glorious future, but without a past. As the nineteenth century went on, however, a*

160

*usable past was something that democratic, republican America,
so frequently under attack from upholders of the much more
conservative anciens régimes of Europe, increasingly felt in need
of. My contention is that it was the Whig Macaulay–ironically
replacing the older, more conservative, Scottish historians
Hume and Robertson–who at last provided Americans with
an English history to which they could comfortably relate, and
even finally adopt as their own.*

I

'Their road lay through a vast and desolate fen, saturated with
all the moisture of thirteen counties, and overhung during the
greater part of the year, by a low gray mist, high above which
rose, visible many miles, the magnificent tower of Ely'. I
opened Macauly's [*sic*] new volume at random two or three
days ago and the very first sentence that caught my eye was
this, describing the march of soldiery through the Lincolnshire
fens. This was at a bookseller's counter, and I at once
closed the volume and went away with a picture and a poem
in my mind; a fine historic painting, framed in a single
sentence.[2]

The date is January 1865; the place, Cambridge, Massachusetts; and the browser at the bookseller's counter is Henry
Wadsworth Longfellow. This letter to his friend, Senator
Charles Sumner, testifies in the precisest manner to the magical,
imaginative potency of Macaulay's historical writing experienced by so many of his readers.

But Macaulay was not admired in America only as an
historian:

Then I borrowed another volume of Macaulay's essays, and
another and another, till I had read them every one. It was like
a long debauch, from which I emerged with regret that it
should ever end . . . I sighed for more Macaulay and evermore

Macaulay. I read his history of England, and I could mea-
surably console myself with that . . .

The place this time is the small village of Jefferson, Ohio, and the
period is the 1850s; the omnivorous Macaulay reader is the
young William Dean Howells. Howells goes on to explain how
for a time Macaulay's influence and example wholly dominated
him:

> Of course I reformed my prose style, which had been carefully
> modelled upon that of Goldsmith and Irving, and began to
> write in the manner of Macaulay in short, quick sentences, and
> with the prevalent use of brief Anglo-Saxon words, which he
> prescribed, but did not practice. As for his notions of literature
> I simply accepted them with the feeling that any question of
> them would have been little better than blasphemy.[3]

Evidence for the American appeal of the third major area of
Macaulay's literary endeavours–his poetry–is to be found in the
work of a writer even more popular than either Howells or
Longfellow. In *An Old-Fashioned Girl* (1870), Polly, Tom, and
Tom's father turn out to share an enthusiasm for Macaulay's
Lays: '. . . he don't care a hang', Tom complains of his father,
'and never even asked if I did well last declamation day, when I'd
gone and learned "The Battle of Lake Regillus", because he said
he liked it'. 'Oh, Tom! Did you say that?' replies Polly, 'It's
splendid! Jim and I used to say Horatius together, and it was
such fun. Do speak your piece to me, I do like "Macaulay's
lays".'[4] It is fair to assume that Louisa M. Alcott had heard very
many such 'declamations' of Macaulay's narrative poems in
New England schools and homes.

These allusions to Macaulay–the Macaulay of the *History of
England*, of the *Critical and Miscellaneous Essays*, and of the
Lays of Ancient Rome by three such diverse American authors as
Longfellow, Howells, and Louisa M. Alcott provide specific
examples to support the familiar generalisation that throughout
a large part of the nineteenth century Macaulay's writing in its
various forms found an immense audience in the United States.

Macaulay and America

More general evidence of Macaulay's American success is also readily available. The most famous testimony is that of Edward Everett who told Macaulay that the sale of his *History* in America exceeded that of every other book save the Bible and one or two schoolbooks. Somewhat solider evidence is provided by Harpers who in 1849, soon after the publication of the first two volumes of the *History of England*, reported that there would be six American editions of the work, that 60,000 copies had already been sold, and that another 200,000 copies were expected to go in the next three months. 'No work of any kind, has ever so completely taken our whole country by storm'.[5] In 1861, when the entire five volumes were out, the 200,000 copy figure was in fact reached within a few months. Finally in 1901 Charles Francis Adams stated that at least twenty American publishing houses 'have brought out complete editions of Macaulay, both his *Miscellanies* and the *History of England*'.[6]

The American triumph of the *History of England* in 1849 is partly to be accounted for by the fact that Macaulay had already established himself on the American cultural scene as a writer of outstanding merit. Like Carlyle, and this is only the first of several significant parallels between the American receptions of the two Victorian sages, Macaulay first came to the attention of American readers through his contributions to the *Edinburgh Review*. The interest aroused by these contributions became so great that American publishers soon began to produce collections of Macaulay's essays; Weeks, Jordan and Co., of Boston, began a five volume edition in 1840, and Carey and Hart followed with a three volume collection in Philadelphia in 1841. These editions forced Macaulay's hand. He had not been inclined to publish his occasional essays in book form, but as he himself described the situation in 1843:

> The question is now merely this, whether Longman and I, or Carey and Hart of Philadelphia, shall have the supplying of the English market with these papers. The American copies are coming over by scores, and measures are being taken for bringing them over by hundreds.[7]

The inevitable consequence was the appearance in England in 1843 of a collected edition of the *Critical and Miscellaneous Essays*. The parallel with Carlyle, once again, is striking: it was in America, thanks to the enthusiasm of his American readers, that *Sartor Resartus* first appeared in book form.

The reputation Macaulay had established in America with his *Essays* was reinforced and extended by the publication in 1843 of the *Lays of Ancient Rome*. The direct, narrative quality of these poems made them appeal to a wider and more popular audience than that receptive to the *Essays*. With the *Lays* Macaulay was no doubt reaching a considerable percentage of that immense American audience for the novels and poetry of Scott, the poetry of Byron, and, more recently, the Roman novels of Bulwer-Lytton. Another factor working in Macaulay's favour was that the American poetry-reading public had already demonstrated its taste for the narrative, ballad-like, poetic genre by its enthusiasm for the poetry of Longfellow: his *Ballads and Other Poems* had appeared in 1842, and over 40,000 copies would soon be sold.[8] Hence the *Critical and Miscellaneous Essays*, and the *Lays of Ancient Rome*, provided the *History of England* with a substantial foundation on which to build. The *History*, however, did raise Macaulay's fame and reputation to a new dimension. In March 1860, the *Southern Literary Messenger* was prepared to express the view that, in America, Macaulay's *History* was 'read and admired by a vastly greater number of persons . . . than on his own side of the Atlantic'.[9]

II

At this point, however, it is necessary to enter a mild reservation or two. In 1942, in his pioneering study of Macaulay's vogue in America, Harry Hayden Clark seems to have taken remarks such as those of Edward Everett more or less at face value. Indeed in suggesting that the 'epic-reception' of Macaulay in America after 1840 makes the earlier success of Scott and Byron seem 'very small', Clark seems to go even further than Everett.[10] But there is no substantial evidence to support such grandiose assertions. Even allowing for the fact that Macaulay's avowed intention was to write a kind of history that would be as popular as any novel, one may find it very hard to believe that Macaulay succeeded so well as to eclipse, in America or elsewhere, the overwhelming triumph of Scott, the most popular novelist of them all. As early as 1823 C. J. Ingersoll asserted that 200,000 copies of Scott's novels had been sold in America; by 1825, John Neal's figure was half a million.[11] By 1840? Two million is not unlikely.

Of course it could be argued that the comparison with Scott is unfair–the number of individual works written by Scott vastly exceeded those of Macaulay. In any event, it is not only with Scott or Byron that comparison has to be made in order to establish the proper scale of Macaulay's popularity. In between the publication of the first and second two volumes of Macaulay's *History* a work appeared n America whose popularity would almost certainly have caused Edward Everett to revise his opinion. In his concern to establish the extent of Macaulay's American vogue, Professor Clark omits to mention it. The work in question is *Uncle Tom's Cabin*, published in 1852: 10,000 copies sold in the first week, 300,000 copies within the year. By 1860 the book had been translated into twenty-two languages and its total sale throughout the world ran into millions. Amazing as the sale of the *History of England* undoubtedly was, one may be sure that it fell well short of that of *Uncle Tom's Cabin*.

The point is not that Macaulay's vogue in America was smaller than Clark and other scholars have assumed. It is simply that Macaulay's success was not unparalleled in terms of copies published and sold. Much more important is the point that while the reasons for the immense interest provoked by *Uncle Tom's Cabin* are obvious enough, explanations of Macaulay's tremendous vogue are much less evident.

One person puzzled by his success was Macaulay himself. He did not understand, he wrote, how his *History of England* 'should be acceptable to the body of a people who have no king, no lords, no established church, no tories, nay, I might say, no whigs, in the English sense of the word'.[12] What is most striking here, perhaps, is the similarity between Macaulay's expression of his sense of the essential differences between England and America and that of Americans writing on the same topic. Henry James, for example, in his account of Hawthorne in 1879, contrasts English and American society simply by repeating and expanding Macaulay's list. However, in the light of Macaulay's more general feelings about America, a topic to which I shall return, both his American success and his puzzlement at it seem more than a little ironic.

However much he was puzzled by it, what is sufficiently clear is that within his own lifetime Macaulay had become a highly significant figure within America's intellectual and cultural life. Like Carlyle, he had become a force to be reckoned with and it is hardly surprising that his death in 1859 did not pass unnoticed. In January 1860, a special meeting of the Massachusetts Historical Society, for example, passed three resolutions on the death of one who had been a distinguished Honorary Member of the Society. The first expressed the Society's regret and sorrow at the news of Macaulay's death. The second affirmed that 'his transcendent qualities and accomplishments as an historian have won for him the very highest rank in his chosen department of letters'. The third regretted that 'his last great work is left unfinished'.[13] After the passing of these resolutions Edward Everett read extracts from his correspondence with Macaulay–an unfinished letter to Everett had been found in Macaulay's pocket after his death. George Ticknor and G. S. Hillard went on to speak of their friendship with Macaulay in England. For these members of New England's intellectual and cultural élite Macaulay's death meant the passing of one of the brightest stars in their own intellectual firmament.

III

Macaulay's American popularity is then sufficiently well-established; but it is easier to quantify book-sales than to explain them. How is Macaulay's vogue in America to be accounted for?

Despite his popularity, Macaulay's reception in America was not uniformly and unvaryingly friendly. Poe, for example, regarded him as over-praised–a logical but not a profound thinker.[14] In fact, at different times, Macaulay came under severe criticism from various power groups within the total structure of America's cultural life. In the 1840s and 1850s he was little to the taste of the American Transcendentalists, arguably the most powerful of cultural pressure groups in New England and beyond. At the same time, and somewhat paradoxically, he frequently came under fire from the upholders of conservatism and religious orthodoxy in America. What the Transcendentalists disliked about him was his materialism, his fundamental lack of concern for what they regarded as ultimate spiritual values. In 1856, for example, Emerson wrote in *English Traits*:

> The brilliant Macaulay, who expresses the tone of the English governing classes of the day, explicitly teaches, that *good* means good to eat, good to wear, material commodity . . . It was a curious result, in which the civility and religion of England for a thousand years ends in denying morals, and reducing the intellect to a saucepan.[15]

What offended the religious conservatives, on the other hand, were Macaulay's views on the Puritans and the Commonwealth as these appeared in the first volume of the *History of England*. The hostility of this group was all the greater in that they had originally welcomed the *Essays* and praised Macaulay as a friend of the Puritans and a modern upholder of those values which they believed the Puritan revolution of the seventeenth century had successfully established. A third group who for a time attacked Macaulay with considerable vehemence may be roughly described as Democrats–men who believed that the future of democracy was ensured by the success of the American experiment. In so far as it emerged that Macaulay did not share their confidence in the bright future of either America or democracy, they disparaged him. After the Civil War the rise of a fourth anti-Macaulay party becomes evident. What this group reflects is the growth of so-called 'scientific history' in America. To Americans such as John Fiske and Charles Francis Adams, Macaulay's kind of history could no longer be regarded as satisfactory: Macaulay was biased, often inaccurate, and he lacked any overall philosophy of history.

These different groups in America attacked Macaulay for different things and often at different times. Hence none of them proved strong enough to have much permanent effect on Macaulay's popularity. Indeed the need to make these criticisms is often itself a testimony to Macaulay's increasing reputation and influence. Just as Andrews Norton, an upholder of conservative religious orthodoxy, had felt the need in the 1830s to counter Carlyle's pernicious influence by violent and sweeping attack, so in the 1840s and 1850s others felt the need not to allow Macaulay's opinions to go unchallenged. In fact Norton's attack did not prevent the spread of Carlyleism in America, and Macaulay's critics were on the whole no more successful. Hence we are brought back to the original question of explaining America's extraordinary taste for the writings of Macaulay.

IV

In the first instance Macaulay was fortunate to come to public notice in America, just as in Britain, as a contributor to the *Edinburgh Review*. Sufficient attention has not been paid to this point. Once again the obvious parallel is with Carlyle whose important early essays also first appeared in the *Edinburgh*. Neither writer could have found a vehicle more likely to gain them respect and attention in America. No periodical, probably not even the native *North American Review*, carried more weight in the American literary and intellectual world than the *Edinburgh Review*. His contributions to the *Edinburgh* gained Macaulay as it were immediate entrée into the cultural establishment of America. Availability of course presented no kind of problem; the *Edinburgh Review* had been reprinted in America from as early as 1810 or 1811. Macaulay, then, was off to an exceptionally good start.

A second point working in Macaulay's favour was the respect and prestige in influential circles in America already attaching to his name. For this happy situation Macaulay was indebted to his father Zachary Macaulay. Through his work as a leading

Abolitionist, and as governor of the Sierra Leone colony in Africa, Zachary Macaulay was well-known in America, particularly in New England. Macaulay undoubtedly benefited from his father's name. Edward Everett, himself, for example, was originally a friend of Zachary Macaulay, though subsequently he was to become, as we have seen, one of the younger Macaulay's most ardent American admirers. Again, in 1852 Harriet Beecher Stowe decided to send copies of *Uncle Tom's Cabin* to men of influence and power who might be ready to promote the anti-slavery cause, such as Prince Albert, Charles Dickens, Charles Kingsley, and, among others, Macaulay. Mrs Stowe knew of Zachary Macaulay as a campaigner against slavery, and in the letter she wrote to accompany the copy of her book she describes how she remembered as a child reading anti-slave trade articles in the *Christian Observer*, which Zachary Macaulay had edited. Of Macaulay himself she wrote:

> One of the most vivid recollections of my early life is the enthusiasm excited by reading your review of Milton, an enthusiasm deepened as I followed successively your writings as they appeared. A desire to hold some communion with minds that have strongly swayed and controlled our own is, I believe, natural to everyone, and suggested to my mind the idea of presenting to you this work.[16]

Macaulay's original American audience was not, however, composed only of readers of the *Edinburgh Review* and New England Abolitionists. Much more important was the welcome Macaulay received from those sections of America's cultural establishment who remained hostile to Emerson, Carlyle, and Transcendentalism. The appeal of Transcendentalism in America had always been to those dissatisfied with the religious, cultural, and even social, status quo. Hence Transcendentalism had always remained offensive to the more orthodox and conservative elements in America's intellectual and cultural world. These elements saw in Macaulay, particularly on the basis of his *Essays*, a welcome and powerful new English ally with whom to oppose Carlyle in particular. Thus in 1840 the conservative *Princeton Review* praised the 'strong common sense' which they felt marked Macaulay's 'every paragraph'; 'there is no puling, there is no cant, there is no transcendentalism'.[17] Similarly the *Christian Review* admired Macaulay because he offered no 'enigmatical sayings, no newfangled philosophy'.[18] One may sense in this praise a suggestion that Macaulay embodied the old Scottish common sense philosophy which had for so long sustained conservative and orthodox feeling in America. Later, in 1856, the *Christian Review* was to suggest that Macaulay was so widely read, at least in New England, because novel-reading was still thought of as immoral, while the reading of history was not. The major point, however, is that Macaulay's lack of any kind of romantic transcendentalism, while offending one category of American reader, positively attracted another, perhaps larger, one.

What has been said goes some way towards accounting for Macaulay's initial American success. But how are we to explain the reputation as an outstanding historian which Macaulay sustained so brilliantly in America for half a century or more? First and foremost, Macaulay succeeded so well in America, just as in the rest of the English-speaking world, because of the magnificent way in which he fulfilled his ambition to write a history which would for a time supplant the latest novel on a young lady's dressing-table. An American audience, delighted by the novels of Scott, Cooper, and Dickens, responded enthusiastically to Macaulay's vivid, narrative history. His character sketches, his attention to detail, and his narrative spontaneity and momentum–it is these characteristics of imaginative writing that made Macaulay's recreation of the past so compelling for countless readers, not least among them his American readers. From the period of his contributions to the *Edinburgh Review* Macaulay had always believed in the virtue of a vivid literary style. In 1838 he wrote to Macvey Napier, editor of the *Review*, 'A bold, dashing, scene-painting manner, is that which always succeeds best in periodical writing'.[19] If Macaulay had gone on to write in a style appropriate to what became known as 'scientific' history, none of the reasons I have adduced would have brought him anything approaching the kind and size of American audience he in fact achieved.

Recognising the universality of Macaulay's appeal, one may nonetheless identify one peculiarly American dimension to Macaulay's American vogue: the simple fact that Macaulay's Whig interpretation of English history was very much to the American taste. Mark Twain may stand as a representative American reader in this connection. All his life Twain was an enthusiastic admirer of Macaulay, responding powerfully to his literary qualities and to his imaginative vivification of the past. He read and reread the *History of England* and, as *Following the Equator* reveals, the essays on Hastings and Clive deeply influenced his view of British colonial rule.[20] But ultimately Twain's enthusiasm was a response to Macaulay's progressive view of history; *A Connecticut Yankee*, for example, is informed by a Whiggish concept of progress whose popular origins are to be found in Macaulay. What this suggests is that before the turn of the century, Twain, as one recent scholar has put it, was:

> as enchanted as any other 'liberal' might have been with the informing thesis of the *History of England*, which, if it did not quite show, as charged, that God was on the side of the Whigs, had at least succeeded in tracing all of the blessings of nineteenth-century life back to the Glorious Revolution and its Lockean innovations.[21]

In other words, Macaulay's *History of England* provided Twain–and, I believe, a host of other American readers–with a perspective on English history which they had often felt the need for, but which had never previously been supplied. Traditionally, the most popular modern British historians in America had been William Robertson and David Hume. But neither of these Scotsmen had been particularly liberal in their views. In 1810 Thomas Jefferson made the point very firmly in a letter about Hume:

> Every one knows that judicious matter and charms of style have rendered Hume's history the manual of every student. I

remember well the enthusiasm with which I devoured it when young, and the length of time, the research and reflection which were necessary to eradicate the poison it had instilled into my mind. [Nevertheless, Hume] still continues to be put into the hands of all our young people, and to infect them with the poison of his own principles of government.[22]

Of course it may be objected that 1810 represents at least an entire generation prior to Macaulay's arrival on the scene. But consider this second opinion:

No historian has been more read than Robertson in this country . . . Hume, too . . . has exercised an unbounded influence over American readers, insomuch, that several years ago, the youth of our country, though sworn friends of freedom, were almost unanimous in favour of the unfortunate but usurping Charles, and were ready to justify transactions in the English history, which were most decidedly opposed to their own feelings and opinions.[23]

This extract is from an article in the *North American Review* published as late as 1832. Nothing appears to have happened to alter Jefferson's 1810 judgment. It is probable, then, that Macaulay's Whig interpretation of English history at last offered Americans an historical perspective broadly in keeping with their own innate feelings, attitudes, and prejudices. In a general way Macaulay saw English history as the Americans wished to see it. The triumph of progressive liberal values that Macaulay saw in the development of English history, Americans saw in the movement of their own history. Hence, however much controversy there may have been over particular points–Macaulay's treatment of the Puritans, or William Penn, for example–it is hardly surprising that Americans as a whole should have so enthusiastically welcomed Macaulay, and taken him, as it were, as their own. Consider, for example, Macaulay's views on the Glorious Revolution of 1688, the Bill of Rights, and the fundamental issues at stake at this crucial moment in English history. Surely no American reader could read Macaulay's pages on these topics without recognising what must have seemed an exact parallel between 1688 and 1776. The freedoms the 'popular element' asserted against the will of the 'monarchical element',[24]–the freedoms apparently so dear to Macaulay's heart–must have struck nearly every American reader as identical with those freedoms the 'popular element' once again asserted in defiance of the 'monarchical element' in 1776. Macaulay himself never made the parallel, and he would not have wished to have it made, but that it could be made goes far towards explaining the essential nature of Macaulay's immense popularity within the United States. In 1853 the *Christian Examiner* described the *History of England* as a 'great historical epic'–an epic of the struggle to achieve and secure free government.[25] Here at last was a view of the English past that Americans as a whole could identify with and embrace as their own. Macaulay, that is, provided America with a usable past. In the tense America of the 1850s–the America of the Compromise of 1850 and of the Kansas-Nebraska Act–Macaulay's *History* must have reinforced in not a few Americans a sense of what they thought of as the true meaning of their own tradition, their own nationhood.

V

The major irony encompassing Macaulay's American vogue has already been hinted at. Macaulay found himself quite unable to reciprocate America's unstinted admiration for him. In fact he saw little to admire in America or in American democracy. It is with Carlyle, once again, that the obvious parallel has to be drawn. In 1849 and 1850 Carlyle expressed views on America and the slavery question which instantly alienated a large proportion of his erstwhile American admirers. While it is true that Macaulay did not express his hostility towards America with anything like the virulence or savagery of Carlyle, he did nevertheless go far enough to disappoint and disillusion many of his American admirers. Ironically America invited Macaulay's criticism. In 1857 H. S. Randall, official biographer of Thomas Jefferson, sent a copy of his new *Life of Thomas Jefferson* to

Macaulay, at the same time inviting the English historian to express his views on Jefferson. In 1860 Randall let the *Southern Literary Messenger* publish Macaulay's reply. Macaulay begins by saying that he has 'not a high opinion of Mr Jefferson' nor of democracy itself. 'I have long been convinced', he writes, 'that institutions purely democratic must, sooner or later, destroy liberty or civilisation, or both'. Jeffersonian democracy in England would inevitably mean either the plundering of the rich by the poor or the preservation of order and prosperity by strong military government at the expense of liberty itself. American democracy had so far avoided such a fate because of the existence of the unoccupied lands of the Western frontier. But once there was no more unoccupied land, then the situation would change. The American future that Macaulay foresees is a dark one:

> Your Constitution is all sail and no anchor . . . When a society has entered on this downward progress, either civilisation or liberty must perish. Either some Caesar or Napoleon will seize the reins of government with a strong hand, or your republic will be as fearfully plundered . . . in the twentieth century as the Roman Empire was in the fifth . . .[26]

In subsequent letters to Randall, Macaulay maintained his position and even went farther, denying that current American progress and prosperity had anything to do with her democratic institutions. That Macaulay's first letter appeared in a Southern periodical in 1860 suggests that its publication had a distinctly political motive. Macaulay's analysis could then be seen as aligning him with a long tradition of English Tory observers of the American scene who had forecast that America's democratic institutions would end in a fine smash. In fact, however, Macaulay's Whig libertarianism was too well-established for him to be accepted as an ally by committed adherents of the South. George Fitzhugh, for example, the apologist for slavery, attacked what he regarded as Macaulay's pernicious doctrines concerning liberty: it was only the institutions of the democratic North that might suffer the fate he had foreseen. In the event the outbreak of the Civil War seems to have muted the immediate impact of Macaulay's critical letters. Reprinted in America in 1877 and 1896, they probably did in the end contribute to the inevitable decline in American enthusiasm for Macaulay. That enthusiasm, it should be remembered, had nonetheless lasted for more than half a century–quite long enough to make Macaulay's contribution to the cultural history of America in the nineteenth century both substantial and important.

Notes

1. Hugh Trevor-Roper, 'The Scottish Enlightenment', *Studies on Voltaire and the Eighteenth Century*, LVIII (1967), p. 1640. And Colin Kidd, *Subverting Scotland's Past, Scottish Whig Historians and the Creation of an Anglo-British identity, 1689–c.1830* (Cambridge, 1993), p. 274.
2. Andrew Hilen (ed.), *The Letters of Henry Wadsworth Longfellow* (Cambridge, Mass., 1972), III, 524.
3. W. D. Howells, *My Literary Passions* (New York, 1895), pp. 116–17.
4. Louisa M. Alcott, *An Old-Fashioned Girl* (London, 1949), p. 51.
5. Harry Hayden Clark, 'The Vogue of Macaulay in America', *Transactions of the Wisconsin Academy* 34 (1942), 238.
6. *Ibid.*, p. 328.
7. See Clarence Gohdes, *American Literature in Nineteenth Century England* (Carbondale, 1944), pp. 43–4.
8. Hilen, *op. cit.*, IV, 5.
9. Clark, *op. cit.*, p. 255.
10. *Ibid.*, pp. 237–8.
11. See *North American Review*, **18** (1824), 162; and F. L. Pattee (ed.), *American Writers* (Durham, N.C., 1937), p. 196.
12. Clark, *op. cit.*, p. 238.
13. *Proceedings of the Massachusetts Historical Society* (January 1860), pp. 426–7.
14. See 'Thomas Babington Macaulay' in *The Complete Works of Edgar Allan Poe* (New York, 1902), VII, 138–43.
15. *Works of Ralph Waldo Emerson* (Edinburgh, 1906), pp. 327–8. Despite his disapproval of Macaulay's materialism, Emerson was an enthusiastic admirer of other aspects of Macaulay's character. In 1848, having dined with Macaulay in London, he wrote to his wife: 'Macaulay is the king of diners-out. I do not know when I have seen such wonderful vivacity. He has the strength of ten men; immense memory, fun, fire, learning, politics, manners, and pride–talks all the time in a steady torrent'. Ralph L. Rusk (ed.), *The Letters of R. W. Emerson* (New York, 1939), IV, 41.
16. John A. Woods (ed.), *Uncle Tom's Cabin* (London, 1965), p. xxxviii.

17. Clark, *op. cit.*, p. 240.
18. *Ibid.*, p. 240.
19. See Asa Briggs, ed., *Essays in the History of Publishing* (London, 1974), p. 124.
20. See Sydney J. Krause, *Mark Twain as Critic* (Baltimore, 1967), pp. 227–45. And cf. Howard G. Baetzhold, *Mark Twain and John Bull* (Bloomington and London, 1970), pp. 186–7.
21. Krause, *op. cit.*, p. 231.
22. E. Millicent Sowerby, *Catalogue of the Library of Thomas Jefferson* (Washington, 1952), I, 157.
23. *North American Review* 34 (1832), 148.
24. Lord Macaulay, *History of England* (London, 1858), III, 410.
25. Clark, *op. cit.*, p. 249.
26. *Ibid.*, p. 256.

CHAPTER TEN

Henry George and Scotland

The voice of Henry George is one that has virtually disappeared from contemporary literary and cultural discourse in the United States. Yet **Progress and Poverty** *(1880) is a great book, a key work in the social, political, and economic history of America in the 1880s, '90s, and early 1900s. An unorthodox, radical, anti-establishment work, no single book did more to focus for masses of readers their growing discontent over what was being done to American life and society by the economic developments characteristic of post-Civil War America. Begun in September, 1877, and completed in March, 1879,* **Progress and Poverty** *was offered for publication to D. Appleton & Co.–the American publishers of the work of the vastly influential British thinker Herbert Spencer. Appleton & Co. rejected the manuscript in the following terms: the work 'has the merit of being written with great clearness and force, but it is very aggressive. There is very little to encourage the publication of any such work at this time and we feel we must decline it'.[1] This was the work destined to appear in over 100 editions, to be translated into almost every European language, and by 1906, to be read, according to some estimates, by around six million men and women.*

To suggest that Henry George and his book have any kind of Scottish context will certainly be seen as surprising. By 1880 almost a century had passed since the Scottish Enlightenment was making its major contribution to American thought and culture; and Carlyleism, like Emersonian Transcendentalism, hardly survived into the more pragmatic America of the postbellum period. Yet in at least two senses, as I argue in this chapter, Henry George is a contributor to the continuing Scottish-American exchange. First, in the quite straightforward

177

*sense that George's voice was listened to with particular atten-
tion in Scotland; and secondly, in that it is possible to discern
Scottish origins for some at least of the key qualities of **Progress
and Poverty** itself.*

Appleton & Co. were right to regard *Progress and Poverty* as an
aggressive work. It is a major onslaught on the capitalist
economic system and its social consequences as these had
emerged in post-Civil War American society. Henry George's
preoccupation with the problem of why it should be that the
increasing wealth produced by economic progress was failing, in
America and elsewhere, to eliminate or even diminish the
existence of poverty, originated in his early life. In 1855, as a
ship's boy, he had seen Calcutta, a city where the contrast
between extremes of wealth and poverty was legendary. In
1869, he visited New York, where in his own words, he 'saw
and recognised for the first time the shocking contrast between
monstrous wealth and debasing want . . .'[2] Back in his native
California, within a year or two he had come up with what he
saw as both an explanation and a solution to the problem of the
coexistence of progress and poverty. Traditional assumptions
about the ownership and valuation of land were the key to
understanding the problem. It was the every-increasing value of
land, and thus the ever-increasing wealth in the form of rental
value accruing to those who owned land, that produced the
constantly growing gap between the rich and the poor. In
chapter five of *Our Land and Land Policy, National and State*
(1871) he published the solution: 'a tax upon the value of land'.
In time this became the 'single tax' policy with which Henry
George's name was above all to be identified.

Progress and Poverty is a detailed exposition of George's
theories. Much of it is written in a mode of cool and rational
analysis. In particular, when he is setting out his fundamental
objections to classical economic theory–from Adam Smith,
through Malthus and Ricardo, down to John Stuart Mill–

George's tone remains that of conventional academic discourse and debate. The issues in question, however, were anything but conventional. Classical economic doctrines were seen as justifying the laissez-faire capitalism of post-Civil war America; classical economic theory, that is, was regarded as confirming the 'there is no alternative' approach to America's social and economic problems. Smith's *Wealth of Nations* was a symbolically revered text, and on December 12, 1876, a hundred leading American intellectuals attended a dinner at New York's famous Delmonico's restaurant to celebrate the centenary of its publication. Afterwards Appleton's *Popular Science Monthly*, a magazine which promoted the doctrines of the English thinkers Charles Darwin and Herbert Spencer more enthusiastically than any other American journal, announced that *The Wealth of Nations* was 'probably the most important book in its influence upon the politics of states and the economic welfare of mankind that was ever written'.[3] Smith and his economist successors were therefore important in post-bellum America; they could be appealed to in order to provide intellectual cover for what the business interest was doing to American society. For George to attack classical economic theory was to signal his total rejection of contemporary American capitalism.

In fact George's careful, academic arguments occur in a context of burning moral and ethical fervour. For George, the failure of orthodox economic thinking is in the end a moral failure. The way things are, justice and liberty are everywhere being trampled underfoot. What is needed is a return to the principles enshrined in the American Constitution; the only alternative, he warns, is a descent into anarchy or revolutionary violence. At the end of the day though, George continues to believe in the promise of America; he is a visionary, still persuaded that the American Dream can be achieved. What is needed, in George's view, for the reinstatement of America's old and best ideals, is a transformation of the economic basis of society. This is why *Progress and Poverty* is a major work of social reconstruction, meriting comparison with Marx's *Das Kapital*. Its overriding aim is to place society's economic ar-

179

rangements on a wholly new footing, and its argument is carried forward with overwhelming certainty and conviction. What is remarkable about *Progress and Poverty*, and an explanation of its popularity, is the cogency of its analysis of the deficiencies and limitations of orthodox economic thinking, and its sweeping confirmation of the feeling of an increasing number of George's contemporaries that what was happening in the economically expanding countries of the world involved unnecessary exploitation, suffering, and poverty; and this in the context of a clear and simple explanation of the root causes of all such problems.

Clarity and cogency of argument, allied to moral and ethical fervour, help to explain *Progress and Poverty's* popularity. An additional factor perhaps counted even more. *Progress and Poverty* appealed because it rejected the doctrines of all those who argued that the sufferings and injustices of the present were inevitable and immutable. Just as he rejected the pessimism of Malthus's theory of over-population, so George rejected the Social Darwinism of Herbert Spencer and his American followers. Crucial here is the point that Spencer was a key figure in the intellectual world of post-bellum America. Indeed it was peculiarly in America that the English thinker's views on the relevance of Darwin's theories of evolution and natural selection to the study of human society had been widely welcomed as basically sanctioning the unchecked operation of a capitalist economic system. George, however, refused to agree that social evolution was a slow and blind process with which man should not interfere. E. L. Youmans, one of Herbert Spencer's leading American disciples, told George that in five thousand years social evolution would have solved the kinds of problem he had seen in New York City. George, and his supporters, were not prepared to wait; if action was not forthcoming, society would collapse into anarchy. By countless readers, then, *Progress and Poverty* was welcomed and revered as a mighty and revolutionary book because it amounted to a comprehensive, philosophical rejection of the whole superstructure of ideas, broadly Social Darwinist in nature, that had come to underpin the post-bellum status quo in America's social and economic life.

In these circumstances it is hardly surprising that Herbert Spencer himself should have dismissed George's book as 'trash'. The alternative was to concede that his own work was based on a fundamental misconception–that evolution occurred within human society just as it did in the natural world. In fact George's dissent from Spencer's postulates was absolute. He rejected utterly the whole theory that the 'progress of civilisation' depended upon a development or evolution which itself proceeded according to the laws appropriate to the genesis of a species: laws, that is, 'of the survival of the fittest and the hereditary transmission of acquired qualities'. The 'hopeful fatalism' of such a 'vulgar explanation of progress', George set aside in favour of the view that society develops and men improve 'as they become civilized, or learn to co-operate in society'.[4] Such an observation was immensely significant. What it means is that George, like Edward Bellamy a few years later, was prepared to argue that society progressed essentially through *peaceful* association; such association was immensely more productive than the impulse towards competitive conflict. Such a view ran counter to one of the fundamental tenets of the ideology of contemporary capitalism, which Social Darwinism had readily endorsed: the idea that competition, and the conflict that competition produced, were essential to desirable social development. George was equally unsympathetic to another of Social Darwinism's fundamental assumptions: the primacy of heredity in influencing the nature and behaviour of the individual. George rejected nature in favour of nurture:

> each society, small or great, necessarily weaves for itself a web of knowledge, beliefs, customs, language, tastes, institutions, and laws. Into this web . . . the individual is received at birth and continues until his death. This is the matrix in which mind unfolds and from which it takes its stamp. This is the way in which customs, and religions, and prejudices, and tastes, and languages, grow up and are perpetuated.[5]

181

George, that is, unlike Marx (who incidentally dismissed *Progress and Poverty* as 'the capitalists' last ditch'), did not regard the means of production as the single factor which determined the life of the individual, but rather, like Gramsci and other twentieth-century Marxists, saw the individual as the product of a configuration of forces, including a superstructure of ideas and assumptions and world-views, which jointly work upon him.

Herbert Spencer and his Social Darwinist followers, however, not Karl Marx, were the key opponents Henry George had in mind in writing *Progress and Poverty*. That is why, in terms of the social, economic, and intellectual orthodoxies of post-bellum America, it was above all a radical, subversive, challenging and influential book. As George's voice became only one among many challenging the Darwinist world-view, as that had been interpreted by defenders of late nineteenth-century American capitalism, so the impact and significance of his book continued to grow.

II

When he learned that Appleton's had decided not to publish his book, and after Harper's and Scribner's had also shown no interest, George decided to go ahead and produce a private edition of his work. Hence *Progress and Poverty* first appeared in an Author's Edition of 500 copies late in 1879. At this point, however, Appleton and Company had second thoughts and agreed to publish the book, making use of the author's own plates. As a result, the first commercial edition of 1000 copies appeared in January 1880. By March the thousand copies had been sold, and an additional 500 were printed. From this point on the pace began to quicken. *Progress and Poverty* was serialised in various New York and Chicago newspapers, and a series of cheap editions followed. In 1881, Kegan Paul brought out an English edition, and translation into French, German, Italian, Swedish and Norwegian soon followed. The book's early reception was, as one would have expected given its unorthodoxy and hostility to accepted attitudes, considerably less than enthusiastic. But George was in no way surprised or dismayed. He was confident that what he had written was a great book, and as the 1880s passed, the ideas propounded in *Progress and Poverty* were indeed received and taken up by an ever-increasing, world-wide audience.[6]

In America the increasing impact of *Progress and Poverty* made its author into a figure of considerable political eminence and significance. George ran twice for the office of Mayor of New York. On his return from his 1882 British tour, he was welcomed by a grand dinner at Delmonico's attended by 170 guests. (This dinner-party was perhaps a response to that at which Herbert Spencer was welcomed by his American admirers during his tour of the United States in the same year.) On American writers, George's impact was substantial. William Dean Howells, who became increasingly aware in the 1880s of the cruelties and injustices permeating American society and its economic system, was powerfully drawn by George's 'solution of the riddle of the painful earth'. (Elizabeth Peabody, a social reformer and educationalist, had written to George on the appearance of *Progress and Poverty* congratulating him on having solved 'the tremendous conundrum of progress and poverty'.) Hamlin Garland, like Howells a major figure in the developing school of American realist writers, became an active campaigner in Boston in the 1880s on behalf of George and his theories. One of the most popular of all of Garland's stories–'Under the Lion's Paw'–was no more than a direct expression in dramatic form of George's view of the massive injustice involved in allowing landlords to raise the rental value of land improved by the toil of others. James Herne, an actor friend of Garland, later a friend and correspondent of George's own, gave successful public readings of this story around the Boston area.

Progress and Poverty showed American writers how their society could be looked at critically. It showed that there was an alternative to an unrestrained capitalist system. It made scepticism about the present, and about current attitudes and philosophies designed to sustain the present, respectable. For a younger generation of thinkers and writers *Progress and Pov-*

erty became a classic anti-establishment statement. It was almost inevitable that someone like Thorstein Veblen (the future author of *The Theory of the Leisure Class*), while still an undergraduate at Carleton College in Minnesota in 1880, should have taken up the book and praised it at a time when established academic economists and philosophers were only too anxious to dismiss it. Orthodox academic opinion is represented by Francis A. Walker, President of Massachusetts Institute of Technology, and author of the period's standard economics textbook for colleges and universities. Henry George and his single tax theory are dismissed as immoral: 'I will not insult my readers by discussing a project so steeped in infamy'. The young Veblen, on the other hand, as soon as *Progress and Poverty* appeared, 'did not hesitate to let it be known that he supported it.[7]

Progress and Poverty is thus a crucial work in establishing a tradition that runs on through *Looking Backward* (1888), Edward Bellamy's anti-capitalist science fiction novel, and into the so-called 'muckraking' activities of the investigative writers and journalists who around the end of the century were prepared to expose directly the scandals and corruptions of the American capitalist system. *Progress and Poverty*, too, was a pioneering expression of that radical critique of America's social and economic life which a new movement in American literature, originating in the 1870s and developing through the 1880s and 1890s, would go on to articulate in more imaginative terms. Newness, in the literary battle that was fought between the literary and cultural establishment and the emergent school of writers, came to be identified with the mode of its expression–realism initially, naturalism a little later–but what the new writing mode increasingly registered was a deepening discontent with the harsh realities of life in post-Civil War America as these were experienced by the great mass of the country's population. What *Progress and Poverty* did was to establish a position, argue a case, that gave intellectual credibility and respectability to such feelings of discontent. Caught up and absorbed in the ferment of ideas and emotions provoked by the increasingly widely-held view in the 1880s and 1890s that American society,

184

as Lincoln had predicted during the Civil War, was in danger of disintegration and collapse, the book also offered a message of hope, pointed a way forward.[8] Social and economic inequalities and injustices, however massive, could, it suggested, be corrected. 'In those days, the solution of the riddle of the painful earth through the dreams of Henry George, through the dreams of Edward Bellamy, through the dreams of all the generous visionaries of the past, seemed not impossibly far off', wrote William Dean Howells in 1911.[9] From 1880 on, *Progress and Poverty*, at once symbol and creator of change, was a kind of time-bomb ticking away beneath the dominant orthodoxies of American social and economic thinking. All that was needed for the book to explode into massive popularity was for the unease, the dissatisfaction, the outrage, over what was being done to America by the business interest, registered by George in the 1870s, to become much more general. In the mid-1880s, and through the 1890s, it happened. As a result, *Progress and Poverty* became one of the great best-sellers of American literature.

III

What, you may ask, has all this to do with Scotland? Henry George's Scottish connection is in fact substantial and significant. The first point to be made, however, concerns the universality of George's message. *Progress and Poverty's* analysis of the ills of capitalism–and their remedy–applied to all industrially developed countries. Thus it was inevitable that his ideas should make their mark across the Atlantic. From the beginning, too, George was determined that his theories should be attended to in Europe: among those who were sent copies of the first, privately-printed, edition of *Progress and Poverty* were Herbert Spencer, Gladstone, Joseph Chamberlain, and the Duke of Argyll. The impact of the Kegan Paul edition of the book in Great Britain was astonishing: *Progress and Poverty* is unquestionably a key work in the development of British working-class politics. According to Beatrice and Sidney Webb, the rise to dominance of the Labour Party in the Trades Union Congress of

1893 was largely due to 'the wide circulation in Britain of Henry George's *Progress and Poverty*'. The 'optimistic and aggressive tone' of the book, they believed, 'sounded the dominant note alike of the new unionism and of the British socialist movement'.[10] It is hardly surprising, then, that George should have visited the British Isles five times in the course of the 1880s, expounding his theories from public platforms in towns and cities up and down the whole extent of the country. Among his British converts was George Bernard Shaw whose attention 'was first drawn to political economy as the science of social salvation by Henry George's eloquence, and by his *Progress and Poverty*, which . . . had more to do with the Socialist revival of that period in England than any other book'.[11] Through Shaw, George's theories passed into the thinking of the Fabian Society. The Christian Socialist Movement also responded positively to George's ideas, while future leaders of the British Left, like Philip Snowden and Keir Hardie, were deeply influenced by him. (George's biographer, Charles Barker, argues that his contribution to Hardie's political career was sufficiently important to signify 'an American impulse behind the Scottish labour movement'.[12]) William Morris reported that when he asked a group of socialists what had given them their political convictions all spoke of reading *Progress and Poverty*. Even liberals–like Joseph Chamberlain–found George's arguments hard to resist.

In the general circumstances suggested by this account of George's pervasive influence on the Left in British politics, it was inevitable that Scotland would be an area in which his presence would be felt. But the second point to be made about George's Scottish connection is that his impact and influence there was greater than would be suggested by seeing George only in a British context. Scotland became his primary British stamping ground. During 1884 and 1885, for example, George visited 39 Scottish towns and cities from Paisley to Wick, and made 50 speeches–double the number he made in England in the same period. As early as 1882 he spoke twice in Glasgow, where his appeal and impact seem to have been particularly strong. At the first of these meetings he had appeared on the platform of the Social Democratic Federation, a socialist organisation then establishing a Scottish branch. The Scottish campaigns of 1884 and 1885 led to the founding of the Scottish Land Restoration League. A foundation meeting was held in Glasgow in February 1884; some 1900 members of the audience signed up for the new organisation. The aim of the League was defined as 'a full and complete restoration of the land of Scotland to the Scottish people'.[13] Existing landowners were to receive no compensation. The arguments for such a takeover of land– arguments essentially derived from *Progress and Poverty*–were set out in a circular addressed to the people of Scotland from the Scottish Land Restoration League. 'In the great and rich city of Glasgow', wrote George, 'can be found poverty and destitution that would appal a heathen. Right on these streets of yours the very stranger can see sights that he could not see in any tribe of savages . . .'[14] The solution of such problems lay in the pro- gramme of the Scottish Land Restoration League. Later the League changed its name to the Scottish League for the Taxation of Land Values–as early as 1885 in the Glasgow municipal elections, supporters of George proposed a four shillings in the pound tax on land values. In the 1890s the Scottish League for the Taxation of Land Values published *The Single Tax*, a monthly paper with an average circulation of 5000 copies. In 1897, 62 assessing authorities in Scotland petitioned Parliament in favour of making land valuation the basis of local taxation. The movement climaxed with the introduction in Parliament of the so-called 'Glasgow Bill' for this form of local taxation.

Even invited to stand for Parliament in a Scottish constituency in 1889, Henry George's Scottish connection is evident enough. The third and most important point to be made about it, concerns its origins. Charles Barker affirms that 'Scotland was particularly Henry George's country', and he cites George's own belief that his ideas would receive readier acceptance in Scotland than in England or Ireland.[15] George's actual visits to Scotland confirmed this view. But the question remains, why should Scotland have particularly been Henry George's country? From Barker we learn that George had a grandfather, John Vallance, who had been brought at an early age from Glasgow to America. From Barker too it emerges that from an early age George, like so many Americans, had a romantic attachment to the Scottish past. Jane Porter's once famous, now forgotten novel, *The Scottish Chiefs*, a romantic account of Wallace and Bruce and the Scottish struggle for independence, was the book George smuggled into his bedroom to read.[16] Perhaps the contrast between the familiar romantic images of Scotland, so well established in America, and the harsh realities of the squalor of so much of Scottish urban and rural life, in some way intensified for George a sense of the fundamental rightness of his analysis of the contradictions between progress and poverty in modern society. On a different level, the economic realities of Scottish life certainly did provide George with fertile ground. The position of the Scottish crofter was not unlike that of the tenant farmer in America; a small number of Scottish landlords owned huge tracts of Scottish land; rents were high in country and city; and the blight, as well as the profit, of industrialism was widely in evidence. In other words the Scottish example could be seen as confirming, in this sense too, the central analysis of *Progress and Poverty*.

That George believed that the positive side of his message would be well-received in Scotland is perhaps also to be related to his belief in the moral strength of the Scottish religious tradition. (This was the tradition which, ironically, Trotsky in the 1920s believed explained the failure of the leadership of revolutionary socialism in Scotland.) Certainly George's own moral idealism might easily have suggested to him that this was a strain in Scottish cultural life to which he might appeal.

Charles Barker makes one other suggestion to explain George's Scottish affinity. George studied with great care the extremely long and detailed chapter, in H. T. Buckle's now unjustly ignored *History of Civilization in England* (1859–61), entitled 'An Examination of the Scotch Intellect during the Eighteenth Century'. Barker's general view of George is that all his work reveals a dichotomy between two sets of attitudes or

188

impulses. On the one hand, he believes, George is a moral idealist, a crusading reformer; in his morality and ethics, that is, he takes an optimistic, progressive view of human nature. In his economics, on the other hand, George seems to accept the classical economists' view that man acts only upon impulses of material self-interest. Barker argues that George would have found this dualistic vision confirmed by Buckle's account of Adam Smith and the Scottish Enlightenment.[17] My own view is that Barker is right to point to the Scottish Enlightenment as an important source of George's thought, but wrong to limit it to the issue of Smith's alleged dualism. George may well have found in Buckle's account the sources of some of the economic arguments with which he was in fundamental disagreement, but in the thinking of the Scottish Enlightenment he may also have found some of the solutions. Admittedly, to a degree that Charles Barker seems not to have been aware of, the naturalised form of Scottish common sense philosophy continued to provide, in post-Civil War America, the best defence of the economic and social status quo. But the Scottish Enlightenment's emphasis on human sociability—on the need for men to cooperate in communities in order to advance civilisation—as opposed to Lockean individualism, may well have appealed to George in the 1870s just as it did to Thomas Jefferson a hundred years earlier. Let me quote again George's crucial formulation of this concept—'men improve as they become civilized, or learn to cooperate in society'—but this time in order to insist that it was above all the thinkers of the Scottish Enlightenment who had popularised such a view. And it is once again in Scottish Enlightenment thinking that George would have found confirmation of his constantly repeated views on the individual's inevitable susceptibility to the customs, beliefs, tastes, laws, and every other aspect of the environment into which he is born.

Scholars who have attempted to pin down the origins of George's views on land values and taxation have frequently come up with Scottish names: Adam Smith, inevitably, but also James Mill and Thomas Carlyle. Less well known, but even more relevant is William Ogilvie, Professor of Humanity at

King's College, Aberdeen, in the later eighteenth century. In 1781 in London Ogilvie published a work entitled *An Essay on the Right of Property in Land* which certainly anticipates George's land taxation policy. George may not have known this work when he was writing *Progress and Poverty*, but he certainly came to know it: in 1889 he commented on Ogilvie's book in an article in *The Standard*, a weekly paper he was then producing.[18] Even more relevant is yet another Scottish text: Patrick Edward Dove's *The Theory of Human Progression and Natural Probability of a Reign of Justice*, published in Edinburgh and London in 1850, and interestingly dedicated to Victor Cousin, the major proponent of the Scottish common sense philosophical school in France. Dove's work is more theologically focused than George's; but there are strong similarities in the two men's views on land ownership and taxation, and in the fervour with which these views are expressed. So much so that George was later accused of having plagiarised Dove's book; he denied the charge, saying he had only learned of Dove's work three years after the publication of *Progress and Poverty*.[19]

Interesting as these parallels between George and earlier Scottish thinkers are, they are less germane to George's Scottish connection than the example of another Scot whose name has already been mentioned in passing: Thomas Carlyle. It is the influence and example of Carlyle that locates George in a recognisable Scottish-American intellectual tradition. In the earlier nineteenth century, Carlyle had been a major influence in America, exciting and inspiring young Americans of Emerson's generation by his visionary philosophy. His American readers responded enthusiastically to Carlyle's denunciations of the crass commercialism and materialism of the present, and his call for a renewal of man's spiritual potential. In post-bellum America, Carlyleism, and the Emersonian Transcendentalism so closely allied to it, soon began to fade. But it is hardly too much to say that in Henry George, the spirit of Thomas Carlyle found a new American voice.

Carlyle does not figure among those thinkers whom George

analyses at length in *Progress and Poverty*. But his name does occur. In a discussion of poverty and its consequences, near the end of the book, he is cited: 'Carlyle somewhere says that poverty is the hell of which the modern Englishman is most afraid. And he is right. Poverty is the open-mouthed, relentless hell which yawns beneath civilized society'.[20] But the point is not really that George is deeply indebted to Carlyle's ideas. Of course George's frontal attack on the evils of unrestrained capitalism has much in common with Carlyle's denunciation of the cash nexus and its consequences; but what links the two writers is ultimately much more a question of tone, of language and style. Both Carlyle and George have in their sights the kinds of thinking, particularly the kind of economic thinking, that attempts to justify the materialism of the present. George, for much of *Progress and Poverty* argues in the language of the economists and their 'dismal science'; but a Carlylean moral fervour keeps breaking through. It is this soaring, Carlylean, prophetic voice, warning of the dangers of the status quo, but insisting that the promised dreams of new world America can still awaken into reality, that so many readers around the world found irresistibly compelling. And this too is the location of the deeper structure of Henry George's Scottish connection.

Notes

1. See Charles A. Barker, *Henry George* (New York, 1955),pp. 312–13.
2. Quoted in Elwood P. Lawrence, *Henry George in the British Isles* (East Lansing, 1957), p. 4.
3. Quoted in Paul F. Boller, Jr., *American Thought in Transition* (Chicago, 1969), p. 71.
4. Henry George, *Progress and Poverty: An Inquiry into the Cause of Industrial Depressions, and of Increase of Want with Increase of Wealth. The Remedy*, (London, 1883), pp. 429–31.
5. *Ibid.*, p. 453.
6. In a letter to his father, George wrote: 'It will not be recognised at first, maybe not for some time–but it will ultimately be considered a great book, will be published in both hemispheres, and will be translated into different languages'. See Barker, pp. 313–14.
7. See Joseph Dorfman, *Thorstein Veblen and His America* (London, 1935), pp. 63, 32.

8. Lincoln's astonishingly accurate sense of America's post-Civil War problems is given expression in a letter to W. R. Ellis:

> I see in the near future a crisis arising that unnerves me and causes me to tremble for the safety of my country. By a result of the war, corporations have been enthroned, and an era of corruption in high places will follow, and the money power of the country will endeavour to prolong its reign by working upon the prejudices of the people until all wealth is aggregated in a few hands and the Republic is destroyed.

Cited in Sylvia E. Bowman, *The Year 2000, A Critical Biography of Edward Bellamy*, New York: Bookman Associates, 1958, pp. 74–5.

9. Howell's comment appears in a new Preface to his 1890 novel *A Hazard of New Fortunes*.
10. See Lawrence, p. 3.
11. *Ibid.*, pp. 75–6.
12. Barker, p. 402.
13. See Elwood, p. 51.
14. *Ibid.*, pp. 45–6.
15. Barker, pp. 401, 530.
16. *Ibid.*, p. 15. Other American admirers of *The Scottish Chiefs* include at least two Presidents–John Adams and Andrew Jackson–as well as Robert Frost and Scott Fitzgerald.
17. *Ibid.*, pp. 267–68.
18. See George R. Geiger, *The Philosophy of Henry George* (New York, 1933), pp. 184–87.
19. *Ibid.*, pp. 165–71.
20. *Progress and Poverty*, p. 411.

CHAPTER ELEVEN

The South, Scotland, and William Faulkner

*Scottish literature is the ultimate source of the romantic image of Scotland. It is out of such works as Allan Ramsay's **The Gentle Shepherd**, John Home's **Douglas**, James Macpherson's **Ossian**, James Beattie's **The Minstrel**, the poems and songs of Burns, the poems and novels of Scott—as well as from a host of minor writers from the end of the eighteenth century on—that the identity of Scotland as above all a land of romance emerges. The increasingly nostalgic, sentimental, and ahistorical elements within that cultural identity have long been emphasised by critics and commentators. Yet in however suspect and debased a form, the romantic image of Scotland seems to have extraordinary powers of endurance.*

What endures, however, may be something less attractive than even sentimental nostalgia; deconstructed, the romantic image reveals, under the lid of the tartan tin of Highland shortbread, a disturbing strain of tolerated violence and prejudice. As I argue in the essay that follows, it is in the history of aspects of Scottish romanticism's impact upon the American South that this darker potential of the land of romance is most clearly revealed.

Scotland's relationship with the South is a topic that has received surprisingly little attention. Any attempt to explain this neglect would focus much more on the question of Scotland's cultural history and diminishing identity in the twentieth century than on the history of the South, but that is not a topic I wish to take up here. Rather I want to begin by focusing on the simple point that in terms of their general cultural situation Scotland and the South have a great deal in common. Scotland's continuing struggle to maintain its own cultural identity in face of the overwhelming political and economic power of England, may be fruitfully compared with the position of the South and Southern culture and their definition in the context of the rest of the United States.

Obvious as the parallel is, I readily concede that there are important differences between Scotland and the South. The economic history, for example, of the two areas is very different: from the later eighteenth and through the nineteenth centuries Scotland became an increasingly industrialised economy. Indeed with the North of England, lowland Scotland was the major focus of the Industrial Revolution in the United Kingdom. The South, at least in the nineteenth century, remained far more of an agricultural and agrarian economy. In terms of social history, there are equally important differences. By the nineteenth century, the Scottish aristocracy had long been relocated, either literally or metaphorically, in England. Southern society, on the other hand, remained dominated by a local aristocracy for most of the nineteenth century at least. Even in cultural historical terms, there are obvious differences between Scotland and the South. For centuries Scottish culture remained divided between the Celtic world of the west and north, and the Anglo-Saxon world of the east and south: the Gaelic-speaking Highlands have had little in common with the Scottish-English speaking Lowlands. In its origins, the South involved Spanish, French, and Creole cultures as well as English, but by the nineteenth century, the dominance of English was such as to produce a broadly unified Southern culture. Whether Scottish culture was ever as unified in the same period is debatable at least.

While there are clearly many ways in which the Scottish experience and the Southern experience are dissimilar, it is still the case that in the broad area of cultural history Scotland and the South exhibit some crucial similarities. The major parallel is the one I began with. Both Scotland and the South have existed as readily identifiable sections or regions or provinces of a larger, political entity. In cultural terms, the result has been an uneasy, uncertain, ambivalent relationship between, as it were, region and nation. Both Scottish and Southern culture have traditionally wrestled with the kinds of issue suggested by terms like assimilation or distinctiveness; union or separation; the Scots or the British, the Southerner or the American. Particularly now, when cultural theory is taking a special interest in the relationship between 'centres' and 'peripheries'–whether these are defined in terms of geography, power-structures, race and ethnicity, cultural traditions, or even gender–and especially when attention is being paid to the radicalising perspective of what used to be regarded as the periphery, then the comparative study of Scotland and the South seems to cry out for attention.

Of course I would agree that, in the terms I have been suggesting, areas other than Scotland could be found for comparison with the South. Canada immediately comes to mind as an obvious example. Yet I wish to argue that two further factors make the parallel between Scotland and the South substantially more specific. One concerns the facts of history, the other the mythopoetic power of the imagination.

In terms of history, Scotland helped to populate the South. Scots and Ulster Scots–the so-called 'Scotch-Irish' who emigrated first from Scotland to the northern part of Ireland, then from Ireland to the American colonies–make up a significant proportion of the white population of the Southern states. Scholars in the field estimate that in the period between the American Revolution and the Civil War the Scottish element in the South amounted to between a fifth and a third of the white population. (The majority of these were of Ulster Scots descent.) As far as the modern South is concerned, the legacy from this period probably does not amount to very much: Scottish family names, sometimes, as we shall see, in corrupt forms; some of the folk-music and folk-songs of the rural South; the Highland Games and Gathering of the Clans held at Grandfather Mountain, North Carolina; and in individual cases a rather romantic attachment to a vaguely Scottish ethnic identity. Only in one area of Southern life and culture do scholars regularly turn to the South's Scottish ancestry to find an explanation and a source. The Southern taste for violence and lawlessness has quite regularly been seen as deriving from its Scotch-Irish inheritance. Whether it is fighting victoriously in the American Revolution, gallantly but less successfully in the Civil War, or engaging in the casual violence of the family feud or the lynch-mob, the Scotch-Irish are seen as leading the field in this particular dimension of Southern life.[1] The prevalence of this view in the literature of the South is, as we shall see, difficult to ignore.

Southern and Scottish literature, in turn, are ultimately the source of the second of the two special factors that underline the parallelism of Scotland and the South. What is in question here is less history than myth. Both Scotland and the South have become visible to the outside world largely as a result of an immensely powerful and highly romanticised version of their historical pasts. In the period from the later eighteenth century, through the nineteenth, and on into the twentieth century, Scottish writers transformed Scotland, its history, its landscapes, its people, into one of the most romantic countries in the world. In the period after the Civil War, Southern writers similarly transformed the history of the Old South; and soon the images of Hollywood were reinforcing the romantic vision of the South and Southern history. Scotland and the South, that is, share a self-produced cultural heritage in which history and mythology, legend and truth are inextricably interwoven. It is hardly surprising that the result for both has often been a peculiarly bitter sense of internalised cultural conflict.

II

I have been arguing that Scotland and the South have enough in common for it to be quite surprising that more work of a comparative cultural studies kind is not already in evidence. But traditional scholarship has attended to at least one aspect of the Scottish-Southern relationship. Ever since Mark Twain in *Life on the Mississippi* identified Sir Walter Scott as the only begetter of the Civil War, Scott's pervasive influence on the Old South has always been recognised.[2] In 1917, in an article in the

The South, Scotland, and William Faulkner

North American Review, H. J. Eckenrode identified the South as 'Walter Scottland', and subsequent scholarship has qualified rather than dismissed what such a title implies.[3] However, even in the case of Scott and the South, what is surprising is the dearth of detailed modern scholarship. Writing in 1986 on the topic of Southern romanticism, Michael O'Brien legitimately notes that it is 'extraordinary' that 'we do not have the research that will accurately tell us about the reception of Scott in the Old South'.[4]

Professor O'Brien's fine essay is concerned with a range of aspects of Southern romanticism, but he is fully alert to the Scottish strain. Indeed his article is one of the few places towards which a student interested in the Scottish influence on the South's literary and intellectual life could usefully be directed. However it is not my intention now to engage either with the particular issue of Scott and the South or with the more general one of Scottish influence on Southern culture. Rather I wish to look at a single aspect of the literary dimension of the link between Scotland and the South, though it happens to be one which Twain's account of Scott underlines.

Twain suggests that Scott's influence on the South was malign. The images of human conduct and manners his work created, accepted by Southerners as models for their own behaviour, led the South, Twain suggests, to self-destruction. Romantic Scottish images, that is, moved the South to violence and civil war. Of course we would all want to argue that the link between art and life has to be more complex than Twain allows. But the subsequent history of romantic images of Scotland in the South shows that such a link can indeed exist, and go on existing, with behavioural consequences just as malign as those Twain identified.

III

The Ku Klux Klan was founded in Pulaski, Tennessee, on December 24, 1865. John C. Lester, the moving spirit in the creation of the new organisation, tells us that the term 'Klan' was included in the title because its founders were 'all of Scotch descent'.[5] Most accounts of the origins of the Ku Klux Klan

197

concentrate on the Greek dimension of the title, but the Scottish connotations may be of greater significance. As everyone knows, the Klan quickly became the main focus of white resistance to Reconstruction in the post-Civil War South. To achieve its aims, it employed violence and terror, elaborate rituals, and, above all, secrecy. The Klan, then, offers a powerful parallel to the Vehme or Secret Tribunal of fifteenth-century Germany, as that organisation is fully described in the Old South's favourite novelist's *Anne of Geierstein*. Unquestionably Chapter 20 of Scott's exciting novel provides an elaborate description of a secret society which both in its methods and rituals, and in the reasons and justifications for its existence, provide an uncanny likeness to the Ku Klux Klan. Scott's character Philipson is forced to appear before the Secret Tribunal in a subterranean vault, lit only by torches borne by men muffled in black cloaks, and wearing cowls 'drawn over their heads, so as to conceal their features'. Set out on an altar are a coil of ropes and a naked sword 'the well-known signals and emblems of Vehmique authority'. Elaborate oaths are sworn binding adherents of the order to unquestioning loyalty and obedience. Probably most significant of all is Scott's explanation of the Secret Tribunal's rise to power: 'Such an institution could only prevail at a time when ordinary means of justice were excluded by the hand of power, and when, in order to bring the guilty to punishment, it required all the influence and authority of such a confederacy'. And Scott continues: 'In no other country than one exposed to every species of feudal tyranny, and deprived of every ordinary mode of obtaining justice or redress, could such a system have taken root and flourished'.[6] The availability of such passages in a popular Scott novel, justifying as they appear to do extra-legal action in the name of justice itself, must at the very least have contributed to the cultural context out of which the Invisible Empire of the Klan emerged. The suggestion is not that *Anne of Geierstein* is the source of the Klan. But it is hard not to believe that a great many Southern readers of the novel found in it a peculiar and reassuring relevance to their own situation.

The South, Scotland, and William Faulkner

It is in a later novel by a Southern novelist, however, that the Scottish dimension of the Ku Klux Klan is explored and embroidered. Thomas Dixon's novel *The Clansman*, remembered today mainly as the source of D. W. Griffith's classic film 'The Birth of a Nation', was published in 1905. Dixon, from North Carolina, and of Scottish ancestry, was intensely proud of what he saw as the South's Scottish inheritance. His earlier novel, *The One Woman* (1903), is dedicated 'to the memory of my mother to whose Scotch love of romantic literature I owe the treasure of eternal youth'. A sequel to 'The Birth of a Nation' called *The Fall of a Nation* (1916), opens with a Prologue exemplifying popular resistance to royal authority and the first example is that of the Scottish covenanting, Cameronian women martyrs, burned at the stake or drowned in the Solway Firth. In *The Clansman*, however, Dixon's Scottish preoccupations move closer to the centre of the novel's landscape.

Dixon's own sense of the story he is about to tell is made clear in an introductory note 'To the Reader':

> How the young South, led by the reincarnated souls of the Clansmen of Old Scotland, went forth under this cover and against overwhelming odds, daring exile, imprisonment, and a felon's death, and saved the life of a people, forms one of the most dramatic chapters in the history of the Aryan race.

What follows in the novel more than lives up to what is implied here. *The Clansman* exhibits a kind of racism so crude and vicious as to make the reader of today almost unable to go on turning its pages. At the same time, there is no denying that Dixon uses a running thread of allusions to a highly romanticised version of Scottish history and traditions to support his selective view of the Reconstruction period. When Mrs Cameron, mother of the novel's Southern hero, hears that her husband is in danger, Dixon tells us that it is her Scottish inheritance that inspires her to act: 'The heritage of centuries of heroic blood from the martyrs of old Scotland began to flash its inspiration from the past'.[7] When Mrs Cameron subsequently appeals to President Johnson, the theme reappears: 'Mr President, you are a native Carolinian–you are of Scotch Covenanter blood. You are of my own people of the great past, whose tears and sufferings are our common glory and birthright'.[8] Senator Ross of Kansas, whose vote saves President Johnson from impeachment, is described as 'the sturdy Scotchman',[9] and Dixon tells his readers that the Ulster Scots settlers of the Carolinas, radicals, revolutionaries, and democrats to a man, composed the largest of all the original immigrant groups in America, and were those who contributed most to the formation of what he calls the American nationality.

But it is in Dixon's account of the Ku Klux Klan itself, that the Scottish theme is most evident. He exploits to the full images associated with the Scottish heritage of clans, clansmen, clan loyalties, clan solidarity–and Presbyterianism. The Presbyterian Rev. Hugh McAlpine is chaplain to the local Klan. And it is Dr Cameron who suggests the use of the Fiery Cross to summon Klan members: 'A sudden inspiration flashed in Doctor Cameron's eyes', writes Dixon, and he tells the Grand Dragon: 'issue your orders and despatch your courier tonight with the old Scottish rite of the Fiery Cross. It will send a thrill of inspiration to every clansman in the hills'![10] Scott had set out the ritual of the Fiery Cross, as the means by which a clan chieftain bent on war summoned his followers in Canto Three of 'The Lady of the Lake'. Dixon follows Scott's description closely. In 'The Lady of the Lake', the cross is set ablaze, then dowsed in the blood of a sacrificed goat. In *The Clansman*, the cross is similarly set ablaze, but dowsed in the blood of the female victim of black outrage. A Klan leader declares: 'In olden times when the Chieftain of our people summoned the clan on an errand of life and death, the Fiery Cross, extinguished in sacrificial blood, was sent by swift courier from village to village'. Now the ritual will be repeated: the 'Fiery Cross of old Scotland's hills'–'the ancient symbol of an unconquered race of men'[11]–will bring forth the loyal members of the new world's Ku Klux Klan. Here Dixon draws upon a set of images from a romanticised, heroical Scottish past to persuade his readers to accept an equally romanticised and heroical version of the recent history of the South.

The South, Scotland, and William Faulkner

We learn from modern scholars that there is no evidence that the Ku Klux Klan in the 1865–1871 period of its existence made any use of Fiery Crosses. But what we have in *The Clansman* is apparently a frightening example of art's capacity to influence life. When the Klan revived after 1915, the burning of the Fiery Cross did indeed become part of its apparatus of intimidation and terror.[12]

IV

At the end of October, 1908, the Opera House in Oxford, Mississippi staged Thomas W. Dixon's dramatisation of *The Clansman*, which had opened to an enthusiastic audience in New York two years earlier in 1906. The Oxford production was performed by forty people, a troop of cavalry horses, and a 'carload of effects'.[13] It is hard to believe that the Opera House audience for such a spectacle did not include the eleven year old William Faulkner. His attendance is all the more likely given the fact that by 1908, Faulkner, a precocious reader, was already familiar with *The Clansman*. A copy of the novel from his library bears the inscription 'Annie J. Chandler 1905'.[14] In 1905, Annie Chandler was Faulkner's first-grade teacher.

The impact of Sir Walter Scott on the South, and the idea that a popular novel called *The Clansman* by a Southern writer of Scottish descent should have a Scottish dimension, bring Scotland and the South together in a fairly obvious way. The notion that William Faulkner–whatever his exposure to *The Clansman*–should play any part in the Scottish-Southern nexus will strike most readers as far less probable. In fact the link between Faulkner and Scotland is real enough, and manifests itself in different ways. I am conscious that much current literary theory tells us to discount a writer's life as irrelevant to his work. Nonetheless, for my purposes, a glance at Faulkner's biography is necessary.

Joseph Blotner begins his standard biography of Faulkner with the following words: '"My ancestors came from Inverness, Scotland", William Cuthbert Faulkner once declared'. Faulkner knew that the 'Falkner' spelling, which his family had traditionally used, was a corruption of the English form 'Falconer', whereas the 'Faulkner' form was more commonly used in Scotland. However, it has to be said that when Faulkner restored the 'u' in his name in 1918 he was in Canada trying to pass himself off as an Englishman! Nonetheless, the evidence is strong that throughout his life Faulkner was always conscious of his Scottish ancestry. Blotner tells us that he told a friend, 'My great-grandfather Murry had his grandfather's claymore which he had carried at the battle of Culloden. My aunt has it now'.[15] In the fiction, of course, this is the claymore that appears in the Appendix to *The Sound and the Fury*, where we are told that Quentin Maclachan 'fled to Carolina from Culloden Moor with a claymore and the tartan he wore by day and slept under by night . . .' And this is the claymore that Mr Faulkner told me he remembered seeing when I met and talked to him in Princeton in 1958. I asked him then if he had ever been in Scotland. 'Yes' he replied. 'Where had he been'? I said. 'Gatehouse-of-Fleet' he answered. I was more than a little surprised. Gatehouse-of-Fleet is a small town in the Galloway area of south-western Scotland. No hard evidence of a Faulkner visit to Scotland exists: the only authenticated Scottish experience is that represented by the landing at Prestwick airport in Ayrshire of the aircraft taking him to Stockholm to receive the Nobel Prize for literature in December 1950. But Gatehouse-of-Fleet is close to the border with England. Is it possible that Faulkner had taken some other opportunity to cross over into Scotland? How else had he heard of Gatehouse-of-Fleet? Blotner tells us that on May 31, 1952, Faulkner flew from Paris to London; he was unwell but determined to set off for England 'and, he said, for Scotland as well, the land of his ancestors'.[16] Blotner says he did not make it to Scotland before leaving London for Oslo on June 4. But I suppose the possibility at least remains . . .

Faulkner's life throws up other 'Scottish' fragments. The house he and Estelle moved into in Oxford in 1930 was named Rowanoak because Faulkner had been reading a passage about Scotland in what Robert Crawford sees as one of the key works in Scottish nineteenth-century intellectual history: J. G. Frazer's

The South, Scotland, and William Faulkner

The Golden Bough.[17] In early 1961 David Yalden-Thomson, a Scot in the Philosophy Department at the University of Virginia, visited Faulkner in Oxford. One day, walking in the town's Square, a Negro girl passed them wearing a ten-cent store tartan made into a dress. 'You don't see that in Scotland', said Faulkner. Yalden-Thomson was surprised at how detailed Faulkner's knowledge was of Scottish Highland history and customs. 'At bottom', he said later, 'I always thought that Faulkner saw himself as a Highlander living in exile in Mississippi'.[18] Earlier, in 1955, Faulkner told a Yugoslavian interviewer that his people were 'of Scottish mountain stock and traditions'.[19] Back in 1938 he bought his daughter Jill a tartan dress in New York, and may even have contemplated buying a kilt for himself.[20]

Much more significant than any of these Scottish moments in Faulkner's life–because it hints at how the Scottish theme might appear in his art–is an episode from 1956. In that year Faulkner collaborated with P. D. East, that uncompromising opponent of Southern racism, and James W. Silver, professor of history at the University of Mississippi, to produce *Southern Reposure*, a satirical paper lampooning Mississippi's Scotch-Irish population as primarily responsible for the state's racial bigotry and intolerance. East himself seems to have done most of the writing, but clearly with Faulkner's knowledge and assistance. In the paper the status quo is comically reversed and it is the Scotch-Irish who are regarded as deserving segregation:

> The average Scotch-Irish is a repulsive and obnoxious creature who is apt, if the notion strikes him to pull a highland fling on the main street of any one of our towns in Mississippi. In addition, they have come to expect to be served oatmeal in our finest restaurants simply because they have the required fifteen cents.

Their behaviour is unbearably vulgar: 'How many times have you heard one exclaim, "Hootman", or "Bergorrah"'! How disgusting'! How could you conceivably want your daughter 'to marry a windbag, highland flinging, kilt wearing creature'?

Another item in the paper refers to a speech given at a segregation rally on 'The Botch Made by the Scotch'. On the last page readers are invited to join the Anti-Scotch-Irish Council and help to keep 'The R Rolling Children Out of Our Fine Southern Schools'. All of this may appear as nothing more than good knock-about fun; but East's aims were wholly serious, and Faulkner clearly did not dissent from the implied view of the major source of racism in Mississippi.[21]

V

If it is possible to argue that there is a Scottish thread running through Faulkner's life, may the same be said about his art? Just about. Two First World War short stories feature Scottish protagonists. 'Victory' appeared in the 1931 collection called *These Thirteen*. However the story derives from scraps of material–two manuscript fragments and two typescripts–written much earlier; probably soon after Faulkner's first visit to England in 1925. The second story 'Thrift' was written in 1927 and accepted for publication by the *Saturday Evening Post* in September, 1929.

'Victory' is the story of Alec Gray, a shipwright from the Clyde, who joins a Scottish regiment in 1914, rises through the ranks to become an officer, wins medals, and is then discarded by the post-war society he has helped to preserve. The story ends with him selling matches on the streets of London. Despite Gray's family background on the Clyde, and references to traditions of ship-building, Calvinism, bible-reading, and Scottish distrust of England, there is only one major episode in the story that seems to reflect Faulkner's sense of distinctively Scottish behaviour. Early in his army career, Gray is punished–unjustly in his own eyes–for appearing on parade unshaven. When his Company takes part in its first attack on the Arras front, Gray seeks out the sergeant-major responsible, stabs him in the throat with his bayonet and smashes his face with his rifle butt. (It is after this that he wins his first medal.) What is striking is Gray's absolute lack of conscience or self-doubt. He had done what he owed it to himself to do. It is an example of the kind of driven intensity of behaviour which will recur again and again when Faulkner turns to the delineation of the society of Frenchman's Bend and Beat Four of Yoknapatawpha County.

The tone of 'Victory' is unremittingly sombre. 'Thrift' on the other hand is essentially a comic tale. It hinges on one of the most familiar of Scottish stereotypes: the mean Scotsman.[22] The protagonist is a Highland Scot called, incredibly MacWyrglinchbeath. At the beginning of the war, leaving his horse and cow in the care of a neighbouring farmer, he becomes an air mechanic. But from the very first moment, the one motive that determines all his actions is the need to remit as much cash as possible back to his neighbour in Scotland. MacWyrglinchbeath's simple-mindedness about this creates a series of grotesquely comic episodes which form the body of the story. But despite accounts of aircraft crashes, dog-fights, deaths, mess-jokes, and the rest, the main issue of the story turns out to have nothing to do with the war at all. MacWyrglinchbeath worries about the cost of the forage for his horse and cow—and for the calf the cow has had in his absence. When he returns home at the end of the war he finds his neighbour has retained the money he sent with an accuracy to match his own detailed accounts.

'Ye'll ha' ither spoil frae thae war-r, A doot not?' the neighbor said. 'Naw'. ''Twas no that kind o' a war-r', MacWyrglinchbeath said. 'Ay', the neighbor said. 'No Hieland Scots ha' ever won aught in English war-rs'.

But there is still the question of the two beasts left behind that have become three.

'Ye'll be takin' away thae twa beasties', the neighbor said. 'Thae three beasties, ye mean', MacWyrglinchbeath said.

He returns home and next day enquires about the value of two year old cattle. That night he sits down and does his calculations. Next morning he returns to his neighbour.

'Weel, Wully. Ye ha' cam' for thae twa beasties'?
'Ay', MacWyrglinchbeath said.[23]

In 'Thrift' it is the Scottish character's obsessive, single-minded,
driven intensity of behaviour that Faulkner again underlines.
Calvinism is not directly present in 'Thrift' in the way that it was
in 'Victory', but various characters in Yoknapatawpha County
make it clear that Faulkner regarded the inheritance of Scots
Calvinism as one of the forces producing the kind of unrelent-
ing, driving, obsessive behaviour so characteristic of many of his
characters: MacEachern in *Light in August* is an obvious,
Scottish-sounding, example.

Commenting on 'Thrift', Professor Blotner suggests that in the
story Faulkner was dealing with familiar subject-matter: the
kind of people who inhabit Beat Four of Yoknapatawpha
County.[24] It is in *Intruder in the Dust* that Faulkner deals most
extensively with such people, so it is here that the Scottish thread
in Faulkner's pattern of the South is most obvious.

In *Intruder in the Dust* Lucas Beauchamp is wrongly accused
of the murder of Vinson Gowrie. Faulkner portrays the Gowrie
family as archetypal inhabitants of Yoknapatawpha's Beat
Four. The Gowries are part of 'a race a species' which

> . . . did not even simply inhabit nor had merely corrupted but
> had translated and transmogrified that whole region of lonely
> pine hills dotted meagrely with small tilted farms and peri-
> patetic sawmills and contraband whiskey-kettles where peace
> officers from town didn't even go unless they were sent for
> and strange white men didn't wander far from the highway
> after dark and no Negro at any time–where as a local wit said
> once the only stranger ever to enter with impunity was God
> and He only by daylight and on Sunday–into a synonym for
> independence and violence: an idea with physical boundaries
> like a quarantine for plague so that solitary unique and alone
> out of all the county it was known to the rest of the county by
> the number of its survey co-ordinate–Beat Four . . .[25]

The physical landscape of Beat Four, incorporating a place

named Glasgow, has something in common with the Scottish Highlands which Charles Mallison, the young narrator in *Intruder in the Dust*, has never seen although his uncle, Gavin Stevens, has described them to him:

> They were quite high now, the ridged land opening and tumbling away invisible in the dark yet with the sense, the sensation of height and space; by day he could have seen them, ridge on pine-dense ridge rolling away to the east and the north in similitude of the actual mountains in Carolina and before that in Scotland where his ancestors had come from but he hadn't seen yet . . .(p. 100)

And again:

> They could see the hills now; they were almost there–the long lift of the first pine ridge standing across half the horizon and beyond it a sense a feel of others, the mass of them seeming not so much to stand rush abruptly up out of the plateau as to hang suspended over it as his uncle had told him the Scottish highlands did except for this sharpness and color . . .

And Stevens goes on to speculate that it was this likeness to the landscape of Scotland which explains why the original migrants to Beat Four chose to live there:

> 'Which is why the people who chose by preference to live on them on little patches which wouldn't make eight bushels of corn or fifty pounds of lint cotton an acre even if they were not too steep for a mule to pull a plow across (but then they don't want to make the cotton anyway, only the corn and not too much of that because it really doesn't take a great deal of corn to run a still as big as one man and his sons want to fool with) are people named Gowrie and McCallum and Fraser and Ingrum that used to be Ingraham and Workitt that used to be Urquhart only the one that brought it to America and then Mississippi couldn't spell it either, who love brawling and fear God and believe in Hell–' (p. 148).

Here once again Faulkner insists on the link between the

violence of Beat Four's inhabitants and the nature of their Calvinist religion. Later in the novel, Charles Mallison reads a similar meaning into Caledonia church itself:

> . . . now in daylight he could see the church, for the first time actually who had lived within ten miles of it all his life and must have passed it, seen it at least half that many times. Yet he could not remember ever having actually looked at it before–a plank steepleless box no longer than some of the one-room cabins hill people lived in, paintless too yet (curiously) not shabby and not even in neglect or disrepair because he could see where sections of raw new lumber and scraps and fragments of synthetic roofing had been patched and carpentered into the old walls and shingles with a savage almost insolent promptitude, not squatting nor crouching nor even sitting but standing amount the trunks of the high strong constant shaggy pines, solitary but not forlorn, intractable and independent, asking nothing of any, making compromise with none and he remembered the tall slender spires which said Peace and the squatter utilitarian belfries which said Repent and he remembered one which even said Beware but this one said simply: Burn . . . (pp. 156–7)

It is clear then that for William Faulkner, Beat Four and its inhabitants encapsulate much of the Scottish inheritance of the American South. What that inheritance is is largely a question of violence and lawlessness, clannishness, distrust of outsiders, rejection of authority, and a taste for home-produced whisky: all held together by a Calvinist ferocity. Faulkner, that is, would probably have been ready to agree with James Lee Burke's Dave Robicheaux that 'John Calvin was much more the inventor of our Southern homeland than Sir Walter Scott'.[26] But in other respects his vision of the Scottish South turns out not to be so far away from Mark Twain's. The Shepherdsons and Grangerfords, despite their social pretentions, would have felt perfectly at home in Beat Four. And when one recognises in the lynch mob confronting Lucas Beauchamp the truth that lies beneath the fiction of Thomas Dixon's romanticised 'Clansmen of Old Scotland', then the Southern inheritance of Scottish literature proves to be a distinctly uncomfortable one.

VI

William Faulkner, however, died in 1962. In the more than thirty years since then much has changed both in Scotland and the South, and thus it might be argued that the Scottish theme must have changed or faded out in the South. But the evidence is rather that old myths never die. The 1990s have seen an extraordinary re-surfacing of traditional Scottish images in popular American culture: I have in mind the amazing success world-wide of Hollywood's Oscar-winning *Braveheart* and *Rob Roy*. Both films reprise an old song: both owe their existence, that is, to that romantic vision of Scottish history which enjoyed an astonishing vogue throughout Europe and America in the later eighteenth and nineteenth centuries. It was then that William Wallace emerged as an archetypal representative of Scotland's grandly heroic and tragically glorious past, and Rob Roy came to be seen as a kind of Scottish Robin Hood. In their Hollywood incarnations both Wallace and Rob Roy remain powerfully mythic figures; but what is truly astonishing is the way in which the myths they represent are once again being manipulated–in the South and elsewhere in America–for less than admirable ideological purposes.

The Southern League is a recently-established right-wing organisation campaigning for a new secessionist South. Founded at Stillman College, Alabama, by Professor Michael Hill, its 4000 membership includes historians and other academics and students from universities in the South such as Texas Christian, South Carolina, Georgia, Alabama, and Auburn. The League's immediate model (because of an objection from the Southern League Baseball Association it is having to change its name to the League of the South!) is the secessionist Northern League in Italy; but its other sources of inspiration include a variety of separatist movements such as the parti Québécois in Canada, Plaid Cymru in Wales, and, inevitably in the South, the

From Goosecreek to Gandercleugh

Scottish National Party. But according to Hill, it is Scottish history in particular that should be inspirational for the League's supporters. The South, he suggests, needs to defend its Anglo-Celtic culture, its history, heroes, songs, symbols, and banners: 'But we should go beyond that to the task of educating our people about their ties . . . the names and deeds of William Wallace, Andrew de Moray, Robert Bruce . . . Sir James (The Black) Douglas [surely he means Sir James the Good] . . . James Graham of Montrose, among scores of others should become common-place'. In such a context it comes as no surprise at all to learn that the League, including its academic historians, regards *Braveheart* as both compulsory viewing for existing members and as a recruiting poster for new ones.

The Southern League, however, is far from being the only extremist American group prepared to capitalise on the *Braveheart* version of Scottish history. The old, far right John Birch Society has urged its supporters to see the film and take its freedom message to heart. Christian Identity, a racist, anti-Semitic, movement, which believes in the purity of the Celtic peoples, has also exploited the film–along with the Declaration of Arbroath – for its own propaganda purposes. Finally–and here the wheel does come full circle–today's Ku Klux Klan has seen Mel Gibson's film as somehow endorsing its agenda: 'This movie may well become a movement pièce de resistance for Christian Patriots' is the reported comment of a Texas Klan leader.[27]

What may one conclude? That there is a clearly visible line of descent from Scott and Scottish literary romanticism through *The Clansman* and *Birth of a Nation* down today to *Braveheart*? Merely that Scottish history is open to exploitation? Or, more disturbingly, that Scottish culture, both aesthetic and political, is complicit in the distortion of its own past? What is clear is that the transformation of art into ideology is a continuing process–and in the case of Scotland and the South the ideology in question may involve something much less attractive than merely a sentimental attachment to the world of Auld Lang Syne.

The South, Scotland, and William Faulkner

Notes

1. In his *Southern Honor, Ethics and Behaviour in the Old South*, (New York, Oxford, 1982) Bertram Wyatt-Brown identifies a Scots-Irish pattern of behaviour as contributing significantly to the South's often violent attachment to notions of honour. Quoting the early Victorian novelist George Tucker, who saw how easily the Scots-Irish assimilated into the culture of the South, he writes: 'Nevertheless, the same violent spirit, inattentiveness to regularity of farming, and clannishness persisted'. (p. 38).

2. Twain's account of Scott's influence on the Old South occurs in Chapter 46 of *Life on the Mississippi* (1883), 'Enchantments and Enchanters'. It is worth noting that the New York writer, J. K. Paulding, had attacked Scott along similar political lines more than a generation earlier.

3. See H. J. Eckenrode, 'Sir Walter Scott and the South', *North American Review*, 206 (October, 1917), 595–603.

4. Michael O'Brien, 'The Lineaments of Antebellum Southern Romanticism', *Journal of American Studies*, 20 (August, 1986), p. 185.

5. See Don C. Seitz, *The Dreadful Decade 1869–1879*, London and New York, 1927, p. 25. According to Wyn Craig Wade–in *The Fiery Cross* (New York, 1987) pp. 34–5–initiates into the Klan in its earliest apolitical days had to recite from Burns's 'To a Louse.'

6. Walter Scott, *Anne of Geierstein*, London, 1899,pp. 250, 254.

7. Thomas Dixon, *The Clansman, An Historical Romance of the Ku Klux Klan*, New York, 1905, p. 101.

8. *Ibid.*, p. 108.

9. *Ibid.*, p. 178.

10. *Ibid.*, p. 324.

11. *Ibid.*, p. 326.

12. See Charles Reagan Wilson, *Baptized in Blood: The Religion of the Lost Cause 1865–1920*, (Athens, Georgia, 1980), pp. 113–18. Wilson argues that it was in fact the success of the film *Birth of a Nation* that led to a new and expanded life for the Klan after 1915; but he agrees that the ritual burning of crosses, then practiced by the Klan, was a Scottish ceremony recalled to Americans by Thomas Dixon's novels.

13. See Joseph Blotner, *Faulkner A Biography*, (London, 1974_), pp. 115–116.

14. *Ibid.*, p. 94.

15. *Ibid.*, p. 3.

16. *Ibid.*, p. 1423. There is one other piece of evidence that may point to a link between Faulkner and Gatehouse-of-Fleet. On the green in one of Gatehouse's streets there is a memorial tree with a plaque in front reading: 'Planted in Memory of B. Phyllis Falkner 1895–1991.' None of today's relatives or friends of Phyllis Falkner have any recollection of William Faulkner. But it seems unlikely that no more than coincidence is involved here.

17. Robert Crawford, *Devolving English Literature*, (Oxford, 1992), pp. 151–175. And Blotner, *Faulkner A Biography*, pp. 660–661.
18. *Ibid.*, pp. 1776–1777.
19. *Ibid.*, p. 1571.
20. *Ibid.*, p. 1002.
21. This account of Faulkner and East derives from Gary Huey, *Rebel With a Cause: P. D. East, Southern Liberalism and the Civil Rights Movement*, 1953–71, (Wilmington, Delaware, 1985), pp. 106–08.
22. Faulkner alludes to the same notion of traditional Scottish meanness in the Appendix to *The Sound and the Fury* when explaining why Quentin Compson waited to the end of the academic year at Harvard before committing suicide.
23. See Joseph Blotner, (ed.), *Uncollected Stories of William Faulkner* (London, 1980), pp. 397–98.
24. Blotner, *Faulkner A Biography*, p. 647.
25. William Faulkner, *Intruder in the Dust*, London, 1957, pp. 35–36. All subsequent references are to this edition.
26. James Lee Burke, *The Neon Rain*, Vintage, 1991, p. 61.
27. See the articles by Diane Roberts, 'Ghosts of the Gallant South' in *The Guardian*, July 22, 1996, and Kirsty Scott, 'The Fatal Attraction' in *The Herald*, August 6, 1997.

CHAPTER TWELVE

The Scottish Invention
of American Studies

Historians would wish to amend, qualify, or refine the view that the War of 1812 between Britain and America was fundamentally a cultural war. Nevertheless, there is a sense in which the armed conflict emerged out of a generalised sense of continuing mutual dislike between the two countries that had long been largely articulated in cultural terms. What American literary historiography calls the 'literary quarrel' between Britain and America had broken out within a few years of the ending of the American Revolution, but it reached boiling-point in the early decades of the nineteenth century, and simmered away for quite a few decades after that. (Has it ever in fact been wholly extinguished?)

*Ironically, the most famous shot fired in this literary war had a quasi Scottish finger on the trigger: Sydney Smith's dismissive little question in the mighty **Edinburgh Review** in 1820–'Who reads an American book'?–echoed as loudly round the United States as the shot fired at Lexington is supposed to have echoed around the world. So much so that in 1824 the **Review** felt obliged to defend itself, as deftly as possible, from the American hostility which Smith's question had helped to inflame. The American reaction was such, wrote the **Review**, that*

> *we really thought at one time they would have fitted out an armament against the Edinburgh and Quarterly Reviews, and burnt down Mr Murray's and Mr Constable's shops, as we did the American Capitol. We, however, remember no other anti-American crime of which we were guilty, than a preference of Shakespeare and Milton over Joel Barlow and Timothy Dwight.*

From Goosecreek to Gandercleugh

As these comments indicate, British criticisms of the limitations of the literature being produced in the new American republic were a major factor in the origins of the literary quarrel. But even more important, as a continuing source of friction, were the published reports of British travellers in America. Nearly every addition to this voluminous literature helped to stoke up the flames of Anglo-American antagonism. Such travel books invariably passed themselves off as the work of neutral observers; in almost every case the truth was that they were heavily politicised. For all those in Britain (and Europe), who upheld the status quo in society and politics, the very existence of the United States was an affront; this American experiment in democracy and republicanism had to be shown to be failing. Hence the most notorious British travellers in America were Tories like Mrs Trollope and Captain Basil Hall, and their books were consequently little more than essays in detraction of American society, American manners, and American culture. We should not underestimate how deeply such right-wing, anti-American feeling could run. Here is the High Tory **Blackwood's Magazine** *writing on America in the highly-charged British political atmosphere of 1832: 'We therefore hope that all true Britons hate American manners, and, to the full extent of their influence, the American people. They must either do that, or hate their own manners and themselves . . .'*

But the anti-American establishment did not have things all its own way. In Scotland in particular–despite **Blackwood's** *best endeavours–there was an alternative Whig tradition, much more well-disposed towards the United States, whose major mouthpiece–here is the irony of American rage over Sydney Smith–was in fact the* **Edinburgh Review**. *The* **Review's** *political sympathies were distinctly Whiggish in nature; supporting change and reform in British politics, its basic stance towards the United States was a positive one. In adopting such a position, the* **Review** *was taking its place in an older Scottish tradition of sympathy for America with its roots in the closeness of the Scottish-American relationship in the eighteenth century. In a 1775 letter David Hume famously called himself an 'American*

214

*in my principles' and others among the Scottish **literati** had
sought for ways of resolving peacefully the dispute between the
American colonies and the mother-country. Thus, despite the
facts that in the Revolutionary period itself many American
patriots regarded the Scots as the most ardent supporters of the
British government's oppressive policy towards the colonies,
and that many of the Scots in America did indeed support the
Loyalist cause, an alternative Scottish tradition of support for
America did survive into the nineteenth century. It was out of
that tradition that what I describe as the Scottish invention of
American Studies ultimately emerged.*

On the face of it, the suggestion that Scotland invented American Studies is absurd. American Studies, as an academic discipline, did not really begin to emerge even in American
universities until after the Second World War. The formal study
and teaching of American literature had begun only a decade or
two earlier. In 1921 the president of the Modern Languages
Association of America was the Chaucerian scholar J. M.
Manly, and it was Manly who reorganised the association into
a series of separate groups for co-operative research and spe-
cialised meetings. A small American literature group managed to
emerge as a sub-division of the English Language section. There
can be no doubting, however, that in this tiny band of MLA
members were the founding fathers of the vast enterprise that
the academic study of American literature has become; and in
due course the exact kind of study of American literature they
originally promoted became profoundly important in the context of the emergence of the new American Studies discipline in
general.

Thus both American literature and American Studies are
relatively recent American creations as subjects available for
academic study. How then can the Scots be seen as contributing
in any way to their invention? The obvious answer is to refer to
the now widely-held view that the origins of what was to

become literary study in the modern sense are to be found in the lecture courses in rhetoric and belles-lettres which became part of the curriculum of the eighteenth-century Scottish universities. If this view is accepted in the context of Britain–and I am not aware that it has been seriously challenged–then it is equally applicable to the development of literary studies in the United States. The Scottish rhetoricians, Blair, Kames, and Campbell, that is, by the end of the eighteenth century and through the early decades of the nineteenth, were as standard a part of the American university and college curriculum as was the case in Scotland itself. Hence there is no doubting the crucial importance of this Scottish rhetorical tradition, with its emphasis both on utility–how to speak and write well–and on moral improvement–the link between literature and moral persuasion–in the development of English as an academic subject both in the USA and Canada.

However, while there is indeed a general relevance of this Scottish background to the eventual emergence of American literature as a subject for academic study, it is not this Scottish tradition that provides the basis for the argument that Scotland may be seen as inventing American Studies. Given its links to moderation in the Church of Scotland, its frequent association with the Scottish common sense school of philosophy, designed above all to refute Humean scepticism, and given too its crucial general contribution to the emergence of modern Scottish civic society, correct, polished, and anglicised, the Scottish rhetorical tradition was broadly conservative in its social and political impact. The Scottish tradition directly relevant to the eventual emergence of American Studies was rather more radical in its nature. In question here is support within Scotland for social and political reform towards the end of the eighteenth century. The 1780s and '90s in Scotland saw the emergence of pressure groups demanding change in the existing power-structure, and pursuing causes likely to bring about reform in society and politics. But it is in the American Revolution, rather than the French Revolution, that the origins of this Scottish movement for political reform are to be located. Thus when the Scottish

The Scottish Invention of American Studies

Whigs famously established a national voice by creating in 1802 the soon powerful *Edinburgh Review*, one of the causes they consistently supported was that of America. The success of the American experiment was proof that major social and political change was in no way incompatible with stability and progress. It is out of this enduring Scottish Whig tradition of sympathy for America that the Scottish invention of American Studies eventually emerges.

The earliest evidence of Scottish academic interest in American literature occurs in William Spalding's *A History of English Literature* originally published in Edinburgh in 1853. Born in 1809, Spalding was an Aberdonian who studied at both Marischal College, Aberdeen, and the University of Edinburgh. A lawyer, he came to know Francis Jeffrey and published articles on Shakespeare and other literary topics in the *Edinburgh Review*. Largely as a result of Jeffrey's influence he was appointed to the Chair of Rhetoric and Belles Lettres in Edinburgh which he held from 1840 to 1845. In 1845 he moved to the Chair of Logic, Rhetoric, and Metaphysics at St Andrews which he occupied until his death in 1859.[1]

Spalding's *History* is presented very much as a textbook 'for the Use of Schools and Private Students'; as such it was eminently successful appearing in no less than fifteen editions, many of them published in the years after the author's early death. Striking is the appearance in the early editions of a section entitled 'Contemporary American Literature'. In some half-a-dozen pages, at the end of his volume, Spalding offers a general account of American literature, focusing almost exclusively on the nineteenth century, and noting that nearly all the important American writers are still alive. Warmly praised are Poe and Hawthorne, while Robert Bird's novel *Nick of the Woods* is preferred to the work of Fenimore Cooper. General comment includes the suggestion that 'In respect of those circumstances which affect style, the position of Americans is much like that of Scotsmen; and the results have not been very dissimilar'.[2] Tantalisingly, the comment is not expanded upon. In the later editions of Spalding's *History*, published after the author's

217

death, the treatment of American literature is more perfunctory: the in-house editors distribute brief comments on American writers across a range of chapters; are on the whole more dismissive of America's literary achievements; and even overturn Spalding's critical judgments. Thus in the revised fourteenth edition of 1877, we are told that Poe's 'weird' stories 'confer upon him a distinction not merited by the unrestrained sensuality of his life'.[3] Despite these posthumous changes, Spalding's own interest in American literature is significant: his is the earliest treatment of American authors in a literary historical context by a British academic, and his influence must explain why, as early as 1874, English students at St Andrews were being invited in their examination to 'give some account of American literature'.[4] How had his interest originated? In my view in all probability through Francis Jeffrey's *Edinburgh Review* and the positive view of American culture which the Scottish Whig tradition it supported tended to adopt.

The relevance of the same tradition to the life and career of the second Scottish academic I wish to discuss is, as we shall see, self-evident. John Nichol was the first occupant of the new Chair in English Literature at Glasgow University created in 1862 in response to the recommendations of the Universities Commission of 1858. Nichol held the chair until 1889, but it would be quite erroneous to believe that it was only with Nichol's appointment that forms of literary study became part of the Glasgow curriculum. Adam Smith had lectured on rhetoric and belles-lettres in Glasgow in the 1750s and '60s, and Smith's pupils such as George Jardine, Archibald Arthur, and William Richardson, ensured that the tradition of literary and rhetorical study at Glasgow continued to flourish on into the nineteenth century. Nichol's appointment, that is, accorded a new authority and status to a subject which had existed previously, as it were, in between more established disciplines. More significantly still, Nichol's appointment was to make possible the Scottish invention of American Studies.

Nichol, himself a Glasgow graduate, grew up in a family context that was at once strongly academic and strongly politicised. His father, J. P. Nichol, had been appointed to the Chair of Astronomy in Glasgow in 1837. Famous as a public speaker and lecturer, Nichol senior was a Victorian of a powerfully liberal persuasion. His son described him as 'a temperate radical' and he was well-known as a campaigner against slavery, and as a friend in Scotland of Kossuth and Mazzini. As a student friend of the young John Nichol put it:

> Dr Nichol was known to be a friend of Kossuth and Mazzini; his sympathies and those of Mrs Nichol were strongly with the Anti-Slavery party in the United States. He did not repress, he encouraged, our zeal for those who in Hungary and Austria, and France and Italy, and America, were for personal freedom . . .'[5]

The Mrs Nichol referred to here was Nichol senior's second wife. His first wife–John Nichol's mother–having died in 1851, in 1853 he married Elizabeth Pease of Darlington. She and her father, Joseph Pease, the first Quaker MP, were prominent members of the British Anti-Slavery Society. It is then not surprising that Nichol senior should have had many American friends and correspondents, including Longfellow and the leading New England abolitionist, William Lloyd Garrison–nor that in 1847–48 he should have undertaken a lecture tour in America. That tour was destined to be of crucial importance–as we shall see–in influencing the direction of his son's major research and scholarship after becoming Glasgow's first Professor of English. More immediately, J. P. Nichol's politics permanently influenced those of his son. At least until the closing years of his life, Professor Nichol's political feelings were even more radical than those of his father. In 1891, three years before his death, looking back on his student days in Glasgow in the early 1850s, he wrote: 'We were all, or thought ourselves to be, keen "Radicals"; believing in the "people", "progress", "free education", "wider suffrage", "rights of man", "rights of women", etc., etc.'[6] Thirty years earlier Nichol had written an account of his early years for his wife's benefit. In this short autobiographical account, Nichol emerges as a fairly typical middle-class radical of the mid-nineteenth century. In his description of his response to the events of the years 1848–49, there is no hint of the ironies present in 1891:

> I have been, of later years, thrown much into the society of men younger than myself, and found it difficult to make them realise the breathless interest with which the friends of liberty in Europe watched every phase of that momentous struggle.

Like his father, Nichol came to know both Kossuth and Mazzini personally. 'My feeling regarding the wars', he went on, 'remains as it was when I ran every morning through the woods to the village, to catch the first tidings from the East'.[7]

In 1855 the twenty-one year old Nichol left Glasgow University for Balliol College, Oxford. Benjamin Jowett, Master of Balliol, became a lifelong friend, but perhaps the most significant event of his Oxford career was the founding of 'Old Mortality', an essay-writing and discussion society. The list of original members of this society makes impressive reading: Swinburne, T. H. Green, G. R. Luke, A. V. Dicey, G. B. Hill, and, most interesting of all in this context, another Glasgow graduate, James Bryce. The society may have owed its name to Walter Scott, but the members did not share that author's Tory politics. Their sympathies rather were firmly on the side of radicalism. Dicey later wrote that by virtue of the strength of their views on such questions as University Tests, Italian nationalism, the policies of Louis Napoleon, and restrictions of any kind on the free expression of opinion–questions which, he says, 'were the subject of daily, I might almost say of hourly, discussion'–'we considered ourselves advanced Radicals, not to say Republicans'.[8]

Some members of the Old Mortality society, however, were soon preoccupied by a new issue, a new challenge to the liberal principles they endorsed: the impending struggle between North and South in the United States. Edward Caird, Jowett's successor at Balliol, recalled that Nichol and T. H. Green were from the first aware of the significance of what was at stake:

The Scottish Invention of American Studies

The great contest of North and South in the United States was then beginning, and Nichol and Green showed themselves from the first well-informed as to the nature of the struggle, and zealously maintained the justice of the Northern cause.[9]

Like Green, Nichol remained a powerful advocate for the North throughout the course of the American Civil War. Back in Glasgow for most of the war's duration as the new Professor of English, he was undeterred by the fact that established opinion in Glasgow, as elsewhere in the United Kingdom, often tended to side with the South: on the public platform and in the newspapers, he energetically supported the Northern cause.

Soon after the close of the Civil War Nichol, like his father before him, made an extended visit to the United States. In the autumn of 1865 he travelled through the New England states and as far south as Virginia. In the course of his trip he visited and was entertained by a range of New England's cultural leaders: Emerson, Longfellow, Oliver Wendell Holmes, Wendell Phillips, and William Lloyd Garrison. Nichol found America enthralling. Experience of the country and its society confirmed all his expectations: the positive view of the new republic, always present in the Scottish Whig tradition represented by the *Edinburgh Review*, proved to be amply justified. 'America', he told his wife, 'is far better than I dreamt of in almost every respect, especially Boston'. Indeed Boston struck him as much superior to Glasgow: 'I would give my left hand to leave Glasgow and come here, but at present there is no opening'. From what he says here, one may reasonably guess that Nichol had talked to his Boston friends about the possibility of exchanging his Glasgow Chair for a Harvard one: 'I must publish a book in England', he writes, 'and get it made known here'. And he concludes with another ringing endorsement of American cultural life:

Everyone I meet in society is sympathetic, literary or metaphysical, refined beyond the refinement of Englishmen, not to say of Scotchmen, and in the van of the world, not tugging at the rear.[10]

From Goosecreek to Gandercleugh

Nichol's dream of becoming a pioneer of the transatlantic brain-drain was not destined to be realised. He never did return to America, but his Boston letter does hint at the direction his scholarly career was going to take. Back in 1848 his father had brought home from America, after his lecture tour, a mass of books including the works of Hawthorne, Longfellow, Bryant, and James Russell Lowell. These were the books which first fired the enthusiasm of the young John Nichol, still a schoolboy in Kelso, for American literature. That enthusiasm he was never to lose. As early as 1861 he was lecturing on American poetry in Edinburgh. In 1867 he published articles in the *North British Review* on American poetry and Emerson. In 1875 he contributed the article on American literature in the *Encyclopaedia Britannica*. In 1879 he lectured on American literature in Cheltenham, and in 1880 on the American novel in Edinburgh. For a senior British academic such as Nichol to choose to specialise in American writing at this time is quite simply extraordinary. Back in 1866, Henry Yates Thompson of Liverpool had offered to endow a lectureship at Cambridge in the 'History, Literature, and Institutions of the United States'; but for a combination of political, ecclesiastical, and academic reasons, Cambridge spurned this offer to appoint a lecturer in American Studies as a dangerous novelty. As I indicated at the beginning of this essay, the formal study of American literature did not begin even in American universities until the 1920s; and in Britain it would be the 1950s and '60s before courses in American literature begin to appear in university departments of English Literature. Yet in 1882, in Edinburgh, Professor John Nichol published the book which was almost certainly already in his mind in the Boston letter of 1865, and which would be the major scholarly production of his career: *American Literature, An Historical Sketch, 1620–1880*. Nichol had earlier published short studies of Byron and Burns, and he would later produce a brief study of Carlyle, but the book on American literature is easily the most important achievement of his research and scholarship. Publishing such a book on a subject so unfamiliar that, in an academic sense, it did not really exist, Nichol must have known that he was taking something of a gamble in terms of his own scholarly prestige. And there is some evidence suggesting that he recognised that in publishing this book he was exposing himself to attack. In November, 1882, he wrote to William Bell Scott in Newcastle alluding to his forthcoming publication:

> I send you a first proof sheet . . . a month old, by which you will see I have not forgotten you . . . The big book to which the sheet belongs will be out very shortly: but *please mention it to no one* till it is out. I have known a little vol. of mine applied for a year before for the purpose of attacking it.[11]

But Nichol never seems to have been reluctant to face up to opposition, and since at least the publication of his article on American literature in the *Encyclopaedia Britannica* in 1875, he had chosen to become the leading British authority on American writing. Again, Nichol's other main academic publications were, as noted above, on Scottish authors: Burns, Byron and Carlyle. Focusing thus on American and Scottish authors, perhaps the Glasgow professor of English literature was already choosing to look beyond the English mainstream in literary study? In any event the motives that led a liberal progressive like John Nichol to write and publish his pioneering history of American literature were in the end probably more social and political than purely academic and scholarly.

So what kind of book is Nichol's *American Literature*? What approach to the study of literature does it reflect? From what standpoint does Nichol address the subject of the history of American literature? The short answer is that Nichol's approach is an historicist one: he believes that a text can only be understood and appreciated within its context. Thus *American Literature* is almost as much social and cultural history as literary history: politicians, orators, theologians, historians, are given almost as much prominence as poets and novelists. The work of individual writers is seen, interpreted, and assessed very much in terms of its social and political background. The American Civil

War, for example, and all the moral and political debates that preceded it, are continually referred to. Nichol makes his approach explicit at the beginning of the book. He tells us he aims to discuss those authors 'who most conspicuously represent' the main periods and areas of American's literary history, but, significantly, he will 'illustrate their position' 'by reference to the history and politics of the time'.[12] This historicist approach extends to what Nichol sees as the continuing problem of Anglo-American cultural relations. English critics of America have always assumed the automatic superiority of the Old World over the New:

> Few are able to divest themselves wholly of the influence of local standards. This is pre-eminently the case when the efforts of a comparatively young country are submitted to the judgments of an older country, strong in its prescriptive rights, and intolerant of changes, the drift of which it is unable or unwilling to appreciate. Our censors are apt to bear down on the writers of the New Word with a sort of aristocratic hauteur. Englishmen are perpetually reminding Americans of their immaturity, scolding their innovations in one breath, their imitations in another . . .

The problem, Nichol argues, is at bottom one of ignorance: both Englishmen and Americans are 'ignorant of their mutual ignorance'. But his emphasis falls on English ignorance of America:

> Untravelled Englishmen know much less of America as a whole–less of her geography, her history, her constitution, and of the lives of her great men–than Americans know of England.[13]

These are the kinds of view the *Edinburgh Review* had been articulating more than half a century earlier, and there are equally traditional echoes in Nichol's apologies for the limitations of America's literary achievements. In America, he suggests, practical activities have had to take precedence over cultural ones; the achievements of American culture exist in the future rather than the past; politics, commerce, material success have so far absorbed the American genius. These are all arguments with a history going back at least as far as the foundation of the new republic. In fact, at the end of the day, one has to say of Nichol's *American Literature* that, however amazingly innovative it is in one sense, in another, paradoxically, it was already out-of-date in 1882. Nichol's book is a celebration of the literary culture of New England in the 1830s, '40s, and '50s–of the work of Emerson, Thoreau, Hawthorne, Longfellow, Bryant, Lowell. It is a celebration of that older America which in fact came to an end with the Civil War. Nichol sees the North's victory in the Civil War as a vindication of America's dedication to the principles and rights and freedoms the Founding Fathers enshrined in the Constitution. Though writing in the early 1880s, he does not see that American history has moved on–and moved on in ways that will further radically undermine the American dreams that the new republic once hoped to embody. Thus he find little of value in the work of more recent writers such as Henry James, W. D. Howells, or–a true *bête noire*–Mark Twain.

In the long term, however, the methodology of Nichol's history of American literature would prove more important than his assessments of individual authors. His commitment to the historical approach to the study of literature remained unshakeable–for him literature and history were inseparable. Thus he believed that an Honours school in English could not be created at Glasgow until the necessary History courses had come into being. This in turn meant the establishment of a Chair in History. Such a Chair, finally created in 1889, was filled in 1893; but Nichol retired in 1889, and an Honours programme in English did not emerge until after the arrival of Nichol's successor in the English chair–the Shakespearean scholar, A. C. Bradley. However, Nichol's emphasis on the link between literature and history proved enduring; only in the 1950s did the Glasgow English Department drop the requirement that Honours students should take a course in British history.

Nichol then was a pioneer in the historicist study of American literature. He was equally a pioneer in two vastly important areas in the history of higher education in Britain: women's education and adult education. Throughout his career, Nichol did everything in his power to promote the cause of higher education for women–as early as the 1860s he was delivering a series of lectures in Glasgow, outside the university, aimed at a female audience, and his was undoubtedly a key role in creating the situation which led to the admission of women to Glasgow University in the 1890s. His commitment to the cause of what would now be called continuing or adult education was equally strong. From the 1860s on, he travelled extensively throughout England and Scotland lecturing on literary and philosophical subjects. Applauded as warmly in Dundee as in Penzance, he did as much as anyone to create what became later in the nineteenth century the University Extension movement. Nichol believed in education for all–and that all included women and working men.

Let us return, however, to the main focus of this chapter. What role did Nichol play in bringing into being the formal academic study of American literature and history, and how can he be seen as a Scottish inventor of American Studies? Obviously Nichol's *American Literature, An Historical Sketch* is of central importance in this connection. What needs to be borne in mind is that, by 1882, not even within America itself had a comprehensive history of American literature appeared: Moses Coit Tyler's *History of American Literature 1607–1765*–to which Nichol acknowledges a debt–had appeared in 1878, but as its chronological span indicates, Tyler's history did not cover the literature of the new republic.

Nichol's history of American literature thus has a justifiable claim to be the first work of its kind in its field. But for a book to count it has to be used–read, studied, assimilated. The evidence here is more equivocal. Many of Nichol's works, including his studies of Byron and Carlyle in the English Men of Letters series, were published in America; the National Union Catalogue identifies frequent reprintings of these and other books by Nichol. But it lists only the original Edinburgh edition of *American Literature, An Historical Sketch*: are we to conclude that American publishers, confident of an assured American readership for studies of major British authors such as Byron and Carlyle, took the view that there was no comparable market for a book-length study of America's own literature? The answer is almost certainly yes. A review of Nichol's volume in the Boston periodical *The Literary World* in fact cites both Adam and Charles Black in Edinburgh, and Scribner and Welford in New York, as publishers of the book.[14] But this is misleading. Through the 1870s, Scribner had built a close relationship with the Edinburgh publishers, importing and binding the printed sheets of such works as the ninth edition of the *Encyclopaedia Britannica*. Even earlier, Scribner and Charles Welford had formed an importing subsidiary specifically for the purpose of bringing British published books to America.[15] Thus the Scribner and Welford Nichol was at best a New York bound version of the original Black edition: but at least the import meant that Nichol was easily available to interested American readers.

So what kind of notice was taken of Nichol's work in America? *The Literary World* reviewer finds in it many errors and inaccuracies, but 'as the work of a foreign critic' it 'deserves reading'; writing on Transcendentalism Nichol is 'in his element, as a Scotchman always is when dealing with philosophy'.[16] C. F. Richardson, of Dartmouth College, who was to publish his own *American Literature, 1607–1885* in 1887–88, writing on the criticism of American literature in the *Andover Review* in 1884, recognised the problem created by the close relationship between English and American literature, and argued that the foreign critic in particular required special qualifications:

> The foreign critic of American literature should be thoroughly acquainted with both English and American political, social, and literary history; should perceive clearly that in England and America is a dominant and assimilating Saxon folk, working out a similar problem on similar lines; and yet should discriminate between variant conditions, aims, methods and results.[17]

Very much, one would have thought, what Nichol had attempted to do. But Richardson is not quite prepared to agree. 'No foreign historian of our literature', he writes, 'has shown himself possessed of all these qualifications. Professor Nichol has some of them, but his book is, after all, only an essay *toward* a history of American literature'.[18] However, when J. J. Halsey reviewed the first volume of Richardson's own history in *The Dial* of Chicago in 1887, he compared it somewhat unfavourably with Nichol's book–even if he was less than clear about Nichol's nationality:

> Professor Nichol has upon the whole demonstrated that a fair-minded and earnest Englishman can come at the very heart of our literature.

'His book', he continues, 'is the first criticism of that literature, and its rank is high'.[19]

Nichol's book, the available evidence suggests, created some ripples in America, but it seems not to have become a major focus for continuing critical or scholarly debate. Late nineteenth-century and early twentieth-century historians of American literature such as Henry A. Beers, Walter C. Bronson, Barrett Wendell and William P. Trent cite Nichol among their authorities–as do the editors of Volume One of the *Cambridge History of American Literature* published in 1917. But the group of MLA scholars, who set about establishing the formal academic study of American literature within the American university system in the 1920s, make scant reference to Nichol. One suspects that the fact that he was a foreigner was a major problem. Fred Lewis Pattee, writing 'A Call for a Literary History' in the *American Mercury* for June, 1924, refers to Nichol's 'now antiquated volume' but returns to it in the context of his discussion of what qualities are required of the American literary historian. Rather like Richardson writing forty years earlier, Pattee concedes that the foreign critic may possess the desirable detachment and impartiality, but will inevitably lack the necessary 'understanding of the American soul':

The Scottish Invention of American Studies

> The Scotch John Nichol's *American Literature*, the most detached history thus far published, falls fatally short at more than one vital point.[20]

What Pattee, like the other young scholars of his generation, was about was a kind of clearing of the ground: their joint aim was to re-establish the study of American literature on a new, modern, professional basis. Past efforts had to be set aside, and a new beginning made.[21] But the problem of deciding how exactly the future study of American literature was to be pursued remained. What Arthur Hobson Quinn, W. B. Cairns, Fred Pattee, Percy H. Boynton, soon joined by Robert E. Spiller and Norman Foerster, decided was that American literature should be presented as an 'expression of national (historical) consciousness' and not as an 'aesthetic offshoot of English literature'.[22] Their view, that is, as Pattee, and therefore one suspects most of the others as well, must have known, was an exact reiteration of Nichol's view; their approach was Nichol's approach. Some years earlier the four volume *Cambridge History of American Literature* had been published (1917–21). But while the *Cambridge History* asserted that as a survey of 'the life of the American people' it was more than 'a history of *belles lettres* alone' it nonetheless announced itself on its title-page as 'supplementary' to the *Cambridge History of English Literature*. This was not the view taken by the first generation of American professors of American literature: for them, just as for Nichol, American literature was distinct and separate, only to be understood within the specifics of the social, intellectual, political and cultural context of America itself.

American Studies, of course, as a subject in its own right, involves much more than the study of American literature. But Nichol's contribution to the invention of American Studies extends beyond his writing of the first history of American literature. I have already noted that the membership of Nichol's Old Mortality society at Oxford in the 1850s included the future statesman and scholar James Bryce. But Nichol's friendship with Bryce was of older date. Bryce became a student at Glasgow University in 1854, and soon came to know John Nichol, only a few years his senior. Given his future career, it is hard not to feel that knowing Nichol must have meant learning of–and perhaps beginning to share–his friend's enthusiasm for all things American. Certainly America seems to have been a shared interest for many members of the Old Mortality society at Oxford. Apart from Nichol himself, T. H. Green, another middle-class radical, was an active supporter of American democracy, and it was in the company of A. V. Dicey, one of Nichol's closest friends, that Bryce first visited the United States in 1870. After that visit, Dicey retained an abiding interest in America. In 1898, as one of England's most distinguished legal historians, he returned to Harvard where he delivered the Lowell lectures on comparative constitutions. And G. B. Hill, who had become a leading scholar of eighteenth-century English literature, visited Cambridge, Massachusetts in 1893 and wrote a well-received account of Harvard College. However, among the Old Mortality group, it is the career of Bryce which is of the greatest significance. Bryce returned to America in 1881 and 1883, and in 1888 he published the first edition of his classic work *The American Commonwealth*. Revised and expanded editions appeared in 1889 and 1893–5, while the final version of 1910 is described by the DNB as 'to some extent a new book'. Like Nichol's *American Literature, The American Common- wealth* was a major pioneering work; but Bryce's searching and critical constitutional history of America was to have an impact far beyond anything achieved by Nichol's study. Particularly within America, *The American Commonwealth* acquired a reputation similar to that of Crèvecoeur's *Letters from an American Farmer* or De Tocqueville's *Democracy in America* and was read and studied with enthusiasm well into the twen- tieth century. Today its classic status would still be generally recognised. Bryce's book included quite extended discussions of American culture, including its literature. His views are not identical to those of Nichol, as he tends to emphasise what American literature shares with English literature rather than what distinguishes the two; but he does agree that American literature, like, as he sees it, Scottish literature, has a kind of dual identity.

In the eighteenth century Glasgow and the Clyde were the main avenues for the export of Scottish influences of every kind initially to the American colonies and subsequently to revolutionary and post-revolutionary America. Hence it is wholly appropriate to find in the nineteenth-century Glasgow scholars John Nichol and James Bryce the original Scottish cultivators of the field that was to become American Studies. In the twentieth century their tradition was re-established by a succession of distinguished Americanists at the University of Glasgow: D. W. Brogan, Esmond Wright, Peter Parish, William Brock. But it is Nichol and Bryce who deserve recognition as the Scottish pioneers of American Studies.

Notes

1. For an extended account of Spalding and his *History*, see Alistair Tilson, 'Who Now Reads Spalding?' *English Studies in Canada* (December, 1991), pp. 469–80.
2. William Spalding, *A History of English Literature* (Edinburgh: Oliver and Boyd, 1853), p. 409.
3. William Spalding, *The History of English Literature*, Revised 14th edition (Edinburgh: Oliver and Boyd, 1877), p. 382.
4. See *The St Andrews University Calendar* (1875–76), p. 97 (Rhetoric and English Literature M. A. Pass Examination, November 1874).
5. Professor W. A. Knight, *Memoir of John Nichol*, (Glasgow, James MacLehose, 1896), pp. 58, 121.
6. *Ibid.*, p. 114.
7. *Ibid.*, pp. 96–97.
8. *Ibid.*, p. 140.
9. *Ibid.*, pp. 151–52.
10. *Ibid.*, p. 276.
11. The italics in the letter are Nichol's own. The letter is part of the Troxell Collection in the Special Collections section of Princeton University Library.
12. John Nichol, *American Literature, An Historical Sketch, 1620–1880*, (Edinburgh: A. & C. Black, 1882), p. vi.
13. *Ibid.*, pp. 2, 7, 12.
14. See, *The Literary World*, (Boston: March 24, 1883), p. 88. Unsigned review. *The American Catalogue, 1876–1884* records no American edition of Nichol's book.

15. See, *Dictionary of Literary Biography*, Vol. 49 (Detroit: Gale Research Co., 1986), pp. 412–14.
16. *The Literary World*, p. 88.
17. C. F. Richardson, 'The Perspective of American Literature', *Andover Review* (November, 1884), p. 480.
18. *Ibid.*, pp. 480–81.
19. J. J. Halsey, 'American Literature', *The Dial* (February, 1887), p. 244.
20. Pattee's article was reprinted in Norman Foerster (ed.), *The Reinterpretation of American Literature* (New York: Harcourt, Brace, 1928), pp. 3–22. See p. 6.
21. Is this why by 1935 Pattee appears to have erased NIchol from his memory? In the Preface to his *The First Century of American Literature 1770–1870* (New York and London: D. Appleton-Century, Co., 1935) he makes no reference to Nichol and describes C. F. Richardson as the 'maker of the first systematic presentation of American literary history' and 'a pioneer scholar'.
22. See Robert E. Spiller, 'Those Early Days: a Personal Memoir', in *The Oblique Light: Studies in Literary History and Biography*, (New York: Macmillan, 1968), p. 258.

Index

Index

Index

Dove, Patrick Edward 190
Drummond, William of
 Hawthornden 98
Drunk Man Looks at the Thistle
 (MacDiarmid) 128
Dumfries 91
Duncan, Douglas 46, 49
Duncan, William 17, 53
Dunlap, William 64
Duyckinck, Evert 154

East, P D 203
Eastwood, Glasgow 46
Easy Club, Edinburgh 31–2
'ebonics' 55
Eckenrode, H J 197
economic theory, George attacks
 178–80
Edinburgh: as cultural capital 81;
 dual appeal 83, 89–90; Franklin
 visits 37; Georgian society 124–5;
 intellectual democracy 81–2, 124–
 5; intellectual groups 30–2;
 medical education 38–9; New
 Town 90; Philadelphia, cultural
 parallels 29–32; population size
 30; problems shared 33; as
 provincial city 29; romanticism 83,
 89–90; ruling elite, freedom 29–
 30; Sheridan's lectures 47, 53–4;
 Silliman visits (1805-6) 83–4, 88;
 Ticknor visits 85, 86–9; tourists 90
Edinburgh Castle 90
Edinburgh Medical Society 39, 80
Edinburgh Musical Society 41
Edinburgh Philosophical Society 80
Edinburgh Review 86, 98, 170; and
 America 213, 214, 217, 218, 221,
 224; American respect for 83,
 139; Carlyle in 139, 168;
 Macaulay in 163, 168; 1755
 edition 30, 44; Sydney Smith in
 213; Whig tradition 214
Edinburgh University 217; and
 American literature 222;
 American students at 79, 80;
 Medical School 38–9, 79;
 Philadelphians at 38–9

Eighteenth Century Scottish Studies
 Society 2, 19
Elements of Criticism (Kames) 51
Elements of Logick (Duncan) 53
eloquence, models of 49
Emerson, Ralph Waldo 5, 109,
 221, 225; Carlyle,
 correspondence with 136–7, 141,
 142, 143, 144, 145; as Carlyle's
 agent 141, 142, 152; and
 Carlyle's extremism 149–50;
 friendship with Carlyle 144–5,
 146; at Harvard 152; on
 Macaulay 167; position in
 American life 145–6; success 146;
 transcendentalism 145–6, 154
Encyclopaedia Britannica 60, 222,
 223, 227
England: cultural dominance 44. *see
 also* Britain
English English language 51;
 correctness 54
English literature: Anglo-centric 4;
 commonality 8
English people, and Scots vernacular
 109
English Studies 4
English Traits (Emerson) 167
Enlightenment: major concerns 47;
 Miller attacks 69; and politeness
 40; Scotland's contribution 73.
 see also Scottish Enlightenment
Enlightenment in America (May) 19
Episcopalian party 34
equality, sexual 72
Essay on Civil Liberty (Ferguson)
 22
*Essay on the Right of Property in
 Land* (Ogilvie) 190
Essay on Truth (Beattie) 28
Essays (Hume) 70
Essays on Fiction (Nassau) 114
'Ettrick Shepherd', Hogg as 124,
 125
European Enlightenment: export to
 Philadelphia 25–7; and provincial
 cities 29
Everett, Alexander 140

Index

Index

Index

Index